MOVEMENT AND PERFORMANCE IN BERLIN SCHOOL CINEMA

NEW DIRECTIONS IN NATIONAL CINEMAS
Robert Rushing, editor

MOVEMENT AND PERFORMANCE IN BERLIN SCHOOL CINEMA

Olivia Landry

Indiana University Press

This book is a publication of

Indiana University Press
Office of Scholarly Publishing
Herman B Wells Library 350
1320 East 10th Street
Bloomington, Indiana 47405 USA

iupress.indiana.edu

© 2018 by Olivia Landry

All rights reserved

No part of this book may be reproduced or utilized in any form or by any means, electronic or mechanical, including photocopying and recording, or by any information storage and retrieval system, without permission in writing from the publisher. The paper used in this publication meets the minimum requirements of the American National Standard for Information Sciences—Permanence of Paper for Printed Library Materials, ANSI Z39.48-1992.

Manufactured in the United States of America

Library of Congress Cataloging-in-Publication Data

Names: Landry, Olivia, author.
Title: Movement and performance in Berlin School cinema / Olivia Landry.
Description: Bloomington, Indiana : Indiana University Press, [2019] | Series: New directions in national cinemas | Includes bibliographical references and index.
Identifiers: LCCN 2018019386 (print) | LCCN 2018043609 (ebook) | ISBN 9780253038043 (e-book) | ISBN 9780253038029 (cloth : alk. paper) | ISBN 9780253038036 (pbk. : alk. paper)
Subjects: LCSH: Motion pictures—Germany—Berlin—History. | Movement (Acting)—History.
Classification: LCC PN1993.5.G3 (ebook) | LCC PN1993.5.G3 L32 2019 (print) | DDC 791.430943/155—dc23
LC record available at https://lccn.loc.gov/2018019386

1 2 3 4 5   23 22 21 20 19 18

Contents

	Acknowledgments	vii
	Note on Film Titles and Foreign-Language Citations	ix
	Introduction: A Cinema against Stasis	1
1	Media, Death, and Liveness	17
2	Theatricality Bleeds, the Presence of Dance	52
3	Between Movement and Affect: The Body's Shared Point of Sense	78
4	Accelerating Performance: From Car Travel to Car Crash	108
5	Nina Hoss's Performance of the Fugitive Body; or, What to Do with Movement	157
	Conclusion: Performance on the Move	181
	Filmography	189
	References	195
	Index	209

Acknowledgments

The energy and spirit of this book are in great part attributions of a study much supported, encouraged, and exuberantly guided, without which this book would certainly not be.

I am extremely grateful to Claudia Breger, who has provided nothing short of unflagging support, brilliantly insightful and engaging feedback, and always positive encouragement. She has been a wonderful mentor and (inter)disciplinary ally, who has gently but persistently nudged me out of my own narrow and ideological corners to see a beautiful world of multiplicity and possibility. Her influence resonates throughout these pages. In a similar vein, I also would like to thank Benjamin Robinson for his enthusiastic support, dynamism, and intellectual curiosity. No matter the topic or question, he has always been ready to provocatively engage and challenge my preconceptions. I am also grateful to Shane Vogel for introducing me to performance studies, which has become my passion and roadmap for navigating so many disciplinary pathways. Further, the rare precision and care with which he approaches any topic or text has also taught me to pace myself and to carefully reflect on the thoughts and ideas I encounter along these pathways. Without Brigitta Wagner, I never would have come around to the films of the Berlin School and recognized their vast scope. For this I am eternally grateful. Her extraordinary knowledge of and passion for German cinema have been an invaluable influence on my work. Alexander Doty, who is certainly much missed, taught me with equal doses of admonition and encouragement how to properly analyze film. For this skill, I am forever in his debt.

None of these wonderful encounters and experiences would have been possible had I not been welcomed to Indiana University and to the Germanic Studies Department as a graduate student. I received nothing but support and encouragement from professors and fellow graduate students throughout my six years as a student there. I can say the same for the two years I spent as a postdoctoral fellow in the German Department at the University of Pittsburgh, where I had the great fortune to dedicate much time to working on this book in fantastic company. Randall Halle typifies, for me, the perpetual mentor. I cannot thank him enough for his tireless counsel, his infectious scholarly commitments, and his friendship.

Tremendous gratitude goes to the anonymous readers for Indiana University Press: their enthusiasm for the project and the abundant time and care each took to read and consider the book have been extremely meaningful and helpful.

At IUP, Robert Rushing's initial interest in the project and ability to see its stakes have had significant consequences for me. For this I am very grateful. I am also thankful to have as my editor Janice Frisch, who has brought this book forth with such acuity, dedication, and energy.

I am equally beholden to all of my friends outside of academia whose very existence has been so grounding and who have offered me such necessary outside perspectives on things and life. Similarly, I am grateful to my parents, especially my mother, Sally Landry, who generously proved to be a wonderful reader of this book in its late stages. As a fellow scholar, my older sister, Christinia Landry, has always been inspirational both personally and academically, and she remains the source for so many of my intellectual passions, because we never cease to learn from our siblings.

Finally, I would like to thank my incredible partner, Ihsan Topaloglu. There is no one to whom I owe so much as I made my way along the circuitous path of writing and revising that lies behind this book. His unflagging love and support have been nothing short of life-giving. I count myself incredibly lucky to have him in my life.

An earlier and shorter version of chapter 2 appeared in *The Germanic Review* and parts of chapter 5 in *Film-Philosophy*. I am grateful to Taylor & Francis and the University of Edinburgh Press for permission to republish some of this work here. Many thanks also go to Schramm Film Koerner & Weber, Heimatfilm GmbH, Iko Freese, Christoph Hochhäusler, Thomas Arslan at Pickpocket Filmproduktion, Komplizen Film, and ZDF for the permission to use images.

Note on Film Titles and Foreign-Language Citations

THE BERLIN SCHOOL films I analyze in this study are all in German. Sometimes the films' titles vary significantly in German and English. Throughout, I employ the German-language titles, but I also include the English title in parenthesis when the film is mentioned for the first time in each chapter. This is also the case for films in other languages. Much of the early criticism of the Berlin School appeared in newspaper articles, interviews, and film critiques. These texts are largely in German. I cite these frequently and offer translations into English in the running text. Generally, if these quotes are long, I give the original in an endnote. Shorter citations I simply place in parenthesis. All translations from German to English are my own, unless otherwise indicated. This includes citations from films, as a number of the DVDs with which I work are not subtitled.

For the sake of consistency and clarity, where an English translation of a text exists, be it secondary or theoretical, I employ and cite the translation. This includes mostly texts originally in German and French. In cases in which I work with both the English and the German versions of texts, I have also listed the German titles in the bibliography. Book or article titles not available in English translation have been left in their original language.

MOVEMENT AND PERFORMANCE IN BERLIN SCHOOL CINEMA

Introduction

A Cinema against Stasis

A SERIES OF crime photographs incites a real-life enactment of murder, dancing erupts at the side of an indoor swimming pool, a long walk to school is nothing more than a long walk to school, landscape images through the window of a moving car swish by, an old jeep careens into a river, a woman cycles to freedom. This is the Berlin School in movement. This is the Berlin School in performance. *Movement and Performance in Berlin School Cinema* trails these swelling gestures, brisk migrations, and mad dashes and makes some sweeping moves of its own.

The title of this book sounds like a paradox. If anything, in our post-cinematic age of digital media and streaming, film has become ostensibly less performance based and even further removed from the influence of live experience. But perhaps precisely in response to this cool and quick transformation of film from analog to digital, from 24 FPS to 70, and from larger-than-life to handheld, live experience has not disappeared altogether; rather, it haunts film like a displaced ghost. Consider for a moment the possibility that the contemporary ambition to create the effect of live experience in film is not unlike the increasingly "realistic" virtual reality games and the touch and voice functions of mobile devices and household entertainment systems. While many scholars (especially in Germany) have tracked, and even lamented, the transformation to the post-cinematic, its claims to flexibility, mobility, and fragmentation,[1] few have sought out the potential signs of life that the haunting of the live yields. Without succumbing to nostalgia for things past, I read the haunting mode of liveness in film instead as a vigorous turning toward a new dynamism and the power of performance. Performance is a concept and discipline duly tethered to the live, to the experience of presence, to interactive spectatorship, and to affective feedback loops.

With a particular focus on the still contemporary German film movement the Berlin School and its significant body of films, I argue in *Movement and Performance in Berlin School Cinema* that in our highly digitalized and mediatized age, narrative film has responded with an inflection of performance. This book attends to the ways in which performance asserts itself in the Berlin School films through the effects of liveness, presence, sensation, and interactivity, all of which are often cited as touchstones of live performance. Mostly it tracks the manifestation of movement over stasis. It concentrates on how abundant diegetic movement, even at its most banal, opens up the possibility for moments of performance. These moments are frequently phenomenological, and at times also theatrical. Outside of specific film genres—such as musicals, documentary, and pornography, as well as early television—treating and tracking the experience of live performance has played only a perfunctory role in narrative film and film scholarship. This book thus proposes a consideration of paths yet unexplored and with it invites us to shift our due attention to the possibility of the imbrications of film and performance, media and liveness, and to how contemporary (German) film asserts itself as more than just an occasion to speculate on our nostalgia for the cinematic.

The films of the Berlin School at once exemplify and engage this performance turn in film. While I recognize the risk of extending this shorthand term to a large body of films and the potentially generalizing approach of performance, it is my aim that *Movement and Performance in Berlin School Cinema* offer a broad contribution and ultimately signal how we can investigate and expand the parameters of film and performance in an effort to figure more intuitive and creative interactions. It is the conviction of this book that the contemporary German film movement, the Berlin School, is this place. That is not to say that no other film movement has engaged performance, nor do I propose that this move toward performance is a precept of the Berlin School. The Berlin School, however, is in many ways shaped by and even shapes film's relationship to performance. The following thus comprehensively examines more than twenty-five films by eleven different German filmmakers associated with the Berlin School. These films date from 1998 to 2014. While not specifically a study on a paradigm of German national cinema, the book does to some extent attend to these films' historical and political grounding within a contemporary German and European context.

Frequently compared temporally and aesthetically to the spate of "new cinemas" that have swept the globe in recent decades (Iranian New Wave, New Argentine Cinema, New Romanian Cinema, New Turkish Cinema, and so-called neo-neo-realism),[2] the Berlin School has an important stake in contemporary global art cinema.[3] This film movement began to develop through the late 1990s and into the early 2000s, specifically with the features of three German Film and Television Academy Berlin (dffb) alumni and colleagues: Thomas Arslan, Christian Petzold, and Angela Schanelec. German film critics coined the name Berlin School in 2001 as a nod to the provenance of these three filmmakers, and it subsequently became an important label for discussing and recognizing their films and those that followed.[4] In the early 2000s, a "second generation" of filmmakers emerged. These included Maren Ade, Valeska Grisebach, Benjamin Heisenberg, Christoph Hochhäusler, Ulrich Köhler, Maria Speth, and Henner Winckler, as well as, to some degree, Elke Hauck and Jan Krüger. Hailing from other parts of

Germany and different film institutions, the movement's affiliation with *Berlin* has become somewhat tangential, but the label has stuck.

Yet this grouping, this so-called Berlin School, as a number of scholars are still dubiously wont to term it, has felt and continues to feel too loosely and arbitrarily contrived for many, including some of the filmmakers themselves. Indeed, the Berlin School has neither a political (such as New German Cinema's Oberhausen) nor an aesthetic (as with the Danish Dogma 95) manifesto to delineate the fixtures and motivations of the movement. Beyond Arslan, Petzold, and Schanelec, even institutional affiliation or geography are not reliable attributes for membership. Further, some critics and scholars have contended that the Berlin School has simply become a designation for art cinema originating from Germany tout court. There is a discernible cohesion and community in the work of the Berlin School that affirm its collective force, however, notwithstanding the potential auteurist styling of this movement. For instance, a number of the filmmakers work with some of same actors (Corinna Harfouch, Nina Hoss, Devid Striesow, Sabine Timoteo, Hans-Jochen Wagner, Mark Waschke), the same editor (Bettina Böhler), the same cinematographer (Reinhold Vorschneider [see Wagner 2010]), and the same production company (Schramm Film Koerner and Weber). In addition to sharing some of the same resources, the movement has also been contemporaneous to a broader revival of film scholarship and discussion in Germany. Already in 1998, filmmakers Christoph Hochhäusler and Benjamin Heisenberg, in collaboration with Sebastian Kutzli, initiated the biannual German-language film magazine *Revolver*. Feeling the dearth of engaged film discussion in German cinema circles at the time, the founders sought to revive film culture both in Germany and internationally. Evidently modeling itself after the famous *Cahiers du cinéma*, *Revolver* consists mainly of interviews with alternative (often European) filmmakers and contributors and has become a platform for both written and live discussion of film in Berlin and elsewhere, as interviews for the journal are frequently conducted in a live forum before they are printed.[5] Much like the *Cahiers du cinéma* was instrumental in shaping the Nouvelle Vague, *Revolver* is considered in many ways to be a journalistic, as well as academic, organ for the Berlin School.

Despite an early self-reflexive and intellectual orientation, scholarship on the Berlin School only started to make waves in academic circles at the end of the first decade of the twenty-first century. Prior to that, thoughtful treatment of this work fell to (mostly German) film critics and journalists, whose inceptive writing I engage at different turns, such as Rainer Gansera, Ekkehard Knörer, Katja Nicodemus, Cristina Nord, Rüdiger Suchsland, and Merten Worthmann, to name just a few. Starting in 2005, the Berlin School began to gain attention in film circles as a new movement when *Cahiers du cinéma* published an article by Elisabeth Lequeret, "Allemagne: la génération de l'éspace" (Germany: The generation of space) (2004), who acclaimed it the "Nouvelle Vague Allemande." This also marked the moment when German film critics began to more seriously consider these new films as an important turn in national cinema away from German cinema's period of Hollywood-infused romantic comedies of the 1980s and '90s, iconically termed the "cinema of consensus" by Eric Rentschler (2000, 265). One of the first articles devoted explicitly to the Berlin School was Rüdiger Suchsland's brief sketch "Langsames Leben, schöne Tage. Annäherung an die 'Berliner Schule'" (Slow life, beautiful days: Approaching the "Berlin School") published in *FILMDIENST* (2005). Taking Suchsland's work as a point of departure, the trend then started to gain momentum in Germany, from the multiauthored 2006 article "'Berlin School'—A Collage" first published in German in *kolik.film* and then in English in *Senses of Cinema*, to Ekkehard Knörer's 2007 English-language article "Long Shots, Luminous Days: Notes on New German Cinema" in *Vertigo* magazine. Therefore, much of the material that exists pre-2008 about the Berlin School consists of interviews and articles from newspapers and film magazines. Marco Abel is widely recognized as one of the first film scholars to write extensively about the Berlin School in a more academic context, starting with his first, much-cited article in *Cineaste*, "Intensifying Life: The Cinema of the 'Berlin School'" (2008b). Others have followed suit, including Hester Baer, Roger Cook, Jaimey Fisher, Gerd Gemunden, Lutz Koepnick, Kristin Kopp, Eric Rentschler, and Rajendra Roy in the United States, and, to a lesser extent, Ilka Brombach, Alisdair King, Sabine Nessel, and Thomas Schick in Germany and Europe.[6] My own work on the Berlin School is beholden to this earlier scholarship.

The present study comes on the heels of four major events and works in the creation and consolidation of the Berlin School as an internationally renowned (German) cinema movement. The first was a film exhibition of the Berlin School at the Museum of Modern Art (MoMA) in New York and an accompanying symposium at New York University in December 2013. In a wide-scale event, filmmakers, actors, a cinematographer, journalists, and scholars from Germany and the United States assembled and publicly discussed the significance, as well as the past, present, and future of the Berlin School. The fruits of this broad discussion were published in part in a display book, *The Berlin School: Films from the Berliner Schule*, commissioned by the MoMA and edited by Rajendra Roy and Anke Leweke (2013). The other three events were the publications of pathbreaking, extended studies on the Berlin School, including the edited works *Berlin School Glossary: An ABC of the New Wave in German Cinema* (Cook 2013), Marco Abel's *The Counter-Cinema of the Berlin School* (2013), and Jaimey Fisher's monograph on *Christian Petzold* (2013). These monographs efficiently laid the groundwork for the Berlin School as an area of German film studies that merits further inquiry.

With *Movement and Performance of Berlin School Cinema* I aim to broaden the scope of the study of the Berlin School and its achievements. No longer burdened with the task of establishing the existence and importance of this movement and its positioning as a national and global cinema paradigm, I seize the opportunity of coming after this initial wave of scholarship to probe Berlin School films as subjects of a new kind of cinema that bends toward performance. The topic of performance is not only new to the Berlin School but also unfamiliar (possibly even antagonistic) to film studies in general. This bend toward performance is a wide one whose figurations range from movement to theatricality, as well as phenomenological affectivity and interactivity, all the while underpinning a telos of live experience. Ultimately, my major claim in this book is that the Berlin School films seize modes of live performance to occasion relational experiences of *being-there* and *being-with*. I read these terms as specifically bearing the phenomenological promise of spatiotemporal presence or presentness—being-there is being present to the experience at hand. (Indeed, this term resonates with Martin Heidegger's phenomenological notion of "Dasein" but is less concerned with ontology, per se). Being-with similarly hinges on the promissory notion of phenomenological presence, only this presence is not specifically spatiotemporally grounded; it thrives on relationality and proximity, a presence with or to someone or something else. Employed in the context of film, and particularly with regard to embodied spectatorship, these terms indicate the gains of Berlin School viewing, which offers the experience of both spatiotemporal presence and relationality with the film world and the bodies that populate it. Such a viewing experience is shaped by phenomenological perception and interaction. Formally speaking, this occurs by way of the Berlin School films' (1) general preference for medium and long shots over penetrating and especially frontal close-ups; (2) frequently (geographically and temporally) undetermined settings; and (3) general (but certainly not exclusive) disavowal of postproduction modifications, including extradiegetic music and classical continuity editing. These films also tend to eschew excessive diegetic symbolism, as well as conventional plot elements to guide the viewer along.[7] Thus, it can be said that the actors' diegetic bodies take on a more prominent role than cinematography and editing in orienting the perception of the viewer in Berlin School films. Often detached from manifest narrative drive, diegetic movement instead assumes both a phenomenological and a performative role in these films. While contemplative in its cinematic reflexivity, I argue that the Berlin School actually defies the recent label of "contemplative" or "slow," attached to much contemporary global art cinema, and especially the Berlin School.[8] Sometimes slow, sometimes fast, movement is not only preponderant in these films but also often the means by which bodily experience is expressed and its effects are activated. For this reason, I prefer to characterize the Berlin School first as a cinema against stasis. Not a wholly negative assertion, I read being against stasis as an affirmation, what Sara Ahmed calls "being for being against" (2010, 162). But this is still not the whole of it. If my first axiom is that the Berlin School is a cinema of movement, then my second catches a slightly different drift, for the dynamism of the Berlin School brings another aspect of these films into relief: Movement is effectively staged for the viewer. It is a mode of performance.

Methods of Film and Performance

Performance is frequently described in the negative, as the anticoncept and the antidiscipline. To this end, Marvin Carlson writes: "Performance by its nature resists conclusions, just as it resists the sort of definitions, boundaries, and limits so useful to traditional academic writing and academic structures" (2004, 206). Or, as Bert O. States similarly opines, "I am convinced that a definition of performance . . . is a semantic impossibility" (1996, 3). Yet precisely in its resistance to definition, disciplinarity, and representation, performance gives rise to the abounding and destabilizing possibilities of interdisciplinarity and praxis-oriented theories. In the most general of terms, my distillation of performance in the present study is as a spectacle of the body (and occasionally the body-cum-object, as in the case of the car in motion) that invites relationality. Therefore, performance cannot occur in isolation. Making a spectacle of the body also entails movement. While the still body can in certain contexts perform, the body on the move readily makes itself tangible and visible to the spectator. Finally, performance might carry intentions beyond mere relationality, but this is not a condition of performance.

When we speak of the performative turn in the social sciences and humanities in the 1990s, which developed hand in hand with poststructural approaches, we generally think about performance via the precept of language performance, influenced by J. L. Austin's (1975) study on the performativity of language and the ability to "do things with words." This turn did not explicitly make it into the folds of film studies. Instead, the 1990s witnessed a definitive turn toward the body and sensation in film scholarship, especially with the work of Steven Shaviro, Vivian Sobchack, and Linda Williams. Thus, while performativity fulfilled a rigorously linguistic project of deconstruction in literature as well as gender and LGBTQI politics and theory, performance's concern with embodiment and bodily movement and practice was actually flourishing in film *avant la lettre*. With the evocative declaration that performance is no stranger to film studies in practice, the present study does not propose a (re)defining of performance and its methods; instead, it adopts performance approaches and figurations as a means of rethinking film and its relationship to performance, specifically the Berlin School films. Cutting diagonally across performance studies, *Movement and Performance in Berlin School Cinema* appropriates performances studies' critical interdisciplinary perspective and a number of its tropes. Liveness, presence, movement, interactive spectatorship, and historical reenactment: these are some of the elements of performance that I explore in the films of the Berlin School.

The performance of the Berlin School films comes into sharper focus as I contemplate their propensity for movement and the attendant fits of immediacy and presence. It is through these vectors that we can track moments of performance. These are moments when film presents itself as mobile, theatrical, interactive, and even visceral. What is on-screen *feels* alive, real, touchable, and the on-screen and off-screen spaces further converge. Throughout, this book engages in close readings of selected events and scenes that heed such moments. To develop these claims, my theoretical mapping begins with a route through questions of mediation and remediation, which I define respectively as mediatic representation and mediatic re-representation (as in the case of a photograph used in film and so forth). This study sets out by asking the ever-relevant question about the ontology of cinema, its status as a unique and fluid medium. It seeks to reconcile the mediated form to qualities of (unmediated) performance, in particular the effects of spatiotemporal liveness. An unexpected path through André Bazin's focus on the photographic elements of cinema and Christian Metz's early semiotic approaches open up this reassessment of the medium. Mediatic effects of liveness are succeeded by a treatment of its qualifiable twin, presence, which, from Hans Ulrich Gumbrecht to Erika Fischer-Lichte, in turn invites an analysis of film's theatrical elements, what I refer to as a "theatricality bleed." This term is a nod to Brigitte Peucker's "reality bleed," which indicates the permeability between two elements that can lead to ontological collapse (2007, 96). I trace presence and theatricality by way of the subtly nuanced influences of the musical and dance genre films. A more explicit examination of movement turns phenomenological and affective when I consider embodied spectatorship anew, it is a precursor to thinking about film and/as performance. This leads to the tracking of perception, orientation, and subject-object reversibility, as lucidly advanced in the phenomenological works of Maurice Merleau-Ponty and those film scholars influenced by him—such takes on the figuration of what I call a "point of sense" in film. If point of view defines a positionality, both physical and ideological, then a point of sense defines an orientation that is forcefully phenomenological and affective. But the gaze returns to some degree later on when I consider what Volker Pantenburg terms the "automobilization of the gaze," which in a slightly more mediated way is also conditioned by movement and orientation and literally becomes a window to a world of shock and awe. Finally, the figure of the fugitive body offers a performative trope for thinking about the body in motion.

Broadly speaking, the methods I formulate and the theories I deploy are part of a longer tradition of reflecting on performance elements in film but have not been brought together in this manner before. This book traces a line in film theory from the early materialists to more contemporary film phenomenologists and finally to the film affect theorists. My archive is diverse and demanding, but also splendidly flexible and mobile. Ultimately, this trajectory limns cinema's established preoccupation with the material, the body, orientation, mobility, the senses, and finally perception over cognition. Working within this capacious framework, my intervention takes these methods one step further and examines what it means and looks like, especially in film's post-cinematic, digital age, as taken up in different contexts by Mary Ann Doane, Adam Lowenstein, Laura Mulvey, and Steven Shaviro, to turn to the discipline of performance studies. Some of the secondary texts I cite throughout address aspects of the body, presence, and affect in individual Berlin School films, but there is no existing treatment of the Berlin School and performance. A turn to performance in film does not necessarily precipitate a disciplinary turning to performance studies, but I argue that such a *tour* spurs film studies in new disciplinary directions. For one, if our aim is to get back to live experience and presence, there is no other discipline so beset by the question of liveness and its foil mediatization than performance studies. Further, performance is exceedingly ontologically anchored in the concerns of the body and its ability to transmit experience, feeling, and even knowledge. Finally, the body in motion as a force of vitality, animation, and affect occupies performance studies' penchant for amplified and augmented bodies. Taking stock of performance, Diana Taylor's brief but succinct guidebook to performance, *Performance* (2016), prioritizes all of these qualities.

Positioned more firmly in film studies, *Movement and Performance in Berlin School Cinema* turns to and grapples with the insights of performance studies in its aim to develop a new episteme of filmic performance. Treating performance topics such as remediation, movement, dance, presence, sensation, and affect in film, this book engages most prominently with persisting debates surrounding liveness and mediatization. For some performance scholars, liveness is not only a part of performance but furthermore a precondition of performance. Certainly, not all performance is live, and liveness is not always an occasion for performance; however, it seems impossible to speak of one without the other. Indeed, performance's guarded precept of liveness has made hitherto investigations of film and performance tricky endeavors. Thus, without overdetermining the role of liveness in performance, heed must be paid and issues of mediatization must be accounted for. The propitious convergences of performance and film is what drives the present study. These demonstrate that liveness does not become a "burden" (as José Esteban Muñoz has also argued in other contexts) that shuts down discussion about reading film as performance. Quite the contrary, I aver that the conceptual contentiousness of liveness serves as an aperture to film and media studies. In the spirit of such proposed openness, I ask what it means for film to be live, present, interactive, mobilizing, and performative. At every turn, I find it is movement that holds these ramified offshoots of film performance together. But beyond the topic of liveness, this book's trajectory of movement also intersects with aspects of utopian queer performance, as most famously delineated by Muñoz, and aspects of historical performance and its becomings, taken up in different ways by Daphne A. Brooks and Oksana Bulgakowa. These more representational explorations of performance in the Berlin School films maintain the corporeal not to mention kinetic esprit of the book, all the while expanding its parameters of content and form. This is a book full of energy and optimism. Throughout its pages, performance manifests affirmation and the embrace of both present and future possibilities. Performance offers a new kind of vitality to film and film studies.

Finally, Elena del Río's thinking about performance and film in her important study *Deleuze and the Cinemas of Performance: Powers of Affection* ([2009] 2012) is informative to my project. She takes film and performance in different directions, however. Her parrying of the death call of cinema entails a revisiting of theatrical and affective-performative moments of classic and new Hollywood and European art cinema. Del Río's project is in tune with the performance of the expressive body of the melodrama. Aside from the obvious distinction in our filmic objects of study, my methodological pursuit of performance and film diverges from del Río's in a twofold manner. First, my account of performance holds to precepts of presence and relationality, whereas hers focuses on artifice and operatics. Second, my focus on the body is more phenomenological than hermeneutic. What performance more generally offers the post-cinematic condition is a self-affirming alternative to the apparent refraction of the embodied spectator, for digital media's fragmentation and individualization ostensibly seem to foreclose the possibility of bodily empathy and proximity. If we begin to look for what appears to be missing, we may actually uncover novel figurations of the lost object wherewith new thresholds can also open up. In many ways, my turn to performance studies' approaches actually mounts itself on the so-called aftermath of cinema.

The Chapters

Movement and Performance in Berlin School Cinema is divided into five chapters, arranged by topic, and a brief conclusion. Each chapter in this book considers an effect of performance and engages in close readings of a selection of films, and in some cases mere scenes and sequences from these films. While the chapters are thematically self-contained, the book's overall topoi of performance and live experience through various forms of movement in the Berlin School nonetheless course through the chapters and form traceable lines of thought. The chapters move sequentially via patterns of presencing and movement, insofar as each chapter to some extent fashions the conditions by way of which the next chapter may be approached. By fusing modes of film with modes of performance, *Movement and Performance in Berlin School Cinema* proposes a radical new epistemology of film as a medium capable of performing. The unexpected quality of movement in these films, its textures and vastness, calls on this performance and bears it out. Berlin School films are accordingly cause and effect of this proposed epistemology: they are simultaneously subjects and objects that create and respond.

To begin to think about film's relationship to liveness and performance with respect to the Berlin School, we can turn to film's relationship with other media. In chapter 1, I propose that it is no coincidence that the Berlin School films broadly employ other forms of visual media. Particular among these are photographs and surveillance camera footage (or CCTV). Remediation of film with these two media underscores the former's ontological drive toward liveness. As Philip Auslander, Jay David Bolter, and Richard Grusin have all averred, the work of remediation is a reckoning with media's potential for the live in our highly mediatized age. Instances of engagement with other media likewise unearth Bazin's ever-pertinent question of cinema's ontology. But all acts of remediation are not the same. The insertion of photography in the diegetic film world of the Berlin School creates a juxtaposition rather than a melding of two media, as photography becomes associated with not only the static but also the dead. Christian Metz (1974), Roland Barthes (1980), and Laura Mulvey (2006), have elucidated photography's affinity to death and its embalming imperative. But the films do not simply reestablish old kinships of realism or binaries of the mobile film image and the still photographic image. Instead, in this collision of the alive and dead, mobile and still, the Berlin School films are curiously incited to perform and reenact. Films such as Christian Petzold's *Toter Mann* (*Something to Remind Me*, 2001), *Gespenster* (*Ghosts*, 2005), and *Phoenix* (2014); Christoph Hochhäusler's *Unter dir die Stadt* (*The City Below*, 2010) and *Deutschland 09. 13 Kurze Filme zur Lage der Nation: Séance* (*Germany 09: Short Films about the State of a Nation: Séance*, 2010); and finally Angela Schanelec's *Mein langsames Leben* (*Passing Summer*, 2001) all employ photographic images that are meant to represent the past—that and those no longer present. Here these *tableaux morts* are given an afterlife through film.

Death and especially crime find mediation through yet another medium in the Berlin School films, namely, CCTV images. The second half of this chapter examines film's remediation with surveillance camera footage. There is a haunting and even mortifying thematic element that connects photography and surveillance. Contrary to photography, however, CCTV images are not presented as film's opposite, but rather as its ontological ally. Through their almost televisual quality of temporal immediacy, the employment of CCTV images in (narrative) film is often to highlight not only what Thomas Y. Levin (2002) has notably called the "reality effect" of film but also its liveness. I argue that this effect permeates pivotal scenes of the films to create a sense of temporal and spatial immediacy. Voyeuristic omniscience is the name of the game in this section and Christian Petzold's films are eminent examples with their complex use of CCTV images. In chapter 1, I examine his insertion of these images in his renowned Ghost Trilogy, including the films *Die innere Sicherheit* (*The State I Am In*, 2000), *Gespenster* (*Ghosts*, 2005), and *Yella* (2007). Two slightly later films, Benjamin Heisenberg's *Der Räuber* (*The Robber*, 2010) and Christoph Hochhäusler's *Eine Minute Dunkel* (*One Minute of Darkness*, 2011), similarly offer noteworthy examples of the liveness CCTV footage imparts to narrative cinema. These remediated gestures traceable in many of the Berlin School films at once open up a dialogue about film's ontology and ascribe its mediatic drive for the live.

The perception of immediacy can be traced beyond the effect of real time to the sensation of presence in the Berlin School films. In chapter 2, I explore this through an unassailable kinetic striving. For a film movement chiefly characterized by static camera work and minimal cuts, it is by no means lacking in diegetic movement. This movement becomes most sentient and theatrical through dance. The Berlin School films abound with dance scenes, which reach the height of spectacles. As a film movement that boasts professional ties with the German theater scene, the Berlin School's propensity for dance makes a historical (re)turn to the bodily animation of very early cinema and its theatrical drive, or what Tom Gunning has famously referred to as the spectacle-based "cinema of attractions" ([1985] 2006) and Miriam Bratu Hansen describes as the "excess of appeals" (1995). Often lasting the entire length of a song, these dance scenes are unexpected, at times excessively extranarrative, and even hinging on the vaudevillian. Similar to the way surveillance camera footage evokes a reality effect, the dance spectacles in the Berlin School films engender a presencing effect. From Gunning and Hansen to Jane Feuer's study of Hollywood musicals and André Lepecki's work on dance and performance, chapter 2 examines the role of dance in film and its critical link to the performance of bodies. The dance spectacle in film wrests what Feuer calls a "'first-person' form, a performance which assumes an active and present spectator" (1993, 23) and thereby infuses the film with theatricality, by means of what I refer to as the theatricality bleed.

From the solipsistic dancers in Valeska Grisebach's features *Mein Stern* (*Be My Star*, 2001) and *Sehnsucht* (*Longing*, 2006) to the unconventionally voyeuristic dance scenes in Angela Schanelec's *Plätze in Städten* (*Places in Cities*, 1998) and *Mein langsames Leben* (*Passing Summer*, 2001), and finally to the campy dance spectacles in Maren Ade's *Alle Anderen* (*Everyone Else*, 2009) and Jan Krüger's *Unterwegs* (*On the Road*, 2004), the placing and pacing of dance in the Berlin School films are variegated. Yet with its exaggerated self-display and gesturing, dance in these films is a performance that like the spectacle of the cinema of attractions has "its accent on direct stimulation" (Gunning 2006, 68) and thus offers the impression of presence and immediacy through an unexpected nod to theatrical performance.

Beyond dance, diegetic movement in the Berlin School films takes subtler but still noteworthy forms. In chapter 3, I expand on this examination of the performance of movement to consider walking and biking. Starting with broad strokes, chapter 3 argues that excessive diegetic movement in these films invites phenomenological and affective engagement through a "point of sense." The body in motion is not only performative as it orients itself through being; it is also highly visible. Its amplification through movement engages the embodied viewer through shared sensory and affective experience. In this chapter, I revisit a well-paved route around the contours of the body and its subjectivity from Merleau-Ponty's phenomenology ([1945] 2007) to film studies' turn to the body and the sensual with the materialists (Béla Balázs), the Deleuzians (Brian Massumi, Steven Shaviro), and the film phenomenologists (Vivian Sobchack, Laura Marks, and others).[9] While some have called for a shift away from film studies' obsession with the embodied subject and the authority of the *touching, feeling* viewer, in the context of the Berlin School films I ask that we abide with this paradigm a bit longer and instead expand on its further potential. A turn to affect is, of course, not a new addendum to the body turn in film studies, yet the dynamically engaging manner with which it reconciles itself to film, form, and mediatization all the while maintaining its exigency to live interfaces is striking. Rounding off with affect theory scholars Lauren Berlant, Eugenie Brinkema, Brian Massumi and others, this chapter contemplates the tripartite force of the Berlin School—movement, embodiment, affect—that distills its promise of live performance further.

Divided into a methodology section and a film analysis section, chapter 3 sets the tone for the next two chapters and their focus on movement. Playing with but also historicizing the loaded practice of flanerie, the film analysis section considers the quotidian movement from A to B in the city. Thomas Arslan's Migrant Trilogy, including *Geschwister-Kardeşler* (*Siblings*, 1997), *Dealer* (1999), *Der schöne Tag* (*A Fine Day*, 2001), figures prominently here as well as Maria Speth's *In den Tag hinein* (*The Days Between*, 2001), all of which appear to be studies on the energetic and omniscient movement of youth through the city of Berlin. Finally, I turn to Christoph Hochhäusler's *Unter dir die Stadt* (*The City Below*, 2010), whose slightly older and wealthier protagonist takes to the streets of the financial capital of Frankfurt am Main in search of distraction and amusement. In all of these cases, the vital and kinesthetic esprit of the actor's on-screen body in motion becomes an important ambulatory trigger of both embodied spectatorship and affective interaction.

Movement in the Berlin School films is not confined to unmediated corporeality, however. In chapter 4, I consider the Berlin School's curious preoccupation with automobiles. This chapter broadly extends from the innocuous experimentation with the road movie genre to the explosive destruction of the car crash. It begins with a consideration of the Berlin School's forays into parts unknown through sundry road trips across the border to Poland in films such as Henner Winckler's *Klassenfahrt* (*School Trip*, 2002), Christopher Hochhäusler's *Milchwald* (*This Very Moment*, 2003), and Jan Krüger's *Unterwegs* (*On the Road*, 2004). The encounter with difference, which becomes projected through Volker Pantenburg's (2010) "automobilization of the gaze" articulates a phenomenological experience of navigating and getting lost in foreign spaces. According to Pantenburg, the automobilization of the gaze is a singular experience of space and landscape facilitated by the moving images within the windshield frame. Thematically, the concept of the automobilization of the gaze inheres in the generic and narrational mode of the early European road movie. But more important, I also propose that this gaze specifically invites viewer participation, as it vividly serves as a citation of how we habitually see the world. The shared gaze of driver-viewer/viewer-driver affectively and perceptually draws us in and puts us behind the wheel, not unlike players of a virtual reality game. I extend my investigation to a host of other films notable for their deployment of the automobilized gaze in different ways. Christian Petzold's films, *Gespenster* (2005), *Yella* (2007), and *Jerichow* (2008), for example, all introduce a mysterious male lead through an uncanny phantom-ride take on the automobilized gaze. In a number of films, this gaze also expressly resists the suture of conventional continuity editing. As such, it engenders narrative ellipsis in Angela Schanelec's *Mein langsames Leben* (2001) and *Marseille* (2004) as well as in Ulrich Köhler's *Montag kommen die Fenster* (*Windows on Monday*, 2006). I argue that by eschewing reverse shots (or at least delaying them), these scenes open up the possibility of an exchange of on- and off-screen positions in their capacity to engage the viewer in spatial, phenomenological, and affective processes of intersubjectivity and reversibility.

The automobile in the Berlin School films is established as a privileged "boîte à regarder" (Nancy 2001, 15, also quoted in Balfour 2010, 36); that is, a space for unrestricted and accelerated looking. It is also, however, a vehicle for and of death and destruction in these films. Indeed, yet another resounding element of the Berlin School films is their quasi-fetishistic predilection for automobile crashes. In the latter part of this chapter, I consider the many scenes of the crash and ask what its overall relationship to the performance of the Berlin School might be. Hurtling across the screen, the powerful violence of the car that crashes is striking. The ubiquity of car crashes in the Berlin School films invites the viewer to (re)experience the assailing shock effects of cinema (as most famously formulated by Walter Benjamin) and to witness at full speed the crossing over and slippage into nonnormative and even counterflows of movement and the resulting liminal spaces of wreckage and destruction. Deterritorializing the film space, the car crash violently hurls the viewer into unchartered modes of experience. At a time when scholars are so engrossed in the aesthetics and politics of slowness, Steven Shaviro has made a curious and duly convincing case for "accelerationism" and "the going through" at full speed (2015), which I explore here. Accelerationism proposes an explicitly Marxian exacerbation of current conditions to the point of explosion, so that it becomes possible to "move beyond them" (2). This is indeed the mode of the car crash. Its transformative jerk has a performance and worldmaking effect that I trace through José Esteban Muñoz's theory of queer worldmaking (1999).

Queer performance theory offers a reparative vitality that helps us to affirmatively embrace the shock of assailing speed and the resulting destructive and disorienting site of the car crash. It transforms these experiences into productive sites of redirection and new worlds. Beginning with a return to Jean-Luc Godard's emblematic film *Weekend* (1967), the latter section of this chapter offers a complex, at times circuitous, path to how film "found on a scrapheap" can perform. For as Karen Beckman has astutely intoned, the car crash is one of cinema's "most persistent self-reflexive tropes" (2010, 1). From Christian Petzold's *Die innere Sicherheit* (2000), with its transformative crash scene that many have cited as the "beginning" of the Berlin School to his circular car crashes in *Wolfsburg* (2003), *Yella* (2007), and *Jerichow* (2008), and finally to the phenomenon of the "primal accident" and its uncanny sexual stirrings in Valeska Grisebach's *Sehnsucht* (2006) and Christoph Hochhäusler's *Falscher Bekenner* (*I Am Guilty*, 2006), this final section of chapter 4 examines how the car crash rejects the here and now and instead opens itself up to something new and yet unknown. This aperture of the crash is a locus of disidentificatory performance, such as that conceptualized by Muñoz as a "ground-level assault on a hegemonic world vision that substantiates the dominant public sphere" (1999, 196).

But does movement only turn into excess and destruction in the Berlin School films? Surely, movement enacts transformation not only on a destructive plane but also in the performative present. In the final chapter, I bring a more directly feminist reading to bear on the performance and movement of the actor Nina Hoss in three more recent films of the Berlin School: Petzold's *Barbara* (2012) and *Phoenix* (2014) and Arslan's *Gold* (2013). Stretching even beyond these three titles, Hoss's contribution to the Berlin School has been significant. She is the putative face of the Berlin School. Indeed, Hoss's performances and star presence, albeit on a minor (national cinema) scale, shape the roles she plays. Without recapitulating the work of star studies, this final chapter considers the co-constitutional relationship of performance and role through the body of a single actor. Encompassing a wide repertoire, the nature of Hoss's roles and performances differ from film to film; they also seem to resonate with an on-the-run motif. In a comprehensive examination of these three films, chapter 5 focuses on the dynamics and implications of Hoss's fugitive performance as representative of a figure perpetually seeking to escape something or someone (even herself). Instead of highlighting the incipient vulnerability and precariousness potentially mobilized in an existence of movement and uncertainty, Hoss's performances characterize an important pursuit of freedom and identity—her discreet lines of flight. Her fugitive body resists the constraints of culturally, politically, and socially mired stasis. A somewhat unlikely source of inspiration for reading Hoss's performances, this chapter ultimately engages performance and African American Studies scholar Daphne A. Brooks's provocative study on movement and fugitive resistance in Pan-Africanist discourses, *Bodies in Dissent: Spectacular Performances of Race and Freedom, 1850-1910* (2006). Without substantively drawing parallels between Hoss's roles in the Berlin School films and the (mostly) African American performances Brooks's study delineates, the method of reading the body in flight as a site of potential and resistance offers a dense frame of reference to the present study. Chapter 5 thus casts a critical eye on the more thematic ties between movement and performance in the Berlin School films. Although it still revels in a mode of movement for movement's sake, it likewise proposes *what* performance does and where it leads in the Berlin School films. While not all performance tracked in *Movement and Performance in Berlin School Cinema* can be subsumed under the figure of the fugitive body, this figure nonetheless offers a compelling thematic basis to contemplate the broader presencing (to some degree, formalizing) of the subject-body in performance in these films. Whether in a more direct (as dance) or an indirect (as automobility) manner, performance with all of its entanglements and possibilities lies at the heart of this book and is that which all of the following chapters will repeatedly return to and bring to bear on the films of the Berlin School.

Notes

1. Notable here is the international conference in Berlin in 2013 on "Post-Cinematic Perspectives" co-organized by the Free University of Berlin and the Institute for Cultural Inquiry. Also, the following texts are quite relevant with regard to this topic: Hagener, Hediger, and Strohmaier (2016); Knörer (2012); Holl (2012); and Elsaesser (2005).

2. *Neo-neo-realism* is a term coined by the *New York Times* film critic A. O. Scott (2009). Scott employs this term to describe a handful of films that emerged contemporaneous to the 2008 financial crisis and address issues of social precarity and disenfranchisement, such as Kelly Reichhardt's *Wendy and Lucy* (2008) and So Yong Kim's *Treeless Mountain* (2008). According to Scott, these films offer a neorealist representation of the new social reality that is akin to that of the postwar Italian neorealist films of Roberto Rossellini, Luchino Visconti, and Vittorio De Sica.

3. In 2015 Marco Abel and Jaimey Fisher organized a seminar, "The Berlin School in Its Global Contexts," as part of the 39th German Studies annual conference. The objective was to

examine the Berlin School and its relationship to other global art cinema movements. Some of the contributions to this seminar have been collected and published as *The Berlin School and Its Global Contexts: A Transnational Art Cinema*, edited by Marco Abel and Jaimey Fisher (2018).

4. Thomas Schick offers an important timeline of the inception of the term. In his words: "There are some discussions about the question [of] who coined the phrase 'Berlin School.' In an additional note to the online version of the article 'Berliner Schule—Eine Collage' (cf. Baute et al. 2010), which initially appeared in the Austrian film magazine *kolik.film*, Rüdiger Suchsland points out that Merten Worthmann used the term *Berlin School* in his review of Angela Schanelec's *Mein langsames Leben* (cf. Worthmann 2001) a few weeks before Rainer Gansera. Nevertheless, most writers on the Berlin School assign the invention of this term to Gansera" (2010, 143).

5. These events—under the auspices of the label *Revolver Live!*—generally occur quarterly at Berlin theaters, such as the Volksbühne or the Hebbel am Ufer.

6. I confine my list to the scholars whose work I quote in this book. This is by no means an entirely comprehensive list, and it does not account for all published articles about individual Berlin School films. I attempt instead to present those scholars whose writing has been significant in shaping the perception of the movement in academia.

7. In his comprehensive study on the Berlin School, *The Counter-Cinema of the Berlin School*, Marco Abel makes the pointed decision not to offer a list of stylistic devices common to these films because, as he claims, this would be very limiting (2013, 297). He makes a valid point, and I do not suggest that the Berlin School films be consigned to their application of these devices alone, but I believe that recognizing formal and aesthetic commonalities among the Berlin School films allows us to approach the films more collectively and with further technical scrutiny.

8. This is a term coined by Michel Ciment (2003) and is often linked to the modes of filmmaking characteristic of Italian neorealism. An expansive range of texts can be cited here on "slow cinema," a rich and ever-growing area of study. Allow me to list just a few: de Luca (2016), de Luca and Barradas (2016), Koepnick (2014), Lim (2014), Jaffe (2014), Flanagan (2008), and Schoonover (2012).

9. It should be noted that these two categories are by no means mutually exclusive. Laura Marks, for instance, also identifies as a Deleuzian.

1 Media, Death, and Liveness

A WOMAN ENTERS a bank. She wishes to deposit a large sum of money on behalf of her crooked new boss. At the teller's counter, she appears stereoscopically in fictional film footage and in a surveillance video image. There is a slight overlapping in action between these two shots. The woman nods to the teller, smiles, and turns to leave. This is a test. She has been given too much money. What will she do with the rest? The grainy, ghostly texture of the surveillance image is at once the solidification of the anonymous alien gaze—structurally extradiegetic in its affect—and the gaze of a dispersed network of authority. This is clearly not her boss's gaze, although she will get caught (by her boss) when she later attempts to mail the extra money to her ex-husband. In Christian Petzold's 2007 film *Yella*, about a woman from the former East Germany in search of upward mobility in the West, a new job, a new start, and a new life mean death. The eponymous protagonist (played by Nina Hoss) is already dead. She is a ghost. But flesh is flesh in film, and in horror films in particular, for as Brigitte Peucker reminds us: "the ghost materializes and is revealed to have a body" (2007, 108). While not a horror film per se, *Yella* takes its cue most notably from Herk Harvey's horror cult classic *Carnival of Souls* (1962). Indeed, Stanley Cavell's conception of the "flesh and blood" actor (1981) assumes full form. In this brief snapshot of surveillance video, death, crime, and liveness intersect in a formal compendium of media modes exclusively meant for the viewer. If anyone catches Yella here, it is us.

Christian Petzold once declared that he works in "the cemetery of genre cinema" (quoted in Abel 2013, 72). I would expand this and propose that he also works in "the cemetery of media." Without being overtly self-reflexive, there is a haunting quality, a play between absence and presence, between life and death, between past and present, that subtends the mediatic entanglements of the films of Petzold and a number of his fellow Berlin School filmmakers. Accompanying this is an awareness of the precarious status of cinema as a dying (perhaps already dead) medium and an urgency to not necessarily resuscitate it but to rethink its place among media, (re)presentation, and imaging. That cinema, or film, for that matter, attempts to reaffirm its status within a culture of new and digital media, is nothing new. As Karen Beckman and Jean Ma assert in the introduction to *Still Moving*, "The issue of the medium specificity has become a central concern for scholars in the field of cinema studies (in response to new media)" (2008, 2). Yet the remediation techniques employed by the Berlin School as a means of mediatic reassertion through the forging of new and old alliances, is a topic that bears its own curiosities. The drive toward performance and therefore immediacy and liveness that this book broadly tracks in the Berlin School films begins thus with the question of the medium, its treatment, and its status. If current media, film included, attempt to, in the words of Jay David Bolter and Richard Grusin, "fulfill our apparently insatiable desire for immediacy" (2000, 5), how do the Berlin School films answer this call? How do they effect a presumable drive toward the live? This is the urgency of the present chapter.

Liveness as a concept is tautological. In the prologue to the second edition of his contentious study *Liveness: Performance in Mediatized Culture* (2008), performance scholar Philip Auslander states that "liveness is a moving target, a historically contingent concept whose meaning changes over time and is keyed to technological development" (xii). Such a teleology suggests that liveness did not exist before the advent of media technology (ibid.); that is, before things could be recorded, everything was live anyway. It was only with the supposed loss of liveness through mediation/mediatization, such as film, television, computers, laptops, tablets, smartphones, and other such handheld (and wearable!) devices, that the existence of liveness and its ontology came into question.[1] Despite the urgency of liveness's charge in our digital age of ever-newfangled devices and new media, the scholarly inquiry surrounding it still has a narrow breadth. It is a concern generally relegated to specialized studies within film, such as documentary, musicals, pornography, and television. Liveness has, however, gained notable traction in theater and performance studies, and it is even considered by many to be a disciplinary touchstone.

To begin to better understand liveness, we must also pay heed to its apparent foil, mediation.[2] José Esteban Muñoz describes mediation as "a text that is not dealing with clouded imperatives to tell what 'really' happened or to give the reader a plastic 'you were there' sensation. The text is instead profoundly evocative, suggestive, and . . . ambivalent" (1999, 58). Muñoz's definition curiously begins by means of exclusion: mediation is not this or that. According to Muñoz, mediation is concerned with neither the hard facts—"what 'really' happened"— nor real experience, "a plastic 'you were there'" (ibid.). Hence, mediation is also not liveness. Instead, mediation, as something "evocative, suggestive, and . . . ambivalent" (1999, 58), is something that entreats interpretation; it is transcendent, even dialectical. Mediation presents not only a temporal and spatial but also a critical remove. What is particularly striking about Muñoz's distinction is the approbational, to the point of defensive, language he applies to mediation, as the "text." It is not "dealing with clouded imperatives" but is rather "profoundly evocative, suggestive." Muñoz has certainly been recognized for his skepticism of performance studies' fetishism of the live, one he has notably referred to as a burden, particularly for minority performance communities. To this end, he has wittingly treated the equally important performance aspects of film, literary texts, and recorded performance in his work.

It is evident through Muñoz's defensive formulation of mediation that liveness has and continues to be a highly contested topic in performance studies—some may even argue to the point of being overwrought. Tavia Nyong'o muses that since the early twenty-first century there seems to be a circular movement of nostalgia for liveness followed by nostalgia for mediation and so forth. Such a pattern marks and shapes performance studies trends (2009, 174). Though rooted in performance studies, the nebulous nature of liveness, as both a conditional concept as well as a historically shifting phenomenon (often an accessory to the advent of new technologies and media), invites the potentiality for more flexible and even cross-disciplinary investigations. Precisely the openness, fluidity, and contingency of the concept of liveness, burden or not, are what the following seeks to highlight in the context of film. Returning to Muñoz's definition of mediation, deduction tells us that liveness implies a spatiotemporal immediacy, a presence—and a here and now. Like the text, film does not readily fit into such an ontological mold. Is it (still) possible for a viewer to experience a film as though it were live, similar to a theater play, that is, as though its characters were standing several feet away, or at least within viewing distance, and its action unfolding at that very moment? Following Muñoz and others, a performance analysis certainly does not strictly hold to an imperative of liveness, as liveness is only one of many discourses in performance studies; yet the challenge that liveness poses to narrative film is more complex and heuristic than it might first appear.

One of the starting points of an investigation of film and liveness is to question the very nature of film in its contemporary role and function. In her study *Death 24x a Second: Stillness and the Moving Image* (2006), Laura Mulvey reposes André Bazin's ever-pertinent ontological question "What is cinema?" with the aim of understanding how cinema—especially contemporary—cinema works. She examines the state of cinema in the context of new media, not least digital film, internet, even post-cinema productions (video installations, and the like). In Mulvey's account, "The specificity of cinema, the relation between its material base and its poetics, dissolves while other relations, intertextual and cross media, begin to emerge" (18). With the digital age came a transformation of the cinematic mode, which developed through a relinquishing of the old mediatic kinships and an embracing of the new. *Movement and Performance in Berlin School Cinema* tracks both. The Berlin School films offer compelling examples of both an ontological distancing from an older media, photography, and the embracing of a co-opting of a new medium, CCTV (closed-circuit television). Thus, the following builds and expands on Mulvey's inquiry by examining how contemporary cinema is shaped by recent forms of remediation that both repel and attract.

Simply put, remediation is the act of repurposing one medium by another. But its function is inscribed by a recent history of new media and the paradoxical move to at once erase media and multiply them—"invoking the twin logics of immediacy and hypermediacy" (Bolter and Grusin 2000, 5). In the context of a "new" remediated cinema, the present study seeks to shed light on the effects of current pursuits of a potentially renewed live culture in the films of the Berlin School. Beyond simply approaching film as a locus of intermediality or a hybrid form of live performance and recorded media, then, I too revisit Bazin's ([1976] 2005) question about the ontology of cinema vis-à-vis contemporary culture's nostalgic pursuit of the live and liveness (returning to Nyong'o's assertion) and ask how this quality has influenced the Berlin School films and the way they may be viewed.

This chapter examines how the Berlin School is shaped by remediation techniques and how these techniques achieve registers of the "real" and the "live." To carry out this task, the following turns to a rather well-seasoned method of exploring film's encounters with other media. But it offers more than a straightforward compare-and-contrast method, and instead draws out the resonance of these encounters. The first section will consider the frequent employment of photographic images in a selection of films. Moving away from Bazin's classic realist claim about cinema's photographic quality (an utterly old kinship), in the Berlin School films, photography is juxtaposed against the filmic image in a forging of mediatic difference. More specifically, this separation of film and photography demonstrates a temporal displacement: a time out of joint and an image out of joint; the past becomes the preserved subject of the photograph and the present emerges as the scene of film. But less concerned with simply reinforcing the binary between photography as a still medium and film as a mobile one, in its remediation with photography, I propose that film accrues new effects, especially that of real time. The second section shifts to another variance of remediation and the inclusion of surveillance-camera footage in a spate of Berlin School films. That both photography and surveillance-camera footage have an intrinsic conjunction to reality and realistic representation is the linchpin that sets up this shift from one form of remediation to another. Contrary to photography, however, surveillance-camera footage has a compelling phenomenological and ideological relationship to real-time experience, aligning it ontologically and epistemologically with live-broadcast television, whose own "promise of presence and immediacy [is] made available by video technology's capacity to record and transmit images simultaneously" (Feuer 1983, 14). The insertion of surveillance-camera footage in a number of the Berlin School films (especially Petzold's features) thematically and formally casts an impression of present time that undergirds the impression of these films' own real-time modality. Surveillance-camera footage, furthermore, transposes the film image into a style of immediate, live broadcast. Along these lines, Thomas Y. Levin reads surveillance-camera footage as a critical "diegetic recasting of cinematic narration as a 'live' and thoroughly televisual multicamera production" (2002, 591). Indeed, in Levin's account, surveillance-camera footage cites the live televisual medium in film. This chapter teases out both the differences and similarities between such distinct processes of remediation and how they literally animate the modalities of film form. Further, the deployment of photography and surveillance-camera footage in narrative film proffers disparate and complex strategies to display the impression and possibility of the liveness of film.

An inquiry into the effects of liveness in the Berlin School also presumes a reading of death and how its ghostly residual power often plays out structurally—that is, mediatically—in these films. Avery Gordon's concept of haunting resonates with the fraught relationship between mediation and liveness. "Haunting," she writes, "raises specters, it alters the experience of being in time, the way we separate the past, present, and the future. These specters or ghosts appear when the trouble they represent and symptomize is no longer being contained or repressed or blocked from view. The ghost . . . is not the invisible or some ineffable excess" (2008, xvi). If haunting is inherently the process of becoming phenomenologically present, then it importantly indicates an experience of modified (or renewed) perception of time and space. Intersecting themes of real and symbolic death and haunting with reflections on liveness and mediation, I argue that the Berlin School films exceed the viewer's perceptions and expectations of narrative cinema. These films enfold theatrical and filmic concepts of the on- and the offstage/screen and effectively throw into question not only the division between liveness and mediation but also those between life and death, presence and absence. In theater, for instance, the dead quite often occupy a place and time somewhere between the on stage and the off stage. These are the spectral figures that haunt the stage; they are what Jacques Derrida refers to as a "coup-de-théâtre" in his *Specters of Marx* (1994), most famously embodied as the ghost of Hamlet's father. Rebecca Schneider explains that these figures are often "staged" and played by live actors (2011, 109); they are, however, theatrically poised in a kind of transcendental off—present but not, dead but also live.[3] The transcendental off represents a space and time distinct from the present one. Derrida's theatrical ghosts, intended as a metonymy for the spirit of Marxism, also thematically overlap with the crisis of old media in the age of new media. He introduces the concept of hauntology, the portmanteau of "haunting" and "ontology," to represent a way of thinking about "Being" as much more than simple ontology (consider, for instance, the complex mystical and abstract nature of the commodity for Marx). Hauntology contains both the real and virtual of the thing as well as the disjunctive character of the two (see Derrida 1994, 10). I recast the concept here to set up mediations on the digital image, which is likewise frequently framed as the site of presence and absence, proximity and distance, potential and loss, life and death.

In the Berlin School films, however, the representation of the dead is assigned not to the digital but to the photographic or (to a lesser extent) surveillance-camera footage. This mediatic displacement of death has a twofold function: it circumvents both the ethical and the real problem of representing death on the screen. By means of remediation, films produce an off, that is, an out-of-frame effect. The insertion of the photograph into the diegesis, for instance, physically marks a metaphysical absence that gestures to a time and place outside of the film. Because the photograph becomes an image framed within an image (the film), this act of inserting generates a transcendental off, which may be considered formally as an internal off. An aperture rather than an interpretative blind spot, the photograph allows us a glimpse of something that is also not there. Under these formal conditions, as Domietta Torlasco proposes, film finds a way "to engage its viewers in the temporality of a death out of joint" (2008, 6). While related research has been done on the films of Petzold, especially his Ghost Trilogy, including *Die innere Sicherheit* (*The State I Am In*, 2000), *Gespenster* (*Ghosts*, 2005), and *Yella* (2007), this study revisits these films, as well as his earlier work in *Toter Mann* (*Something to Remind Me*, 2001) and his later feature *Phoenix* (2014) with the endeavor to integrate their thematic affinity for death and ghosts, into a broader conversation about the Berlin School and its many guises and minutiae. Broadening the scope of this study, I also turn to narratively disparate films: Angela Schanelec's *Mein langsames Leben* (*Passing Summer*, 2001), Christoph Hochhäusler's *Unter dir die Stadt* (*The City Below*, 2010), *Deutschland 09. 13 Kurze Filme zur Lage der Nation: Séance* (2010), and *Eine Minute Dunkel* (*A Minute of Darkness*, 2011), and finally Benjamin Heisenberg's *Der Räuber* (*The Robber*, 2010). To varying degrees, all of these films pore over the power of death and the challenge of its representation in film, which has traditionally been perceived as a medium that gives life to dead things. In these films, the representation of the dead ostensibly displaces the boundaries between real and imaginary, on- and off-screen, as well as the boundaries of the film medium itself. In sum, remediation serves to incite and animate film beyond its own conventions of representation in the direction of liveness.

Enlivening the Image; or, What Film Can Do for Photography

Tracing the encounter between film and photography is a path much taken. A return to the photographic is a perennial project of film scholars in the unrelenting probing of film's ontology. From the various returns of earlier film theorists (André Bazin, Christian Metz, Roland Barthes) to more recent travelers (Garrett Stewart [1999], Laura Mulvey [2006], and Karen Beckman and Jean Ma [2008]), the following notes its place in a longer film scholarly tradition. At the same time, it moves in slightly different directions and attempts to offer new points of entry to thinking about the juxtaposition of film and photography. The Berlin

School films explore—and to some extent even exploit—the mediatic distinction between cinema and photography; they are also concerned with the possibilities to be found in this mediatic rift. This section recites and recasts the leading question already posed by Katrin Peters (2005) in the context of Angela Schanelec's film *Marseille* (2004): "What does cinema want from photography?" More specifically, then, what does the Berlin School want from photography? Despite photography's epistemological relationship to a removed time and place, as Roland Barthes has thoroughly explored in *Camera Lucida* ([1980] 2000), with its indelibly indexical ties to the referent it is often considered a more faithful representation of reality compared to film. In "Photography and Fetish," Christian Metz states that "photography . . . remains closer to the pure index, stubbornly pointing to the print of what *was*, but no longer *is*" (1985, 82–83, emphasis in original). Riffing on Bazin in his opening chapter of volume 1 of *What Is Cinema?*, "The Ontology of the Photographic Image," it can be added that photography similarly possesses a mortifying effect, one that temporally and spatially embalms a time and place. While many have disputed the indexicality of the photograph—and certainly the advent of the cut and paste of Photoshop and digital-image manipulation have given reason to disclaim the charge of photography's direct relationship to reality more generally—the present investigation of Berlin School films suggests that within the embedded context of narrative film the photograph typically maintains its rather unproblematic status as a rhetorical marker and record of reality.[4] When a photograph appears in a film it tends to index a true event—that is, something that really happened. It prompts the historical reckoning that lends truth to events. Even when a photograph is imported into the diegetic world of film, photography cannot, "escape this pure deictic language" (Barthes [1980] 2000, 5). Further, photography's alliance with death through what Barthes has notably called the "spectrum," or the spectacle of the return of the dead (9), seems to distance it from the medium of film in an added way. In his famous analysis of the photograph of the convict Lewis Payne, who awaits execution, Barthes declares that in every photograph death is at stake. This is by virtue of the intensity of time that links all photographs as a manifestation and representation of the future anterior of "*this will be* and *this has been*," namely, "*that* [which is featured in the photograph] is dead and *that* is going to die" (96, emphasis in original). Sedimented in a time now passed, photographs are ontologically implicated in the potentiality of death.

As the medium of both indexicality and of mortification, photography thus distinguishes itself from film. This distinction, furthermore, remains firmly in place through remediation with film. Representing a time and space now in the past, the photograph begets an outside or off-effect within the film (Peters 2005, 5). Inserted into the diegetic film world, the photograph is an image within an image. Yet this effect is not a direct doubling; inside the film frame the photograph physically and transcendentally sets itself apart from its host film image, what Barthes referred to earlier as the "diegetic horizon" (1977, 66). Contained within its own frame, the photograph functions, first and foremost, as a distinct internal off. If it bears qualities of a mise en abyme, this is not an express mirroring effect but rather an ambiguous recasting that curiously heeds dramatic interpretation, that is, reenactment. As the Berlin School film examples here will demonstrate, in a number of cases the film becomes a space of performative reenactment of the image represented in the photo. While not antagonistic, here and elsewhere the distinction between the photographic image and the filmic image is not undone but upheld.

Notwithstanding its relationship of reenactment, the juxtaposition of photography and film mobilizes a phenomenological perception of difference via stasis and movement. That the Berlin School films maintain this distance between the two media does not propound indissoluble tension but rather a resistance against reducibility: these media do not bleed into each other—not in the Berlin School films, in any case. Film uses photography. The presence/presencing of the mobile diegetic hand that can often be seen grasping the photograph asserts the fluidity and mutability of the film frame in comparison to that of the photograph. Film affirms its quality of a-liveness. Contrary to photography, Metz observes in the introduction to his early text *Film Language: A Semiotics of the Cinema*, cinema has a certain "presence" ([1971] 1974, 4). Film presents an experience of liveness in contradistinction to the static image of the photograph. Indeed, Metz would further assert in his essay "Photography and Fetish," that "Film gives back to the dead a semblance of life, a fragile semblance but one immediately strengthened by the wishful thinking of the viewer" (1985, 84). Although not a phenomenologist, Metz's brief text stands out as utterly phenomenological in its appeal to the inherent a-liveness of film—its ability to give life back to the dead. Whether echoing the materialists or anticipating a later turn to phenomenology in film theory, Metz avers that film seeks to bring images to life. Liveness is evoked in the Berlin School films not only through a preconceived remediation of photography and film, that is, of still versus mobile media, but also via the viewer's perception of this difference and the underscored possibility of film's ontology as generating an embodied experience by means of, for instance, the mobile hand, and more broadly the moving image extraneous to the borders of the photograph. Metz's formulation of the weightiness of the viewer's "wishful thinking" emphasizes *Movement and Performance in Berlin School Cinema's* extensive pursuit of an audience-driven intersubjectivity. This chapter takes up how the viewer's projected "wishful thinking" undergirds an experience of liveness in these films.

Consider Petzold's neo-noir thriller *Toter Mann* (2001) about a woman who seduces a lawyer to procure information about the whereabouts of the man convicted (and recently released on parole) of brutally raping and murdering her sister. In this earlier Petzold feature, photographs play a subtle yet crucial role. At various pivotal moments in the film a series of photographs appears. These are black-and-white crime-scene photos of the brutal rape and murder that occurred fourteen years prior; Leyla (Nina Hoss) stole them from the lawyer (André M. Hennicke). Despite being crucial to the film story and to the identities of the central figures in the film, particularly Leyla and the convict Blum (Sven Pippig), this crime is revealed to the viewer only in mediated fragments through these photos, and never through a flashback scene. On the one hand, these forensic photos are objects of evidential or even archival proof; they are even officially numbered as though directly taken from a police archive. More important, their embedded frame and photographic (re)mediation in the film, on the other hand, distinguish the photos both temporally and spatially from the surrounding image of the film. The photographs seem to transcend the film, just as, according to Diana Taylor in her monograph *The Archive and the Repertoire* (2003), archival photos, in their suspension and crystallization of an event or action transcend the live (19). In its contrasting position to these photos of a death (literally of a murder scene and a corpse), the film footage seems to emerge ever forcefully as a medium of action and even liveness, or at least as a kind of performance space.

In a strikingly climatic scene at the close of *Toter Mann*, Leyla attempts to reenact the crime scene represented in the photos as a means of avenging her sister's death, in a performative play of giving life to death and death to life. Indeed, the scene presented in the photos is abstracted through these black-and-white taxonomizing images: a lacerated hand, a splattered bed, a pair of darkly stained scissors. Leyla constructs an ad hoc torture chamber, complete with blacked-out windows, an interrogation lamp, and the rickety frame of a cot. Further, she mounts the photographs in a montage on the wall. To execute her plan, Leyla lures her victim (the original murderer) to her apartment and drugs him. He awakens to find himself tied at the ankles and wrists to the frame of a metal cot. Narrating from the shadows, she then walks her victim through the steps of his crime with the visual aid of the photographs—literally, in an attempt to give life and presence to them. Against the backdrop of the photomontage, Leyla declares to her victim that he will now experience a reenactment of his crime: "Now you will get everything back, your entire crime." ("Jetzt kriegst du alles zurück, deine ganze Tat.") Although Leyla is ultimately incapable of executing the entire performance of the crime—torn by her simultaneous hate and pity for the rapist and murderer of her sister, the feeling of live performance in this scene is compelling. The setting of the reenacted crime scene in *Toter Mann* is also peculiarly reminiscent of the interior of a cinema. The room is dark with the exception of a single spotlight projected on the photographs positioned together into a large square formation on the wall, resembling a movie screen (see figure 1.1). Blum, the murderer-turned-victim in this scene, is forced to be

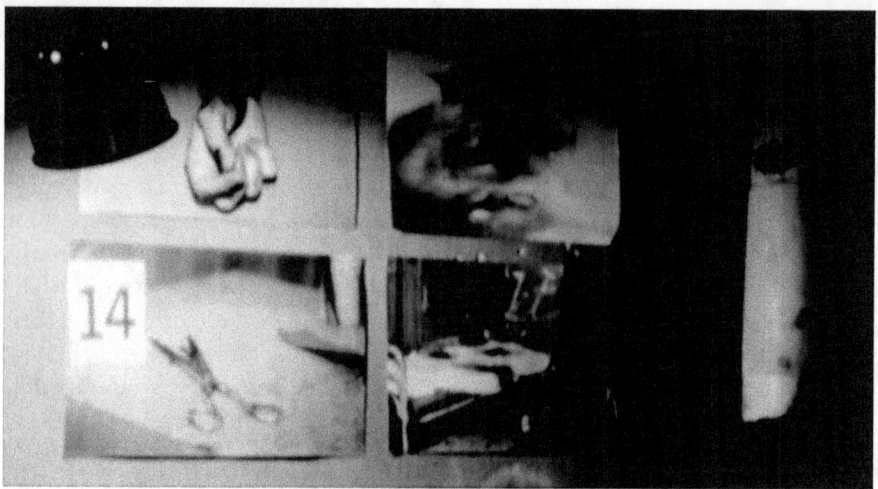

Figure 1.1. The cinema-style torture chamber in *Toter* Mann, 2001. © ZDF

a spectator of the crime he committed whilst simultaneously reliving it in real ("time") life. The complex ontology of film as both photographic and theatrical, in terms of its reliance both on the absence and the presence of the actor, as Bazin and others have observed, finds its analogy in this scene. More germane to the present study, however, is that the relationship between film and reality is highlighted via the overlaying of media and performance. The film that the (external) viewer is watching, *Toter Mann*, demonstrates its closer ontological kinship to liveness and to the theatrical (as opposed to the photographic) by the end of the scene when Leyla intercepts and terminates the photographic narrative because she is ultimately incapable of carrying out her revenge through this replay and recasting of the violent images. In the end, she does not reenact the entire crime, and Blum's lawyer and the police arrive.

In what is a possible allusion to the indexical photographic images of a crime scene in *Toter Mann*, Christoph Hochhäusler's later film *Unter dir die Stadt* (2010) reveals an analogous photo collage of torture and murder. A brief plot synopsis would reveal that this film is about a young investment banker and his wife who move to Frankfurt am Main for his work. Things begin to unravel when the bored and reckless housewife has an affair with her husband's boss. Some have averred that the narrative follows an updated version of the biblical story of King David and his affair with Bathsheba. Distinct from those in *Toter Mann*, the photos in *Unter dir die Stadt* bear less discernible narrative weight. Represented in the photos is (at least we are given to believe) the gory corpse of a Frankfurt investment banker, who had been assigned to a Jakarta branch, where he met his untimely and violent demise. What is visually pronounced in these photos is their sensationalism: not simply indexical, they are also performative. These images are not part of a police archive of evidence; rather, they are intended as a message from the torturers. The viewer is struck with the colored gloss of pure haptic horror. Five photos obliquely depict the bloody and brutalized corpse of a man. The performative force of these photos, their embedded message (perhaps to blackmail or invoke the feeling of insecurity and fear among the bank CEOs) is supplanted by a certain degree of ambiguity, however. Indeed, the bank manager Roland (Robert Hunger-Bühler) appears unaffected by the photos. One earlier scene shows Roland on his cell phone mentioning them in a nonchalant, business-as-usual tone to someone in English: "Yes, I've seen the photos—terrible, just terrible." Roland's apparent ambivalence toward the gruesome photos thematically finds its context in the film by means of his explicitly fetishistic pursuit of the real and the live, which, contrary to Peggy Phelan's claim in her eminent monograph *Unmarked: The Politics of Performance* (1993), apparently does not escape market value in the high-finance world of *Unter dir die Stadt*. Twice Roland has his private driver pay drug addicts so that he can watch them shoot up. He sets only one rule: no eye contact. Perched on a plastic chair (meticulously positioned and wiped clean by his gloved driver beforehand) in an abandoned office space of a vacant building, Roland indulges his voyeuristic fantasies through a live performance designed exclusively for him. He almost all-too-directly embodies the desensitized cinema viewer in search of the live and the real. On one occasion, this live spectacle affects him so viscerally that he almost passes out and has to be ushered away by his driver. By no means a sentimentalist or a man given to oneiric fancy, Roland's pursuit of live experience and performance plays out in explicit but enigmatic ways. One such example of this is his restaging of an old photograph of his murdered and tortured employee as a child.

Although the murdered man in the photo series does not appear in the film prior to his death, soon after the revelation of the torture images Roland goes to the house of his former employee to inform the man's wife. Stoically poised, as though not entirely surprised by the news of her husband's death, the widow proceeds to nostalgically show Roland unordered old photos of her husband. This montage unfolds in a series of shots from the point of view of the widow, who holds the photos and occasionally passes them to Roland. As though presented in contrast to the earlier torture photos, these appear to (or at least attempt to) displace the horror with sentimental pleasantries. These photos offer a record of the happy moments of a man's life: birthdays, vacations, graduations, weddings. This viewing is supplemented by the widow's embedded narration of the life story of her late husband. Well into this photographic narrative, the two stop at an old black-and-white one of the dead man as a child on his first day of school— evidenced by his clutched *Schultüte* (a cone of candy traditionally presented to children on their first day of school in Germany). In the photograph, the child stands in front of his family's home in a working-class neighborhood of Mannheim. The image has all the fixings of a photo plucked straight from Barthes's *Camera Lucida* collection. Roland is particularly struck by this photo and takes it with him. Subsequently, the photo makes repeated appearances in the film, not least as the motivation for another pursuit of the real.

In an altogether bizarrely and superfluously orchestrated reenactment of the widow's narration of her husband's life, Roland goes to the childhood home in Mannheim represented in the photograph. Unlike the reenactment in *Toter Mann*, this is not a reenactment of the dead employee's torture and murder but rather of his childhood. Motivated by sexual desire and not revenge, Roland takes Svenja (his new employee's wife, played by Nicolette Krebitz), his soon-to-be paramour, along. Temporarily displacing the current owners (an elderly Turkish-speaking couple who seem completely baffled by the situation) from the apartment with financial incentive, Roland enters the home with Svenja and begins to re-narrate the story of his deceased employee's childhood, but in the first person. Roland co-opts the story as his own and tells Svenja this was *his* childhood home. His re-narration/reenactment even includes details about his supposed father and brother, and is supplemented by contrived personal anecdotes about his father having to work late. It all seems quite natural; Roland even shows her where he says he slept as a child. It is not clear to the viewer why he does this. Perhaps he believes he will appear more alluring to Svenja as a man who originates from a simple, working-class background, as this modest and rather austere apartment seems to evince. Svenja, however, appears largely indifferent to Roland's performance and eventually exits the home prematurely to have a cigarette on the street. It is possible that Roland, despite his detached demeanor, actually harbors a guilty conscience about his murdered employee.

In the concluding two shots of the sequence, the black-and-white photo of the murder victim as a child reappears. Now alone in the apartment, Roland attempts to place the photograph in a door frame, first in front of an already present photo of a young woman, then behind it, and finally above it. Moving in for a close-up, the camera captures the photo one last time before it is slid completely beneath the edge of the doorframe and disappears. One can only speculate whether this protracted concealing of the photograph is related to the fact that the deceased man's identity has essentially just been stolen; in other words, the photo as indexical proof against Roland's story must be concealed, not dissimilar to concealment of the photos of the tortured corpse of the deceased employee, which, as discussed by the bank CEOs in an earlier scene, may not be leaked either to the bank employees or to the public. Another possible reading of this scene could be as a gesture of goodwill (indeed, Roland does develop as a character throughout the film, and eventually leaves his job at the bank). To this end, Roland symbolically returns the deceased man to his home. In either case, the photograph is dramatically and literally eclipsed by the live performance in his scene, as the former slowly disappears within the wall—a veritable slipping through the crack—and does not materialize again in the film.

Toter Mann and *Unter dir die Stadt* offer vivid instances of film emerging as a locus of reenactment of the dead and past events. The photograph is presented as performative only within the context of the film. In this sense, Rebecca Schneider's claim that photographs, in their capacity as what Barthes has called "Tableaux Vivants" (Schneider 2011, 32), that is, as the site of reenactment and performance, must be reconsidered for these films, whose performance evidently lies in the (at least) attempted (re)enactment of photograph. In her book, *Performing Remains*, Schneider refers to reenactment as a syncopation of time—of one time punctuating another time (2011, 6). By focusing on the "againness" of reenactments, "the double, the second, the clone, the uncanny" (ibid.), Schneider takes issue with the widely held view that performance is an ephemeral and singular event. She avers, instead, that performance is not a vanishing act but actually "remains" precisely because it occurs in the "meantime." In other words, performance occurs in between acts, where there is an encounter in the act of repetition (88). In a rereading of Barthes's *Camera Lucida*, Schneider analogously underscores photography's possible link to theater as a space of reenactment. Incidentally, Schneider does not explicitly distinguish between photography and film, apparently, making this argument for both visual media. In this interstice, I seek to emphasize the division between the two media in these films and to demonstrate the way in which they work both together and against each other as two distinct media, and to what extent this frayed intersection transmits effects of liveness. In the above film examples, photography is employed as a past record of representation, and film as a quasi-live reenactment thereof. Affirming the distinction of archive and repertoire (Diana Taylor) along media lines (of photography and film) precisely as I endeavor to open up performance discourses to make a space for film may seem counterintuitive; this striking treatment of photography in many Berlin School films brings forward such an investigation. A closer look at the role of reenactment in *Toter Mann* and *Unter dir die Stadt* suggests that film legibly takes up this role in its drive to both bring life to and to disturb the deictic practice of the photograph. This is made possible insofar as the films manipulate the photographic narratives through live reenactment. As a result, the photographs lose their resonance in these films as potential agents of action against the mobile and durational medium of film, which, as Mary Ann Doane posits in her study *The Emergence of Cinematic Time*, contrary to photography, "has the ability to inscribe duration [and] temporal process" (2002, 208). That is, unlike photography, film can engage the viewer in an unfolding of the event through its performance of time.

A slightly later film by Christian Petzold, *Gespenster* (2005), reintroduces the possibilities of the remediation of photography in film along exceptionally different lines. Similar to the two previously examined films, a photographic collage is the denouement (or possible counterdenouement) of this film narrative. Yet contrary to those in *Toter Mann* and *Unter dir die Stadt*, the photos in *Gespenster* crop up only once, in the ultimate scene. A film about confused identity, trauma, and the desire for female love and attachment, both sapphic and maternal, *Gespenster* is the least generic of the examples explored thus far. The main protagonist Nina (Julia Hummer) is a teenager without parents, who lives in a group home in Berlin. Her daily garbage collecting in the Berliner Tiergarten (Berlin's central park) also implicates her previous trouble with the law. Over one eventful summer day, Nina meets and falls for the rebellious and capricious Toni (Sabine Timoteo) and encounters Françoise (Marianne Basler) who pathologically searches for her long-lost daughter and believes Nina to be this object of maternal desire. In the end, however, Nina loses both her lover and the mother she never had. The final scene of *Gespenster* distills this drama of loss; alone and rejected, Nina returns to the garbage bin where Françoise's stolen wallet (the handy work of Toni) was discarded in an earlier scene. Nina inspects it and finds inside an original color photo of an infant, together with a computer printout of four slightly different black-and-white photos. These are computer-generated photos of a young girl through consecutive ages. Matching the accompanying colored photo, the first of these images is assumed to be Françoise's daughter Marie, who as the viewer has learned was kidnapped shortly before her third birthday. The subsequent photos are representations of what Marie might have looked like as she grew up. As Petzold states on the official website for the film: "A good year ago, I was in Ardennen, Sedan and Charleroi, and in a post office there, I saw photos of girls who had disappeared from Belgium and France. They had been gone a long time. There was always the last photo of them, and then a series of computer-generated images. The images showed the girls as they might have looked three and two years ago, and how they might look now. The computer-generated portraits were strangely ghost-like. In them, you saw visages without any traces of social experience, strangely pale, not of this world. In reality, dead. Ghost portraits" (2004).

Pictured as a teenager in the last photo of this collage, Marie's "ghost" looks uncannily like Nina. But as Françoise's husband, Pierre (Aurélien Recoing), reveals to Nina in the preceding scene, Marie is long dead. The exposition of these "ghost portraits" at the end of the film nevertheless seems to support the possibility that Nina is Françoise's long-lost daughter, and thereby casts a shadow of doubt on the authenticity of Pierre's claim and the fact of Marie's death (all the while invoking Michelangelo Antonioni's 1966 film *Blow-Up* in more ways than one). At the same time, however, the mise en abyme created by the embedded photographs—here indisputably an enigmatic mirroring effect—may alternatively question Nina's identity. Is Nina (as Marie) also dead? Has the viewer been watching a ghost this whole time? Certainly, from the very beginning the title of the film reckons with such a reading as more than just a possibility.

In the case of these computer-generated images in *Gespenster*, photography still strongly presents a contrasting mediatic juxtaposition to film as in *Toter Mann* and *Unter dir die Stadt*; however, in contrast to the two earlier film examples, the deictic function of these computer-generated images may not be taken for granted. Since these images cannot fully index a real event—or even a real person for that matter—we must ask what precisely their function in the film is. As Nina unfolds each picture in a sequence, like a flipbook, not only does a mediated narrative unfold via these pictures—the life of a young girl from infancy to young adulthood—but so does a virtual one. According to the film's diegesis, and Pierre's claim, this narrative never existed. If the photos are external to the film story in terms of their (un)reality, then they necessarily occupy the space of the *off*. Yet this off is not a typical filmic off-screen, what Pascal Bonitzer refers to—citing Barthes—as a kind of "replete off-screen space" ("*hors-champ étoffé*") of film where the life of the characters continues simply out-of-sight (1980, 6).[5] In *Gespenster*, the off (of the photograph) is the "other"—that is, of another time and space and utter possibility. The computer-generated photographs in *Gespenster* present a dilemma to the authenticity of photography, as they clearly index not a real but a virtual event (and identity) generated by technology. In their potentially performative function as acts of subjectivity, that is, the very existence and possibility of what is in the image is dependent on the image itself, the computer-generated photographs serve more as possibilities than as indices and records. Failing to reference anything or anyone in particular, these photographs offer fitting examples of Bazin's description of the photographic image as the object itself, also quoted by Mulvey, as "the object freed from the conditions of time and space which govern it . . . [the photographic image] shares, by virtue of the very process of becoming, the being of the model of it which it is the reproduction: it is the model" (2006, 56).

By the same token, the computer-generated photographs in *Gespenster* seem to serve an additional function of reenactment in the film. The film, or at least the mother-daughter story of Françoise and Nina, retrospectively emerges as a site of the reenactment of the ghost-like photographs. As it turns out, they serve as Françoise's incitement to search for her daughter, who, according to these images, not only possibly still exists but furthermore strongly resembles a living person—Nina. Françoise, then, like Leyla in *Toter Mann*, repeatedly attempts to bring these images to life and to find her long-lost daughter as a way of subduing and displacing the trauma of losing her only child.[6] Her pursuit of Nina in the film is a direct result of Nina's photographic likeness to Françoise's—potentially still living—teenage daughter, as simulated in the images. Although the status of these computer-generated photographs remains ambiguous even by the close of the film, they are perceptibly and curiously displaced by the filmic image in this final scene, which in some ways echoes the symbolic repression of the photo of the deceased employee as a young boy in *Unter dir die Stadt*. After inspecting the computer-generated images in *Gespenster*, Nina seems to evaluate them as dross; she brusquely tosses them back into the garbage can and walks away into the fleshy, untamed greenery of the Berliner Tiergarten. The viewer is not afforded even psychological disclosure of Nina's face in a reverse shot. The film's message is manifest: contrary to the photographs, in this diegetic world the realm of transcendence and sheer possibility is replaced by the harsh physical world of perceptible reality.

As demonstrated especially in the preceding two film examples of *Unter dir die Stadt* and *Gespenster*, the medium of photography is used not only to portray death as such but also to portray the dead as *dead*—that is, embalmed in the photograph. This form of representation is commonly employed in Berlin School films. From Angela Schanelec's *Mein langsames Leben* to Christian Petzold's *Wolfsburg* and Jan Krüger's *Unterwegs* and *Auf der Suche* (*Looking for Simon*, 2011), photography often mediates past lives in a way that would pose a challenge to film as a medium of presence. For instance, after resisting the impulse to show the death of Valerie's (Ursina Lardi) father *on-screen* in her film *Mein langsames Leben*, Schanelec ends her film with a penultimate close-up shot of a photograph of Valerie as a young girl with her father on a boat. The viewer sees Valerie's hands as she pins this photograph onto the wall. Simultaneously, Valerie's voice can be heard in voice-over narration: "He also wasn't there [at the funeral] anymore. I had the impression that he had been gone for a long time."[7] Invoking absence through his photographic presence, Valerie's father appears ghost-like in this old picture. The photographic medium offers an alternative to film here inasmuch as Schanelec forgoes both a conventional flashback as well as an image of the dying father in the hospital, who in an earlier scene remains blocked by a tempered glass door. As Schanelec asserts, "I don't think it's possible to film someone when one wants to say that that person is fatally ill. That doesn't work, it's a lie" (2001).[8] Schanelec's declaration clearly underscores not only the ethical dilemma associated with showing the dead in film but also the ontological dilemma associated with the limits of representation of cinema as a medium of, if not explicitly, liveness, then at least of an indispensable *liveliness*.

In this brief scene, film does not so much become the site of reenactment of the photograph as the frame and even condition of photography's deictic role. The film presents the photograph as the representation of the dead father. Framed not only by Valerie's hands (she literally opens them up to reveal the photograph she has just pinned on the wall) but also by her voice, she commands it to point and "speak"; she gives the photograph its name, as she states in voice-over narration, "This is (was) my father." In his essay "Fotografien sind wie Namen" (1995), Martin Seel posits that photographs are denotative rather than connotative; that is, indexicality is an effect but not necessarily a direct function of photography.[9] Only within the film's diegesis does the photograph of Valerie's father actually function as a photograph of Valerie's father. This is indeed a real photograph of a man and a young girl on a boat (perhaps it is an image of the filmmaker herself as a child with her father); however, its referential quality is limited to the context of the film. Put differently, the performative function of the embedded photograph is reduced to its assigned role in the film. Finally, Schanelec's move in *Mein langsames Leben* to show the father in the past, not only dead but even "phantomlike" in this black-and-white family photo (Bazin 2005, 14), instead of through a flashback, stresses the comprehensive pursuit of the authentic and the real of the filmic medium that this study suggests permeates many of the Berlin School films. Since a flashback would betray the effect of the temporal authenticity of film, the Berlin School films seem to alternatively portray events in the past, especially death, through the medium of photography.

Even in Petzold's more recent historical feature, *Phoenix* (2014), in which it is evident that the events of the film have occurred in the past, the film generally maintains its assertion of temporal authenticity. This is a film about a Jewish Holocaust survivor who returns to Berlin shortly after the war with a facial injury. Nelly (Nina Hoss) was shot in the head and presumed dead. This attempted execution by the Nazis shattered her facial skeleton, leaving her essentially without a face.[10] Indeed, for the first quarter of the film Nelly is masked in an orthopedic skull cast. In an effort to reconstruct her face, the clinic procures two photographs of Nelly, presumably from before the war and her deportation. She discovers these images one night in the office of the surgeon who performs her surgery. One reveals a group of women seated blithely in a row. Two of the women's faces are circled and penned over each of three others hovers a foreboding cross. The circled are the Nazis and the crossed are the deceased. In the same image over Nelly's likeness also hangs a faded cross, which bears empirical as well as metaphysical truth. She was shipped to Auschwitz, the horrendous byword for death, where she was ultimately shot in the head and left to die. While not physically dead, Nelly—the Nelly in the picture—is dead. Unrecognizable to friends, her husband, and even to herself, Nelly dejectedly declares to her friend Lene (Nina Kunzendorf): "I don't exist anymore" ("Mich gibt's nicht mehr"). In this same scene, Nelly recovers the two photographs pinched from the clinic and exclaims to her friend and savior Lena: "This is me!" ("Das bin ich!") This absent "I" in the picture is an utterly ambiguous subject, as she too has no face. In both photographs, the one of her and old friends and the other of her and her husband, Nelly's face is obscured by a curtain of hair. This drape of opacity—an exegetic blot—generates a blind spot that turns on the narrative question of the film: who was Nelly? These photographs appear only on two occasions; in a film about the desire to reenact the past, however, they are instrumental.

Incapable of conquering this blind spot and thus of reenacting the photographs on her own, that is, recovering her identity, Nelly seeks out her husband, Johnny (Ronald Zehrfeld). Although he does not recognize her as his deceased wife, she reminds him of her and he coerces her into a ruse of elaborate measures to swindle his wife's (indeed, her own) estate. All Nelly has to do is play the role of herself—become the woman pictured in the photographs. In a plot hauntingly reminiscent of Hitchcock's psychological thriller *Vertigo*, Johnny transforms Nelly into *his* (sublime) image of this former wife. In her desire to rediscover herself and also rekindle their love, Nelly (not unlike Judy in *Vertigo*) complacently collaborates in the planning of this elaborate performance. Yet this is not a case of mortification via sublimation, as Slavoj Žižek argued in the context of *Vertigo* in *Looking Awry* (1991). Nelly's reenactment of herself is not a photographic embalming. It does not lead to an inevitable death; instead, it gives her life. The film closes with a grand scene of denouement, when Nelly initiates her own powerful performance of her former self (the celebrated singer and stage performer) and sings the classic show tune "Speak Low" to a shocked audience of old acquaintances, including Johnny, which is confronted with the reality of her live presence.

The phantom objectivity of the photographs that must be both reckoned with and met with live performance in *Phoenix* is particularly remarkable and complex. As a victim of Nazism in a period when blindness and repression are, to borrow Avery Gordon's words in the context of sociological haunting, "the national pledge of allegiance" (2008, 207), Nelly is the living ghost that returns in order to remind us of the violence of the recent past. Whereas the photographs can do no more than serve as mere vestigial evidence of a life torn asunder by hate and violence and are ultimately incapable of approximating real life, Nelly's performance spectacle in the final scene glossed above, which I explore at length in chapter 5, steps in and summons memory and death into a vital state of evocation and confrontation. But what is perhaps most striking is the self-reflexive nature of the photographs that already contain a congealed mediatic truth—that the photographic image is simply not enough.

As a final example of the deployment of photography in Berlin School films, I turn (and chronologically return) to Christoph Hochhäusler's short film *Séance* (2009). This film was released as the final episode in a collection of short films under the title *Deutschland '09-13 Filme zur Lage der Nation* (Germany '09-13 Films on the State of the Nation, 2009). More of an essayistic, even poetic, exploration of the haunting power of photographic images as specters of a passed time and space, the film is manifestly influenced by the work of avant-garde German filmmakers Harun Farocki and Hartmut Bitomsky, who have also worked extensively with the effect of photography in film and the relationship between the two. As they are former instructors at the German Film and Television Academy (dffb) and important collaborators on a number of film projects, the tutelage of Farocki and Bitomsky, has been crucial to Berlin School filmmakers, and such influence is noted throughout this book. One of Farocki's most prominent films, *Bilder der Welt und Inschrift des Krieges* (*Images of the World and Inscription of War*, 1988), explores history and violence through, for example, ambiguous aerial photographs of Auschwitz taken by Allied powers during the Second World War. Hochhäusler's film likewise tells a story in a series of still images and objects. *Séance* shows photographs plucked from the archive of Germany's tumultuous past. Such images as the infamous shots of infinite piles of eyeglasses and shorn hair taken from the victims at Auschwitz are paired with benign images of a couple kissing and a woman sunbathing. This visual track is set to a dramatic musical soundtrack and voice-over narration that relates a futuristic tale, presented as history. The deep and aged voice of the actor Hans-Michael Rehberg solemnly tells the story of how the German people began a colony on the moon and were forced to forget about their homeland. Through this combination of photographs from the past and the tale of a fantastical future, *Séance* presents a powerful commentary on the current state of German nationalism and memory. Loosely based on Chris Marker's classic film *La Jetée* (1962) (stills from which are also shown as catalogued photographs in *Séance*), this film presents itself in the vein of a science-fiction fairy-tale comprising photographs.[11]

Even without live actors present in the film—save for a single diegetic hand that appears in one shot as it turns the pages of a large picture book of astronomy—it is still possible to make an argument for the contrasting juxtaposition of still photography and the mobile film image in *Séance*—even of film's reenactment of the photographic image. Perhaps such a distinction becomes ever more palpable in this film. As the camera moves over the archival still images in pans or scans across their surface, the very temporal and spatial frame of each photograph appears to shift and even becomes mobile. The dead begin to move. Further, editing uproots these photographs from their historical positioning and recasts them somewhat arbitrarily into a continuous relationship—a narrative of cause and effect. A story is not only retold but also told in a new way. The use of accelerated montage and the layering of shots of photographs that dissolve into one another at intermittent moments in the film imbue the still images with a sense of movement and elusiveness. This film is perhaps best described through Mulvey's writerly formulation of the differentiation of cinema and photography: "Like running water, fire or movement of trees in the wind, this elusiveness has been intrinsic to the cinema's fascination and its beauty. The insubstantial and irretrievable passing of the celluloid film image is in direct contrast to the way that photograph's stillness allows for the presence of time to emerge within the image" (2006, 66).

The photographs in the film begin to adopt precisely the qualities of cinema that Mulvey postulates in the citation above. The photographs as a sequence of still tableaux become *tableaux vivants* under the enlivening lens of film. The life with which the photographs are infused is that of the film itself. As such, the photographs exhibit cinematic qualities of mobility and ephemerality. That is not to say that the qualities of film and photography collapse; on the contrary, *Séance* underscores the differences between photography and film, the latter being a medium that gives life back to the dead—"fleshes it out," to cite Vivian Sobchack (2004, 146)—precisely through this layering of the two media. Photographs offer the possibility of visually presenting events in the past and persons now dead, while film animates the photographs into a story and even a performance. The reenactment of the photographs through cinema is directly addressed in the title of the film: this film is a séance—a haunting enlivening of the dead (photographs).

The pervasive presence of photography in the Berlin School films and its metonymical not to mention indexical kinship to death is striking. In all of the examples examined here, remediation juxtaposes photography and film in their enunciatory, ontological distinctiveness. Photography embalms and stills a past gaze, whereas film unfolds a moving and present event. Although this section has aimed to demonstrate that photography certainly has the capacity to motivate reenactment, contrary to Schneider, I argue that photography is not the site of theatrical performance (at least not in these films). Instead, it is film that bears out the possibility of live performance through reenactment of the (dead) people, objects, and events crystallized in the photographs. These Berlin School films seem to stress photography as more tangibly the medium of a kind of archival indexicality, which even in its ambiguity can merely document and point, as Susan Sontag also ascribed in *On Photography* (1977). In its ontological and operational distancing from photography and the photographic medium with which it has been traditionally classified, then, film gets a new lease on life and emerges more acutely as a theatrical and performance-based medium. Film performs: it intervenes, it moves, it fleshes out. In a sense, it lives. Film's liveness plays out further over its connection to the televisual medium of surveillance-camera footage in the following section. It is film's ontological and epistemological kinship with the medium of surveillance that accentuates its qualities as a medium capable of presenting a live event with live actors.

The Televisual Liveness of Surveillance-Camera Footage

All cinema is a form of surveillance. But cinema cosmeticizes the image—gives it depth, dynamism, resolution. Cinema sanitizes surveillance, like it sanitizes voyeurism; it renders the act of viewing effortless, harmless, and innocent. What happens, then, when the film viewer is reminded of film's ontological extractions? Uncanny, uneasy, unhinged: these are the registered reactions that mark the sensory apparatus unleashed by cracks in the cinematic aesthetic. No film provides such a cunning example of this as Michael Haneke's 2005 thriller *Caché (Hidden)*. In the establishing shot of the film a still image of the exterior of a residential city street endures a bit too long and unease promptly sets in and lingers for the entire length of the film. Of course, cinema's relationship with surveillance as more than just a legacy best left undisclosed predates Haneke's provocative unmasking. Yet new studies of cinema and surveillance continue to emerge, indicating that we still have much to learn on the subject. Chronologically, Sébastian Lefait's *Surveillance on the Screen* (2013), Garrett Stewart's *Closed Circuits* (2015), Catherine Zimmer's *Surveillance Cinema* (2015), and Martin Blumenthal-Barby's *Cinema and Surveillance* (2016) make up the recent scholarly turn to surveillance in cinema studies. A dense archive, all of these monographs ultimately carve out a path back to Thomas Y. Levin's 2002 ur-text "Rhetoric of the Temporal Index: Surveillant Narration and the Cinema of 'Real Time.'" Well-trodden as this path may be, I too join this ritual of return to Levin, whose brief study effectively formulates the conditions of surveillance video on the cinematic screen as a rhetoric for the live and the real that gestures toward television. The parameters of Levin's initial focus on 1990s Hollywood films, and a mere handful at that, have certainly been expanded in the recent literature. Yet beyond the pale of explicit film genres, the idiom of surveillance video in cinema still poses unaccountable not to mention fascinating questions. That surveillance video has the capacity to reelaborate and reinscribe cinema's live impulses is the argument I intend to earn here.

Following up on the relationship between film and photography in the Berlin School films and the machinations of remediation spent to liven up film, I now turn to surveillance-camera footage, commonly referred to as CCTV (close-circuit television). While Berlin School films do not employ surveillance-camera footage as frequently as they do photography, its insertion is a trademark quality in Christian Petzold's films, most prominently in his Ghost Trilogy. He himself has even suggested that "making films is always like surveillance."[12] Additionally, Benjamin Heisenberg's films *Schläfer* (*Sleepers*, 2005) and *Der Räuber* (*The Robber*, 2010) explicitly and narratively take up issues of surveillance. With a focus on Petzold's films *Die innere Sicherheit*, *Gespenster*, and *Yella*, as well as Heisenberg's *Der Räuber* and Christoph Hochhäusler's made-for-television film *Eine Minute Dunkel*, this section seeks to theorize how surveillance-camera footage forms a continuity of liveness in film. Distinct from photography in its closer mediatic kinship to film, surveillance-camera footage still expressly has a selfsame stake in the telos of death, or at the very least to the spectral that makes it a potential kinetic replacement for photography. Evangelos Tziallas cannily calls surveillance-camera footage "reality's uncanny" (quoted in Zimmer 2015, 85), Daniel Eschkötter's "phantom images" (2007). The haunting mark of slow speed and a two-dimensional configuration of space of surveillance-camera footage indisputably infect film with a spectral sense of reality.

Surveillance in cinema may speak for a whole range of cinematic techniques that do not as a matter of course imply the insertion of CCTV footage. Cinematography boasts an impressive repertoire of surveillant moves from illicit shot angles that artfully convey the impression of surveillance, such as, for instance, the archetypal bird's-eye view in the establishing shot of Francis Ford Coppola's *The Conversation* (1974) or its offshoot, Tony Scott's *Enemy of the State* (1998). For the sake of specificity, this study will narrow its scope to a reading of surveillance-camera footage images. Albeit often faked in cinema, the simulated low-resolution, low-pixel, low-frame-rate, grainy, black-and-white quality of surveillance-video images are identifiably distinctive. To this end, I encourage the reading of surveillance footage as an aesthetically and epistemologically different kind of (filmic) medium. Such a reading aims to recover and expand on Dietmar Kammerer's intuitive assertion at the close of his essay "Video Surveillance in Hollywood Movies" (2004) that "There is no simple cause-and-effect relationship between these two [surveillance and film texts]" (473). My argument follows that the complexity of surveillance-camera footage and its remediation in film extends over a confluence of ideological and phenomenological effects for which I will round up the usual suspects: Jean-Paul Sartre, Maurice Merleau-Ponty, and Michel Foucault. But first an attending to the question of medium is in order.

More than a decade ago, Levin averred that photographic indexicality in cinema had been replaced by surveillance footage. The latter, he wrote, is "an important new idiom of cinema's 'reality effect'" (2002, 592). The declared *new* cinematic idiom of reality, surveillance footage is distinct from photography in important ways. As a mobile medium, surveillance video is of course ontologically closer to film than photography. In terms of medium specificity, however, surveillance-video footage should not and cannot simply be synthesized into film montage. Its intermittent appearance marks a mediatic shift that demands the viewer's attention. This footage is more than just a formal additive to heighten suspense or diegetically set a scene, what Catherine Zimmer has convincingly referred to, riffing on Tom Gunning, as the "caught in the act" phenomenon of surveillance video (2015). Instead, a medium-driven inquiry urges us to take into account surveillance-camera footage's kinship to the televisual medium. The etymology of "close-circuit *television*" (CCTV) certainly invokes this gesture, if only nominally. Surveillance-camera footage's reel-to-reel phenomenon of temporal immediacy subtends its televisual quality—the impression of the immediacy of live, real-time broadcast. A number of scholars, including Levin, have drawn compelling comparisons between surveillance video and television, particularly (but not exclusively) reality television, *Big Brother* being the most notable example. Although television is seldom watched by a live audience (in a studio) anymore, and even live broadcasting has been relegated almost exclusively to the news and talk shows, it has retained its rhetorical marker of liveness that is instantiated through its pretense of directness. Philip Auslander calls this the "essence" of television, that is, its explicit capacity "to transmit events as they occur" (2008, 12). Mary Ann Doane makes a similar albeit reverse observation when she writes that "the 'liveness' of the televisual image ensures its adhesion to the referent just as the index adheres to its object" (2002, 208). Television's unsevered link to liveness by virtue of its ostensible instant stream is taken up by surveillance video's instantaneity and logic of directness. Taking due advantage of this network of liveness, the appropriation of surveillance video in film is, in Levin's words, the "appropriation of the rhetoric of 'live' televisual broadcast" (2002, 592).

The twice-framed photographs in the Berlin School films that render a cinematic transcendental off are thus displaced by surveillance video's extradiegetic quality—a medium self-contained within its own frame. Surveillance video images do not generate mise en abymes but rather stereoscopic occasions where two disparate images—surveillance and film—are not only inverted, as Lefait observes (2013, xvii), but also fill each other out, offer depth and expand parameters, in other words, become contiguous. The work of remediation in film in general and in the Berlin School films in particular is reflexive. Surveillance-camera footage employed in narrative film creates what Levin calls "a certain kind of intermedially-displaced cinematic reflexivity" (2002, 581). It forges an intrinsic relationship between the cinematic and the surveillance image. Whereas the juxtaposition of photography and film demonstrates a disconnect between two distinct forms of media, the use of surveillance-camera footage actually accentuates the liveness register of the film medium insofar as it converges two indexicalities into a continuous whole—the heightened temporality of surveillance and the spatiality of diegetic film. Media distinctions are maintained but not alienated. Thus, I take issue with the assertion presented by several contemporary scholars that surveillance video in the Berlin School films creates an effect of both distancing and poststructural emptiness. Eric Rentschler argues that the surveillance video images in the Berlin School films "lack affect" and "do not speak until people speak for them" (2013, 638). Carsten Strathausen's reading of the remediation of surveillance video in the Berlin School construes it as a process which "accentuates—rather than dissimulates—the gap between the diegetic and the extradiegetic world" (2013, 256). Such a semantic claim that these two media are ultimately incommensurable is not without value. However, it both dismisses the ontological similarities of surveillance and film and neglects the complex montage sequences of these media, which I intend to explore here further. In my reading of remediation in these films, surveillance actually powerfully sutures rather than accentuates the gap between the diegetic and the extradiegetic. If anything, an *inter*-diegetic world opens up; it is where the on and the off begin to converge. At such a convergence, film appropriates the effect of liveness transmitted by surveillance-camera footage—a liveness forged through its kinship to television.

The first film of Petzold's Ghost Trilogy, *Die innere Sicherheit*, was also one of the earlier most commercially successful of all the Berlin School films.[13] Most attribute the film's success to its subject matter, namely, the demise of fugitive Red Army Faction (a left-wing terrorist group in West Germany that was responsible for a number of political murders and bombings in the late 1970s) members and their teenage daughter. As Marco Abel elucidates in his interview with Petzold for *Cineaste* (2008b), the film was released when there was a renewed public debate about the RAF in Germany. From such a film the expectations for surveillance-video images are high. There are in fact three instances of the employment of surveillance footage in *Die innere Sicherheit*, the first of which I put to close scrutiny. This example of surveillance video consists of a single shot sutured into a scene as Klaus (Günther Maria Halmer), an old friend of the mother (Barbara Auer), arrives at a gas station to meet with the fugitive family and give them money so they can leave Europe. As he exits his car and removes a brief case from the trunk a young woman approaches him and asks for a ride. He refuses but seems to feel bad and gives her some money instead. As he hands her a few bills there is a cut to surveillance footage with a match on action from a different angle and closer up (see figure 1.2 and 1.3). This subtle and seemingly insignificant instance of editing radically effects the power of suture and continuity, insofar as two otherwise distinct moving images temporally and spatially coalesce to tell a story that could not be told otherwise. What just seconds prior appeared to be a simple gesture of goodwill in the standard film footage now appears clandestine and criminal through the lens of the surveillance footage. It raises the stakes of Zimmer's "caught in the act" to the very condition of the criminal act itself; it even has a performative function. No sooner is there a cut back to the standard film footage than several police cars rush on the scene and the police arrest them both. The film discloses neither the reason for this arrest nor its direct consequences. Klaus and the young woman simply disappear from the film. Lasting a matter of seconds, this brief surveillance shot thematically evinces the apparent pervasiveness of the police presence and surveillance in Germany, which provocatively echoes the zeitgeist of late-1970s West Germany during the so-called German Autumn (*Deutscher Herbst*, also represented in the omnibus 1978 film *Germany in Autumn*), when in 1977 the RAF kidnapping of a public official resulted in the transformation of West Germany into a police state.

Figure 1.2 and 1.3. Surveillance match on action in *Die innere Sicherheit*, 2000. © Schramm Film Koerner & Weber

Surveillance evokes the ideological dimension of film viewing that, as Thomas Elsaesser and Malte Hagener have formulated via Michel Foucault's theorization of the panopticon, is more concerned with "the fact of 'being seen'" than "with the active look" (2015, 117). Particularly in this scene in *Die innere Sicherheit*, surveillance becomes the locus of both the controlling mechanisms of the panoptic power of omnipresent surveillance and the subject-forming social mechanisms of docile bodies that reflexively self-discipline through the internalization of the gaze. In his *Discipline and Punish* (notably titled *Surveiller et punir* [*To Survey and to Punish*] in the original French), Foucault famously theorized not only the birth of the prison system but also its aligned beginnings with the nascence of modern surveillance. Surveillance was and continues to be key to the mechanisms of disciplinary power. Foucault writes: "[Surveillance] was also organized as a multiple, automatic, and anonymous power; for although surveillance rests on individuals, its functioning is that of a network of relations, from top to bottom, but also from bottom to top and laterally; this network 'holds' the whole together and traverses it in its entirety with effects of power that derive from one another: supervisors, perpetually supervised" ([1975] 1977, 176–77). The violently automatic and anonymous surveillant gaze in this scene of *Die innere Sicherheit*, which immediately incurs disciplinary intervention but whose provenance is never revealed forcefully cites the machinations of the disciplinary panoptic gaze illuminated by Foucault. Cinema's shift from a voyeuristic emphasis of "looking" to an objectifying "being seen" is an inversion with which the employment of surveillance images confronts the viewer.

Considered from a phenomenological angle, on the other hand, the surveillance shot in *Die innere Sicherheit* concomitantly evokes the register of Levin's "cinema of real time" (2002, 593), inasmuch as it conveys an immediacy of action. Its insertion offers a slice of temporal transparency that permeates the entire scene. The viewer has the impression not only of suspense—that *someone* is watching this scene—but furthermore that this scene is unfolding before the viewer's eyes. The intersection of surveillance and phenomenology generates a situation of direct experience of what Maurice Merleau-Ponty might call the "alien gaze," characterized not only as the stranger's gaze but also as the objectifying even disempowering gaze of an-other: "Usually man does not show his body, and, when he does, it is either nervously or with the intention to fascinate. He has the impression that the alien gaze which runs over his body is stealing it from him, or else, on the other hand, that the display of his body will deliver that person up to him . . . in so far as I have a body, I may be reduced to the status of the object beneath the gaze of another person" ([1945] 2002, 193).

The alien gaze is the powerful gaze whose provenance remains hidden. Such a formulation likewise fits to the surveillant gaze. Unaware of the origin of the surveillant gaze, the viewer is at once implicated in surreptitious surveying and becomes the object of this gaze herself, not dissimilar to the phenomenon described by Jean-Paul Sartre in his essay "The Look" in *Being and Nothingness* ([1943] 1977). Sartre's voyeur at the keyhole is in fact the one being watched—ashamedly "caught in the act" *of looking*. The affective invasiveness of surveillance-camera footage and its anonymous yet omniscient observer phenomenologically conjures its paranoid reciprocation—that is, if I am looking at someone, then someone (else) is probably looking at me. Reversibility's presentness of film viewing as an oscillating phenomenon that repeatedly loops back engenders an experience of lived time (and possibly space), as the embodied viewer, the sense-sharing body, comes to anticipate the response of an-other. A sense of liveness emerges from surveillance's intensification of this now-ness and here-ness, not dissimilar to performance's being-there and being-with, and in its wittingly reflexive presence imbues this entire scene of *Die innere Sicherheit* with a dimension of reality and immediacy. Surveillance thus gives film a new lease on life.

The relationship between film and surveillance thickens. Blending idioms and layering aesthetics, Petzold's 2005 film *Gespenster* explored in the earlier section about a mother desperately searching for her teenage daughter, who was kidnapped as a child, offers a striking sequence that sutures surveillance-camera footage with the film's own internal surveillant gaze. Exemplified in this sequence is Levin's assertion that *"surveillance has become the condition of the narration itself.* In other words, the locus of surveillance has thus shifted, imperceptibly but decidedly, away from the space of the story, to the very condition of the possibility of that story" (2002, 6, emphasis in original). In Levin's account, surveillance not only is an added feature of a film but also shapes the manner in which the film story is told. I take this one step further and propose that surveillance-camera footage also (re)shapes the manner in which the film is viewed. The sequence from *Gespenster* sutures surveillance footage with standard film footage to construct a congruity of images that not only narratively complement each other but also phenomenologically align. A germane opening, the bird's eye view from the window of the Marriott Hotel next to Berlin's Potsdamer Platz ideologically and geographically establishes this montage of seeing and being seen.[14] In this shot from the hotel room window atop the Potsdamer Platz Françoise (Marianne Basler) spies Nina (also played by Julia Hummer) and Toni (Sabine Timoteo) as they pass by on the street below. The bird's eye view from the perspective of Françoise indicates a potential diegetic bearer of the surveillant gaze. To follow is a series of various-angled medium shots of Nina sitting in a fitting room of the H&M clothing store in the shopping Arkaden in Berlin's Potsdamer Platz. In these images, she is shown as she extracts the tags from clothing, in what is evidently the disclosure of shoplifting. Structural and ideological anticipation is finally met with the proceeding set of surveillance video shots of Toni and then Nina swiftly moving toward the exit of the store with their stolen clothing. The whole sequence concludes with a return to film footage and classic shot-reverse-shot convention: in a medium close-up, Nina exits the store at an increasingly fast pace, followed by a medium shot of Françoise as she watches Nina start to run away. As Nina exits the store, Françoise reaches out to touch her shoulder from behind. Nina's paranoia, incited by the axiomatic internalization of the surveillant gaze in her anticipation of repercussion for her crime, is fleshed out in this set of shots. She appears to believe that Françoise works for H&M and that she has been caught shoplifting. This would at the very least explain her sudden impulse to run away and to then later confess her crime to her pursuer. Nina's paranoia is brought to extradiegetic form in this scene through the employment of surveillance video in the preceding shots. Its remediation permeates the film sequence with an inundating doom of the disciplinary gaze.

By no means randomly placed, the surveillance-camera footage in the middle of this sequence does not, however, directly invoke the authoritative and performative intervention it does in the scene examined from *Die innere Sicherheit*. In the earlier Petzold film, the surveillance shot immediately leads to police intervention—a literal case of "caught in the act." The surveillance-camera footage appears to have a direct operational function in this earlier film. In *Gespenster* the surveillance-camera footage is more indirect but remarkably Foucauldian in its function of the internalization of the gaze. Surveillance video shows Nina and Toni as they move to exit the store (in the midst of executing an actual crime, as opposed to the mere speculated crime scene in *Die innere Sicherheit*), but it belies its own ideological intention and does not lead to their apprehension by the police. Instead, when the standard-film-footage image returns with a close-up of the back of Nina's head at the store's exit, it is a point-of-view shot from the perspective of Françoise and not from the security guard positioned at the door of the store, who is visible in the surveillance footage. The work of montage creatively draws an association between these shots and positions Françoise as the agent of this surveillant gaze, both in the first shot from the upper-level hotel room window and in the penultimate shot of Nina leaving the store.

That the surveillant gaze has a possible provenance and that there is one recognizable agent of the gaze in this sequence of *Gespenster* is notably evocative. The film's employment of surveillance-camera footage as a function of both ideological and phenomenological evocation is richly and complexly developed in this sequence, whose composition not only engenders a cause-and-effect pattern but even generates a critical relationship of codependence of seeing and touching. Françoise's gaze transforms into a disembodied hand that reaches out and orients itself toward the object of her gaze. This scene in *Gespenster* and the materiality of the gaze are reminiscent of Merleau-Ponty's discussion of the reversibility of the visible and the tangible in *The Visible and the Invisible* ([1964] 1968). According to Merleau-Ponty, the flesh of the world binds the visible and the tangible into an "intercorporeal being" as a kind of perceptual mesh of communication and exchange (143). Invoking Merleau-Ponty's "flesh of the world" in the context of surveillance, Petzold draws the viewer in as part of this world— an altogether intersubjective dynamic of seeing, being seen, touching, and being touched. Therefore, the relationship of the shots in this sequence and the play on the gaze troubles a straightforward connection between the surveillance camera and state power as well as the anticipated distinction between the cold and objective gaze of the surveillance camera and the embodied gaze of Françoise, which albeit traumatically (she still grieves the loss of her daughter) also lovingly and full of hope reaches out for Nina. Petzold's film exerts a keen interest in how the play with the ideological dimension serves the function of highlighting the phenomenology of the image.

Shaping the way in which the viewer perceives film images and sequences, *Gespenster* manipulates the expected positioning and articulation of the gaze in this sequence. As a result, one function of the "reality effect" of this surveillance sequence is to wrest the viewer from the passivity typical of narrative cinema spectatorship. Realistic (re)presentation is distinctively less teleological than the direct cause-and-effect relationship present in much narrative cinema. Therefore, *Gespenster*'s complex use of surveillance-camera footage further underscores a confluence of the ideological and the phenomenological as it directs the viewer's experience of the film images to a perceptual here and now—the place of liveness, presence, and performance in all of its temporal and spatial excess. The surveillance video images in this sequence concretize both the paranoid and the ineluctably embodied perception of and for the omniscient presence of the alien gaze. My argument is that surveillance video in this film enfolds an experience of intersubjective time and space that yields the promise of being-there and being-with for the viewer. This heady promise of phenomenological presence and proximity is condensed in these films' ability to contrive a shared sense of space and especially time, in effect, a sense of liveness that engages, excites, and enthralls.

The multiplicities and complexities of surveillance video and its affects and effects in the Berlin School films certainly expand beyond Petzold's oeuvre. Another trilogy of death forms the context for Christoph Hochhäusler's film *Eine Minute Dunkel*. Part of *Dreileben (Three Lives)*, a series of intersecting stories in three films respectively directed by three different filmmakers (Christian Petzold, Dominik Graf, and Christoph Hochhäusler), *Eine Minute Dunkel* portrays one perspective and story of a serial murder set in a picturesque fictional small town in the province of Thuringia, in east central Germany. The first installment of the trilogy, *Etwas besseres als den Tod (It Beats Being Dead*, 2011) by Petzold also employs surveillance video images; Hochhäusler's final installment, however, is duly a film grounded on the question of surveillance video's register of real-time production and its attendant injunction of liveness. The title of the film, *Eine Minute Dunkel*, promptly evokes what is to be revealed as the surveillance video's blind spot, the ultimate failure of its visual field. In all three films, at least one young woman has been murdered and the suspect is at large. Ostensibly, "the minute of darkness" indicates the structural black screen in a prerecorded surveillance-footage video that the detective charged with solving the murder investigation repeatedly and frantically watches in a desperate search for clues.

Thus begins the film. The actual murder has not been caught on video surveillance, as the critical camera feed malfunctioned just seconds prior. This footage reveals the moments leading up to the young woman's murder but in medias res cuts to black. Formal darkness becomes epistemological here; it is not only the tired form of the utter lack of knowledge but also sets up the question of surveillance as a reliable visual field in the first place.

Casting a shadow of doubt on the guilt of the murder suspect, the blot of this video surveillance, as prerecorded videotape footage with an internal viewer, fails to reveal sufficient evidence of the crime that would convict the suspect. Incited by this surveillance blind spot, the detective must reexamine the murder case. While this archival instance of surveillance blindness opens the film, it is ultimately eclipsed by an exquisitely textured and detailed surveillance-camera sequence at the close of the film. In this later instance, there is no visible internal viewer and the actions—depicted in the here and now—align with the film diegesis. It is noteworthy that these surveillance-video images are distinct from the previous, which is watched repetitively by the detective through a continuous loop of play-pause-rewind and is clearly a piece of prerecorded evidence. In the later sequence, which I will examine in further detail, there is a sense of a present and spontaneous unfolding of events via the suturing of surveillance-video footage and standard film footage in an intricately complex montage. This configuration of images almost undeniably exposes the suspect as guilty of yet another (attempted) murder. As an occasion of narrative veracity, the presence of what appears to be a live-feed broadcast—that is, real-time footage of a murder—is effectively accented as a more reliable narrative source that ultimately trumps the validity of the previously shown prerecorded surveillance-camera footage.

This final sequence has a duration of roughly two and half minutes and combines a diverse range of shots. It begins with an altogether voyeuristic scene—an ominous counting of filmic snapshots of female passersby. "Eins (one). . . . (cut). Zwei (two). . . . (cut). Drei (three). . . . (cut)." The shots hail from the point of view of someone (there is no reverse shot) surreptitiously gazing out through a street-front window. It can be assumed (based on the extradiegetic voice that accompanies these shots) that this is the perspective of the escaped murder suspect, Molesch (Stefan Kurt), whom the film has been tracking. A ponderous male voice sadistically counts the women, from one to seven. Once seven is reached the scene changes and the woman (who may be recognized as Ana from her more central role in Petzold's earlier installment of the trilogy) identified as number seven—apparently, his new target—is pursued by the suspect. Jarring extradiegetic music punctures the scene in stutters, as sound itself fades in and out—not uncommon for Hochhäusler's films (Miller 2012, 56). Suspecting that she is being pursued, the young woman quickens her pace. The scene develops into a full-blown chase scene. There is an auguring cut to a surveillance video image of a secluded road in a menacingly high angle shot. The young woman dashes in and out of the frame and is followed by her pursuer, who keeps a steady pace behind. A cut back to the diegetic film footage reveals the already-assumed identity of the pursuer—the fugitive murder suspect—from behind brandishing a large kitchen knife. Horror film mode sets in. This shot is then followed by a medium-long frontal shot of the suspect. Again, there is a cut to surveillance video from the same direction and angle as the previous one. Real-time mode and spatial distension in this footage are underscored by the sheer continuity of the shots and the precision of the consecution and coordination of time and action. The figures are still moving within the same larger surveillance-footage frame in this second shot. In two other surveillance-footage shots, this time from different angles, the same young woman can be seen running away. There is a final shot of surveillance-camera footage at the end of this sequence—and subsequently the end of the film—that appears to be broadcast on a television monitor (in the film). It is framed in black and the image is slightly askance. Present on this image in the top right-hand corner are the date and time. Although the screen goes black mid-action, the viewer still glimpses the murder suspect raising the knife to stab his new victim in a final act. The image presents an all-too-generic final trope of slasher horror, an almost overwrought citation of the horror cliffhanger. It may be possible to also view this last shot as a recorded (past) image of the crime, as it appears physically internal to the diegetic film frame. Yet its consecutive place (temporally and spatially) within this longer pursuit scene seems to indicate instead that this footage is live-feed and that no security guard appears to be watching. If someone had been watching the footage, we can assume that this person would have intervened and prevented the murder. Instead, the critical connection between what is presented through the standard diegetic film footage and the surveillance-camera footage relies on temporality and demonstrates a match on action. This produces a crucial omniscient viewing experience that not only troubles typical film-viewing practices but also underscores the film's potentiality to show events in real time.

An even more complex surveillance sequence than in *Gespenster*, this sequence in *Eine Minute Dunkel* effectively merges what Levin refers to as "classically omniscient narration" and "*a diegeticized surveillant omniscience*" to create "a spectacle of real-time CCTV tracking" (2002, 589, emphasis in original). The interweaving and temporal and spatial agreement of several sequential surveillance shots and the diegetic image yield a pervasive sense of liveness enacted through a real-time effect in this sequence. Surveillance's ontological affinity to television as a live medium finds contextual frame in the case of this film, which was indeed originally designed as a television broadcast. The fact that the trilogy *Dreileben* was made for television offers an additional frame to the examination of surveillance and liveness in Hochhäusler's film. The trilogy, of which

Hochhäusler's *Eine Minute Dunkel* was the last installment, was a television-film experiment supported by ARD Broadcasting Service that was featured one Monday evening (August 29, 2011) on the German national channel *Das Erste*. The experiment was a huge success and offered a challenge to the claim of many critics that television had been rendered artistically obsolete.[15]

As a final example of the operative presence of surveillance-camera footage in the Berlin School films, Benjamin Heisenberg's film *Der Räuber* bears scrutiny. Based on the true story of the Austrian bank robber and marathon runner Johann Kastenberger (fictional name: Johann Rettenberger), this crime-action film provides yet another example of the Berlin School's complex employment of surveillance montage. Perhaps more directly than all of the other examples, this film explicitly mobilizes the relationship between surveillance video and live television broadcast. Midway through the film there is a dynamic montage sequence of varied audiovisual media. While this film about a bank robber deploys only one sequence with surveillance-camera footage, Heisenberg has called this the most important sequence in the film. It begins in a standard diegetic mode with Johann (Andreas Lust) in a sport shoe store testing running shoes on a treadmill. Positioned in front of the machine is a television screen that monitors the steps of the runner. The black-and-green screen visually resembles an x-ray machine, as it shows the spectral-like disembodied feet of Johann on the running surface. Gradually swelling to fill the frame, the ghostly shoes confront the viewer directly. As the humming of the running machine continues in the background, there is a cut to surveillance-camera footage of a man (also Johann) in a Ronald Reagan mask entering what appears to be a bank with a shotgun. Gradually, the background sound transitions to a suspenseful extradiegetic drum beat. The surveillance-camera footage consists of seven different shots from various positions. Notwithstanding its black-and-white and high-angled compressed images, the surveillance-camera footage in *Der Räuber* appears to have a higher pixel count than the other examples considered in this section. While still distinctly surveillance video, the sharper images in this latter film aesthetically mimic standard diegetic film images more closely. Aesthetically and structurally, the sophisticated composition of these shots appears to close the gap between the different media further.

The series of surveillance images of the bank robbery is followed by the live news footage of a marathon in Vienna in which not only the fictional Johann Rettenberger but also the real "flesh and blood" actor Andreas Lust participate. As Heisenberg explains in the DVD voice-over commentary, Lust actually runs the last leg of a marathon in Vienna for the film. The organizers were aware of the actor's presence and the film crew, but the bystanders and spectators of the race were not aware that Lust was not a "real" participant in the marathon. Despite the fact that the film employs stock television footage of the race acquired from

ORF Austrian News, the shots of the marathon are meant to appear live (and certainly were when they were first broadcast on television) through their lower image quality, as the footage would have been compressed to facilitate quick and easy data transfer—for a live broadcast. Further, the original "Live ORF 1" logo is present in all the shots of the race, including those with Lust. That television has an imperative to temporal liveness has been established in this section. This final example representationally articulates Auslander's claim that "television's intimacy was seen as a function of its immediacy—the close proximity of viewer to the event that it enables" (2008, 16). In the latter part of this sequence in *Der Räuber*, the live television shots of the marathon are cut with film footage of the same race. Suturing standard film footage with surveillance-camera footage and television footage into a single sequence underscores their mediatic and onto-logical resemblance. Indeed, the entire sequence mimics a documentary mode in its true-to-life design. *Der Räuber* is infused with a sense of real time here by virtue of film's pronounced relationship to surveillance and its added dimension of televisual liveness that directly infuses the transmedial capaciousness of this sequence. Yet media do not ontologically converge in this and other instances considered in this chapter. Creative remediation rather fleshes out cinema's aesthetic and structural multiplicities and complexities.

The aesthetic ghostliness of surveillance-camera footage, whose typically black-and-white and grainy image is already phenomenologically and ideologically linked to voyeurism and surreptitious looking, becomes an ideal medium for the representation of transgression—death and even murder—in film. Heightening the phenomenological suspense of the film, surveillance-camera footage adds a startling register of eerie reality. What is more, its ontological proximity to the live medium of television conveys an effect of lived time and space. It is a citation of reality and real time that undergirds not only the authenticity but also the presence of the action in the film. In all five of the films examined in this section, surveillance-camera footage and its live qualities are utilized by narrative cinema as a means of playing with realistic representation and experience. In these elaborate mediations of diverse audiovisual forms of surveillance video and diegetic film, narrative cinema is reconstituted as live experience through a heightened sense of the here and now. Liveness is generated through the viewer's perception of surveillance video, whose rich phenomenological, ideological, and ontological properties have been effectively co-opted and executed by these filmmakers.

In this twin study of both photography and surveillance video, and their respective relationships to film, I propose that the Berlin School films offer a possible response to Schneider's insightful query about remediation: "How can we account not only for the way differing media cite and incite each other but for the ways that the meaning of one form *takes place* in the response of another" (2011, 168, emphasis in original)? While I resist purist views of media, as different media invariably, and certainly ever increasingly, intersect and flow into one another, I also do not hold that the Berlin School films propound what Rosalind E. Krauss has famously referred to as the post-medium condition (2000). This chapter has been chiefly concerned with the complex ways in which different media influence and shape each other in their interaction and remediation while still maintaining their mediatic specificities. Such relationships and interplays of various media can and do provide productive frameworks within which to examine the possibilities and qualities of the film medium in its myriad articulations. Here I draw out film's potential to an unexpected experience of liveness.

Brought to life through creative strategies of overlaying and suturing disparate media, the effects of liveness in these films rely on film's capacity to simulate sensations of the here and now. As observed in the first section, this capacity lies in film's inherent relationship to motion and can be emphasized through its contrast to the still medium of photography. But without simply restating clichéd binaries of still versus mobile media, I investigate film's ability to bring photographs to life through performance. In the second section of this chapter, I demonstrate in what way the Berlin School's trend of deploying of surveillance-video images serves to ideologically and phenomenologically link film to live media, specifically to the televisual medium. Television's tradition of live broadcast in front of a live studio audience has maintained its resonance as a characteristic of this medium, even if it is no longer in practice. (Consider for instance the inclusion of laugh tracks applied to sitcoms—vestiges of the live audience preserved for the viewer's imaginary.) The Berlin School's insertion of surveillance-camera footage into and next to the diegesis structures the film (or at least parts of the film) around a compelling synchronicity of the present time and the film time. Such synchronicity suffuses a form and a sense of liveness. This suffusion of liveness in mediated forms is comparable to a reverse process of mediatization commonly adopted in live performance. It represents the anticipated reaction to our overall mediatized culture. It nostalgically and temporarily fills the voids left by mediatization and hypermediality in our everyday—bringing us back, as it were, to the experience of contingency, proximity, and relationality of being-there and being-with, of presence and intercorporeality. Liveness is the intangible element that makes bodies tangible and real for the viewer, places them within our field of perception, coordinates points of tension and connection.

Notes

1. The ontology of liveness as one of loss may also be traced further back to the advent of writing technology and its marked loss of the oral tradition. This particular study focuses more specifically on the conceptualization of liveness and loss within the field of performance studies and its common dichotomy of liveness and mediation.

2. I endeavor to distinguish between "mediation" and "mediatization" (used by Auslander [2008]), the latter being a term used to describe the more general trends toward and privileging of mediated experience and culture.

3. In a 2008 production of *Hamlet* by Thomas Ostermeier, which continues to be reprised, at the Schaubühne in Berlin, Hamlet's father appears as a bloody image on a screen. Although the spectators in the audience see that this is the mediated image of an actor standing behind the transparent screen and being filmed, it is clear that the larger-than-life mediated image is meant to yield a certain ghostliness of presence and nonpresence as well.

4. Christian Petzold's film *Gespenster* (2005) is one important exception to this case, which I will also consider in this section.

5. I am indebted to an anonymous reader for the excellent translation of this phrase into English.

6. There is evidence in the film that Françoise has pursued other young women in the belief that they could also be her long-lost daughter. In fact, this is precisely what brings Pierre to Berlin in the opening scene. Although the details are unclear, it seems that Françoise has been treated in a clinic after falling victim to assault while approaching a young woman with her story, and Pierre must come and collect her.

7. "Er war auch nicht da. Ich hatte den Eindruck, dass er schon lange weg war."

8. "Ich denke man kann jemand nicht fotografieren [with this verb she implicitly means to film; though, she seems to possibly equate the two], wenn man erzählen will, daß er todkrank ist. Das geht einfach nicht, das ist eine Lüge."

9. I am indebted to Gertrud Koch for pointing out this more nuanced reading of this scene in *Mein langsames Leben*, as well as for her suggestion to consider Seel's article in connection with this reading.

10. For more on *Phoenix*, see chapter 5 and Landry (2017).

11. It may be noted Vivian Sobchack refers explicitly to the film *La Jetée* in her book *Carnal Thoughts* (2004) as an example of how photographic images can be animated by film.

12. Incidentally, one of the few films by Petzold's that does not contain surveillance-camera footage is *Barbara* (2012), about a woman in the former GDR who is constantly under surveillance by the *Stasi*. In the context of this film, Petzold stated in an interview that he "never wanted to see Barbara through the eyes of the state" (D. Lim 2012).

13. According to the German Wikipedia page for the film, *Die innere Sicherheit* pulled in 120,000 cinema viewers; other sources, suggest this number is closer to 200,000. It also won the Federal Film Prize in Gold for Best Feature in 2001. Comparably, on average the Berlin School films have 5,000 to 10,000 cinema viewers (Suchsland 2005). Even Petzold's later celebrated film *Yella* drew in a mere 77,000 viewers. Only two other Berlin School films have surpassed *Die innere Sicherheit* in terms of viewer numbers: Maren Ade's *Alle Anderen* (2009) with 190,000, and *Barbara* (2012) with more than 300,000 viewers in Germany alone.

14. An important topographical location in the new Berlin Republic, the Potsdamer Platz has a loaded history. Andrew J. Webber called it the new agora for Berlin, insofar as it "is one that also flourished in the reality and mythology of the Weimar years, was struck, apparently fatally, by history, and has been resurrected at the millennium." (2011, 72). At present, it is considered a swank and touristy landmark for eating, shopping, and cinema-going.

15. The trilogy was celebrated by critics and journalists as the "Hochform des Fernsehens" ("high form of television"). (See Haupt 2011.)

2 Theatricality Bleeds, the Presence of Dance

IN HER ARTICLE "Workshopping for Ideas: Jacques Rivette's *Out 1: Noli Me Tangere*," Laura Marks makes the following curious remark: "Like most cinephiles, I abhor the theater. The incantatory treatment of presence, and the performers' straining to be raw and in the moment, embarrass me. My role as an audience member to witness and complete the performance makes me cringe" (2016, 1). She follows up, however, arguing for the possibility of presence, and proposes that a film about theater might offer a "middle ground on which to work out these prejudices" (ibid.). While I personally disagree with Marks's distaste for the theater, as I am an equal admirer of both cinema and theater, her aim of reconciling the two aligns all too well with the ambition of this book, and this chapter in particular.

Presence, dance, theatricality: these make up the bleeding nexus that will drive this chapter's pursuit of performance in the Berlin School. First of all, speaking of presence in film, much as in the previous chapter's exploration of liveness, demands a carefully and critically laid out point of departure. As in the preceding chapter, we must begin by asking if it is even possible to speak of "presence" when referring to film. For what exactly is "mediated presence"? Is there such a thing? It is important to note at this early point that presence can develop from and ultimately adopt different forms. As Hans Ulrich Gumbrecht explains in the brief "User's Manual" that opens his influential book *Production of Presence* (2004), the "'production of presence' points to all kinds of events and processes in which the impact that 'present' objects have on human bodies is being initiated or intensified" (xiii). Such notions of the intensification and the possibility for presence to resonate from "all kinds of events" are crucial to understanding the creation of presence in the Berlin School films to be investigated in this chapter. Accordingly, if film as a mediated form presents a challenge to conventional productions of presence, which generally entail a certain degree of liveness, and temporal and spatial immediacy, then it also can upset these parameters.

While she is an unlikely proponent of the production of presence in film, the performance and theater scholar Erika Fischer-Lichte's conceptualization of presence as the force which "brings forth humans as that which they always already are: embodied minds" ([2004] 2008, 100), is germane to this inquiry. Although Fischer-Lichte claims that "real human bodies, objects, or landscapes actually remain absent anywhere on the movie, television, or computer screen" (ibid.), she does concede that electronic and digital media have the power to create "presence effects." Such effects, she claims, "create the *impression* of presentness without actually bringing forth these bodies or objects as present" (ibid., emphasis in original). In what some have called a culture of "diminishing experience of 'presence' within a simulated environment" (Kaye and Giannachi 2011, 90), the present-day inflow of mediatization also, curiously, makes concerted efforts to recover or re-create live presence through simulation. That is, the more mediatized and digitalized our world becomes, the more we seek out compensation for the loss of liveness and presence. Echoing the twin logic of remediation that proceeds from the idea that the more mediatized we become, the more we seek to supplant this mediatization and utilize it to erase itself. As advanced by Jay David Bolter and Richard Grusin (2000), the simulation of live presence is the paradoxical goal of modern technology. Most evident examples of this are the touch screens and voice-activated devices of our smartphones, tablets, and home entertainment systems. These developments, I suggest, have also had significant impacts on film—how it is made and how it is viewed. Indeed, we cannot speak of new media (digital film included) without engaging the topic of gaming. Not dissimilar to the preceding chapter's examination of surveillance-camera footage, one could make the argument that recent film also has been influenced by virtual reality video and online games. Likewise, human-computer interaction (HCI) designs and haptic interfaces have ushered in new and highly interactive modes of technology that leave indelible marks on how film is made and received in the present age. Direct responses to this have been film experiments, such as the interactive Google-sponsored film and experimental music video 3 *Dreams of Black* (2011) by Chris Milk, which candidly take to task the challenge of the interactivity of film viewing, or any number of immersive video installation works, including David Aitkin's six-channel video installation THE SOURCE, which launched at the 2014 Sundance Film Festival. Three-dimensional filmmaking subsequently has grown in popularity, from action flicks to slow-paced dramas. A host of scholars have likewise turned their attention to the relationship between film and gaming. Some draw a clear distinction between the two, while others, such as Adam Lowenstein in his study *Dreaming in Cinema* (2015), are eager to chart their intersections.

 The paradox of the swelling proclivity for liveness or presence within mediatization finds its foil in the increasing mediatization of/in live performance. Approaching this query from another angle, then, theater provides a reverse and well-established (certainly since the days of Erwin Piscator's documentary theater) example of how live (theater) performance regularly employs film and recording techniques to add a dimension of mediation, and in some cases a sense of "reality," to its performance. In theater, mediation may serve to create two different but not mutually exclusive effects. On the one hand, the presence and liveness of theater may be disrupted by mediation; on the other hand, the presence of film and other forms of mediation may actually be underscored. The general dominance of media in cultural production has not completely prevailed over theater, as Theodor W. Adorno and Max Horkheimer had rather pessimistically predicted ([1987] 2002, 99–100); it has in fact been put to creative and productive use in the theater space. There are many such examples. Even Christian Petzold's own theater debut, an adaptation of Arthur Schnitzler's tragic play *Der einsame Weg* (*The Lonely Path*, 2009), offers a compelling illustration of this. Apparently unwilling to completely sever himself from the cinematic medium, or simply intent on asserting the overlap of cinema and theater, Petzold, together with the stage designer Henrik Ahr, designed a mise-en-scène that resembled an inverted film projection, literally a theater set-cum-camera obscura (see figure 2.1). It consisted of four slanted intersecting planes to create a perspectival view. This ramp-like stage was then set against a large screen on which real-time footage of a night scene in front of a Berlin Hospital (*Vivantes Klinikum am Urban*) was projected (see Slevogt 2009). Such a display of mixed media, or remediation—in this case, a direct citation of what Philip Auslander refers to as "the representation of one medium in another" (2008, 6)—is common practice in theater and performance spaces. Auslander argues that "almost all live performances now incorporate the technology of reproduction, at the very least in the use of electric amplification, and sometimes to the point where [live productions] are hardly live at all" (158). Petzold's application of real (the projection screen) and symbolic (the stage itself as a constructed film projection) remediation in his play presents just one case in many wherein a live event self-reflexively becomes more mediated. If live performance such as theater can and has quite cogently adopted elements of mediation, such as film and prerecorded music, then this chapter explores matters from the opposite angle, namely, how the ephemera of presence can also permeate mediated performance, such as film. Tracking this phenomenon as a cultural zeitgeist, Claudia Breger makes a convincing claim for the turn to presence in contemporary (especially German) visual media, not only in theater but also in film and literature (2012). Returning, then, to film, I call for a reading of film and its increased presence not through its relationship to other media, as I explored in the preceding chapter, but by way of its recovery of its legacy of theater and theatricality through the presence of dance.

Dovetailing with chapter 1's focus on the Berlin School cinema's effects of liveness through techniques of layering and juxtaposing of film with photography and surveillance-camera footage, this chapter will demonstrate how the Berlin School cinema develops compelling effects of both temporal and spatial

Figure 2.1. The theater stage as camera obscura in *Der einsame Weg*, 2009. © Iko Freese / drama-berlin.de

presence, or what Breger has referred to as "an aesthetics of presence" (2012, 253). This is made possible through its rich employment of the theatricality of dance, which as I suggest further emphasizes cinema's close relationship to the tradition of spectacle and absorptive attraction. In the films of the Berlin School, the setting of the dance floor, in all of its makeshift incarnations from abandoned clubs to poolsides and cluttered domestic interiors, becomes an important stage for the playful display of bodies and their movements.

Berlin School as a Cinema of Theatrical Spectacle

To speak of the pervasive presence of dance in the Berlin School seems like a contradiction in terms, as it implies a charge of excess and kinetics that directly goes against the heretofore widely received aesthetics of the Berlin School as slow and minimalistic. These films are frequently analyzed under the banner of "slow cinema," in which, as Karl Schoonover has indicated, the only excess appears to be that of time passed and time wasted (2012). Certainly, initial scholarship on the Berlin School has emphasized this direction. Characterized as slow-paced, phlegmatic, and devoted to a minimalist "aesthetics of reduction,"[1] this cinema ostensibly bears all the traditionally off-putting fixtures of the art film, what Steven Shaviro decried as "contemplative cinema" (2010, citing Tuttle, 177). Within such an aesthetic regime, dance spectacles seem oddly out of place. I do not disagree that many of the Berlin School films adhere to qualities of slow cinema, with its conventions of open-image aesthetics (long takes and austere editing practices), which emphasizes the role of mise-en-scène over editing and with it the possibilities of the diegetic space and characters' relationship to this space. There arises, however, a tendency to brush over the many other moments in these films that seem to go in disparate directions. Of the twenty-five films examined throughout this book, roughly half have dance scenes.[2] Consider the lengthy dance scene in Angela Schanelec's *Mein langsames Leben* (*Passing Summer*, 2001). This scene features the thirtysomething protagonist, Valerie (Ursina Lardl), and her brother (Devid Striesow) as they bounce around in an almost moshing style to a dance-mix hit in a virtually empty dance club. Their movements are free and clearly unchoreographed as they spontaneously disappear from and reappear in the frame. Faithful to Schanelec's style, their dancing is captured in one static long shot that lasts nearly two and a half minutes. According to Schanelec, this is her way of making movement visible, forcing the viewer to follow the bodies on-screen directly and not by way of the mobile camera (Schanelec and Vorschneider 2012, 417). Yet this outburst of movement "made visible" is also what makes this scene so striking. It offers an intense contrast to the film's overall lethargic flow and pace—its "slowness"— immediately invoked through its suggestive title (in the German), literally translated as "my slow life." The scene thus dramatically diverts from the film's overall temperamental pacing. The 1999 hit single "Genzora" by the Maltese indie-rock band the Beangrowers provides the musical track. A typical late-nineties rock song, it sustains a dynamic change during the chorus. The two dancers automatically adjust their movements to the altering pace of the music, from very fast agitation to slow rocking and back again. Further, the static nature of the shot and the lack of a reverse shot until the very end of the scene suggest a spectacle and staging that are primarily meant for the sake of the film viewer. But this dance scene does not yield visual pleasure for the viewer so much as it does perplexity. With its palpable air of exhibitionism, the directness and unpredictability of the spectacle force the viewer into a position of unease.

Such troubling and out-of-sync dance scenes commonly turn up in the films of the Berlin School. The argument I pursue in this chapter thus moves to the following beat: these dance scenes present theatrical intervals of spectacle of unbounded movement, exhibitionism, and heightened bodily presence. The dancing bodies of the Berlin School are akin to what Elena del Río would call "shock waves" in the films that elude mimesis and even narrative (2012, 10). What follows is an examination of six of these dance scenes and their performance as souvenirs of the spectacle of early cinema. The scenes considered in this chapter are taken from Valeska Grisebach's feature films *Mein Stern* (*Be My Star*, 2001) and *Sehnsucht* (*Longing*, 2006), Angela Schanelec's *Plätze in Städten* (*Places in Cities*, 1998) and her previously cited *Mein langsames Leben*, Maren Ade's *Alle*

Anderen (*Everyone Else*, 2009), and Jan Krüger's *Unterwegs* (*On the Road*, 2004).[3] By examining the dance scenes in these films, I seek to shed light on alternative and even unexpected dimensions and influences of the Berlin School that connect this cinema quite convincingly to traditions of cinematic spectacle and theatricality.

The Berlin School in fact has an explicitly practical connection to theater that is frequently sidestepped in the scholarship about the movement. Berlin theater and film are quite notably and importantly intertwined. Petzold's brief foray into theater with *Der einsame Weg* provides one example. Angela Schanelec worked extensively in theater as a director, writer, and actor, before turning to filmmaking. Further, although a number of Berlin School films, especially the earlier 1990s films, use nonprofessional actors "who," as Marco Abel declared, "appear to be chosen for who they 'are' rather than for whom they could be" (2008b, 5), just as many, if not more, Berlin School actors come from the theater. Actors such as Corinna Harfouch and Maren Eggert are part of the ensemble at the Deutsches Theater (Berlin); Nina Hoss, Lars Eidinger, Judith Engel, Mark Waschke, Ursina Lardl, and Angela Winkler are at the Schaubühne (Berlin); and Birgit Minichmayr, Katrin Angerer, and Sandra Hüller were at the Volksbühne (Berlin), to name just a few. In a 2017 interview podcast with West German Radio (WDR 3), filmmaker Maren Ade directly called for more collaboration between Germany's distinctly rich theater scene and its national film scene. According to Ade, Germany might not have the film culture and tradition of its European counterparts such as France and Italy, but its theater culture is unparalleled. The celebrated theater tradition in Germany (especially in Berlin) offers an important context within which to consider German cinema movements.[4] Acting style in the Berlin School films has been shaped by Brechtian acting aesthetics; a number of prominent actors (Lars Eidinger, Corinna Harfouch, Nina Hoss, Devid Striesow, and Mark Waschke) received training from the Ernst Busch Academy of Dramatic Art, which is celebrated for its Brechtian influence and legacy. Indeed, acting in the Berlin School relies heavily on theatrical gesture, albeit subtle. To say that these films are altogether theatrical would be an overstatement; there is a compelling charge of theatrical and gestural exhibition in a number of Berlin School films, which bids closer attention, however.

At the 2012 German Studies conference, during a panel on the Berlin School, Eric Rentschler offered the rather bold suggestion that this cinema takes us back to non-narrative moments of the "cinema of attractions."[5] Similarly, Sabine Nessel claimed that the Berlin School films seem to be less interested in cinema as a storytelling medium than as a medium of kinetic exhibition and gesture. Nessel pursues this possibility with the argument that "the dialogue with film of the early cinema of attractions opens up our perception to forms that do not immediately attribute to narration, but rather, that yield event-driven operations like showing (pointing), performing, presenting" (2009a, 106).⁶ Historically, the cinema of spectacle and exhibitionism, of course, did not disappear into obsolescence with the growing dominance of narrative cinema. Instead, as Tom Gunning observes in his now legendary piece on early cinema "The Cinema of Attractions," it "[went] underground, both into certain avant-garde practices and as a component of narrative films, more evident in some genres (such as the musical) than in others" (2006, 382). While neither Rentschler nor Nessel cited the Berlin School's numerous dance scenes as possible exemplary fragments of this founding cinematic paradigm, clearly these scenes render precisely such anachronistic bursts of what Gunning has famously referred to as the "cinema of attractions," or what Miriam Bratu Hansen called an "excess of appeals" in her study on cinema and the public sphere, "Early Cinema, Late Cinema: Transformations of the Public Sphere" (1995, 138).

I propose here and in later parts a brief return to film's "historical turn" and its enthusiastic preoccupations with the materialist film tradition, from Béla Balázs to Walter Benjamin and Siegfried Kracauer, which underpinned film's ontological concern for the shocks and agitated rhythms of the body brought on by modernity. Early cinema proffered, in Hansen's words, "a particular aesthetics of display, of showmanship, defined by the goal of assaulting the viewers with sensational, supernatural, scientific, sentimental, or otherwise stimulating sights, as opposed to simply enveloping them into the illusion of a fictional narrative" (137). These could be characterized as moments of direct engagement that possessed an elliptical quality of excess often at odds with the narrative. But rather than suggesting that the Berlin School films follow such a course and thus present themselves essentially as throwbacks to the preclassical and prenarrative cinema that Gunning and Hansen notably treat, I propose a view of the Berlin School as a postclassical cinema that combines the spectacle-based "cinema of attractions" with unique narrative structures. That is, contrary to Hansen's view that there is a clear trajectory from preclassical to postclassical cinema, divided simply chronologically by classical narrative cinema's "historical interlude" (149), postclassical cinema is much more complex. For example, the Berlin School films demonstrate a vital tie to preclassical cinema but still admittedly draw on the inescapable formative influence of classical narrative cinema (especially the later films of the Berlin School).

Although *postclassical cinema* is a term often applied to post-1960s Hollywood film (frequently referred to as "New Hollywood"), whose task it was to challenge the producer-driven filmmaking system of the past, the term may also extensively characterize film that stylistically cites the traceable reminders of the "cinema of attractions." These citations can range from the modest dance spectacles of European art cinema, such as those found in the Berlin School, to the special effects of Hollywood blockbusters, such as Stanley Kubrick's *2001: A*

Space Odyssey (1978) or James Cameron's *Titanic* (1997). Noting, of course, that spectacle functions very differently at these two ends of the continuum, the critical difference is that the Berlin School cinema employs spectacle as a means of creating a sense of theatrical presence, whereas the spectacle of the Hollywood blockbuster presents an encounter with the hyperreal (G. King 2000). To understand how theatricality works in the Berlin School, I turn to Fischer-Lichte, who cautiously describes theatricality as the phenomenological sense of embodied "presentness" framed by contingency and openness of action ([2004] 2008, 100). By employing this definition as my anchor, I urge a shedding of the weight of artifice and extravagance of mise-en-scène often associated as the precondition for cinematic theatricality (as, for instance, in the films of Rainer Werner Fassbinder and Peter Greenaway).

In the case of both Hollywood blockbusters and the films of the Berlin School, however, spectacle and narrative must negotiate new terms of engagement. In his examination of Hollywood cinema, Geoff King (2000) avers that narrative and spectacle are crucial to postclassical cinema, but that these two elements must also be masterfully interwoven. This may be true for the Hollywood blockbuster, but the integration of spectacle and narrative in many of these Berlin School films remains (effectively) troubled. An ineluctable disjointedness between spectacle and narrative permits—even encourages—the viewer to perceive the boundary, or at least the possible tension, between the two. This in turn makes the appearance of the dance spectacles all the more shocking and spectacular. In a sense, the Berlin School cinema offers another layer of complexity to Walter Benjamin's description of (early) cinema's "shock effects" (*Chockwirkungen*), meant to phenomenologically, even viscerally, shake the viewer out of complacency. It is the unexpected display of kinetics through dance and its intervention of exhibitionism in these otherwise "unspectacular" Berlin School films that heightens the shock effect. Presenting the contemporary viewer with an added dimension of sensuous experience within postclassical cinema, the Berlin School's striking deployment of the theatrical element of the dance spectacle creates compelling effects of presence, which, like the "cinema of attractions" post-factum, earnestly destabilizes the voyeuristic charge of classical narrative cinema (Gunning 2006, 64), such that the viewer may not easily forget that she is on the other end of a spectacle.

Conceptualizing Dance in the Berlin School

Dance in the Berlin School cannot be characterized as artistic or choreographed, which generally distinguish dance from other types of movement. Moreover, these instances of dance are wholly unprofessional, in contrast to the skillfully improvised "bricolage" of the masters of the Hollywood music-and-dance films of Gene Kelly or Fred Astaire, as Jane Feuer notably illustrated in her 1993 study,

The Hollywood Musical (see 4–5). As such, the display of dance in the cinema of the Berlin School distinguishes itself at least aesthetically from that of popular musical and dance film genres. Surrendering choreography and artistic craft, the following thus attends to dance in its relationship to corporeal movement, as a display of bodily excess and presence. Through its unhinging improvisation in the Berlin School films, dance simultaneously frees the body from stasis and carries off new movement by supplanting habitual kinetics.

Distinct from the classic musical and dance film for one because of its lack of virtuosity, the dance scenes in the Berlin School films nonetheless do share the formers' quality of presence. In Feuer's account, "The Hollywood musical worships live entertainment because live forms seem to speak more directly to the spectator. To make a verbal analogy, live entertainment seems to be a 'first-person' form, a performance which assumes an active and present spectator" (23). Musicals and dance films have habitually undertaken efforts to appear live and thereby capture the qualities of a stage performance by including, for example, an embedded audience engaged in watching the spectacle. Feuer calls this a "reflexive form" that works to overcome any potential divide between live performance and the illusion of film (30).

While many dance scholars have argued that recording disrupts the presence, corporeality, and immediacy of dance, film scholars counter that dance actually confers precisely these qualities on film. Erin Brannigan lucidly and extensively addresses this debate in her book *Dancefilm: Choreography and the Moving Image* (2011), in which she proposes that the advent of cinema is in effect intrinsically linked to the development of modern dance. Echoing Peter Sloterdijk's kinetic ontology of modernity as a "being-toward-movement" (2006, 38), dance scholar Gabriele Brandstetter also posits that "[dance] is the symbol of modernity and the key medium of all arts, which seek to reflect on the new technical age as one defined through movement" (1995, 35).[7] Cinema's early years actively celebrated the kinesthetic possibility of the body through dance and especially its intensified gesturing, as witnessed in the early films of the "cinema of attractions," including the work of the Skladanowsky brothers, the Lumière brothers, and Georges Méliès. The potential of cinema as a medium was in many ways the potential of the body in motion, driven by the desire to know more about the body. Linda Williams astutely proposes that this drive to understand the body more fully, the mechanics of its movement, "underlies the very invention of cinema" (1999, 36). What better way to observe bodily movement than through dance? In varying ways, both dance and film changed the status of movement, challenging old habits and developing new forms. Gilles Deleuze observed in *Cinema 1* that "... art, ballet and mime became actions capable of responding to accidents of the environment; that is, to the distribution of the points in space, or of the moments of an event. All this served the same end as the cinema" ([1983] 2006, 7). This coincided with the abandonment of poses and figures. Film and modern dance launched movement a priori as the figuration of spatial (and I would add temporal) reckoning. Taking up Deleuze, Brian Massumi adds that "position no longer comes first, with movement a problematic second. It is secondary to movement and derived from it. It is retro movement, movement residue" (2002, 7).

As a crucial component of cinema's emergence, then, dance follows an important trajectory above and beyond its more self-evident role in certain film genres, such as the musical. The dance scenes found in Berlin School cinema may also be compared to the striking unchoreographed dance scenes found in a selection of 1960s and '70s European art films, such as Dino Risi's *Il sorpasso* (*The Easy Life*, 1962), Jean-Luc Godard's *Band à part* (*Band of Outsiders*, 1964), François Truffaut's *La peau douce* (*The Soft Skin*, 1964), Pier Paolo Pasolini's *Uccellacci e uccellini* (*The Hawks and the Sparrows*, 1966), and Federico Fellini's later *Amarcord* (1973).[8] The Berlin School examples likewise catalyze unusual ruptures that are distinct from the utopian or escapist moments of the Hollywood musical, whose music and dance interludes constitute a dimension of the imaginary in the film that is eventually synthesized into the "reality" of the film narrative (Feuer 1993, 77). In contrast, the dance scenes in the Berlin School cinema are diegetically embedded in the film but remain affectively and often narratively sidelined. Further, they frequently disorient the viewer as to their purpose, insofar as they seem to serve neither a narrative function nor even as a titillating diversion. The ruptures these dance scenes generate are subtle but striking. Such generative forces produce and engage phenomenological outbursts of movement and gesture that vividly underscore the potential for theatricality in these films. Theatricality leads us back to Fischer-Lichte and to the aleatory and the contingent. Riffing on choreographer and composer John Cage (also a significant figure in the development of modern dance), Fischer-Lichte defines theatricality as "the very lack of intentionality and planning; openness for what could occur; the impossibility of control; coincidence, transience, and perpetual transformation without any outside intervention" ([2004] 2008, 124). I also move away from Platonic notions of theatricality as artifice, illusion, and lie. Instead, theatricality is about breaching the fourth wall and opening up the possibility for presence and even authenticity. This definition of theatricality is almost directly echoed in Angela Schanelec's description of how film should be categorized—namely, as "transience, unintentionality, precision, amazement" (2012, 36).[9] Adopting a similar kind of theatricality, then, the dance scenes in the Berlin School yield moments of contingency in which there is an impression not only that the action before our eyes is without plan or choreography but also that it sways in the act of becoming—an unfinished performance of being—and continuously unfolds before our eyes. Through its thrust of spontaneous action, in a kind of inversion of what Brigitte Peucker insightfully calls the "reality bleed" in her book

The Material Image (2007), here it is actually *theatricality* that brings the image on-screen temporally and even physically "closer" to the viewer in a symbolic disturbance of the fabled fourth wall—a "*theatricality* bleed," if you will. This proximity subsequently proffers a sense of presence and direct address.

Both the proximity and spontaneity of dance—its spatiotemporal disregard—are at work in the creation of presence in the Berlin School films. The body engaged in dance extends itself over space and calls attention to its presence and its physicality. Dance intensifies occasions of sensorial perception, much like the "events and processes" described by Gumbrecht, "in which the impact that 'present' objects have on human bodies is being initiated or intensified" (xiii, 2004). What is more, through its theatrical spontaneity, dance in the Berlin School films has the capacity to invoke unexpected and unprecedented affects to which the viewer may only be able to corporeally respond. In its refusal of reflection and its structure of intensity, the spectacle of dance fosters the viewer's visceral response to visual forms directly charting us back through body and phenomenological film theory, which I explore at great length in the following chapter. The visceral presencing of dance in the Berlin School forecloses or at least precedes the viewer's ability to "read or interpret them as [mere] symbols" (Shaviro 1993 26). Finally, it heightens what Vivian Sobchack has referred to in other contexts as the "prereflective bodily responsiveness to films" (2004, 63), one which assumes a sensual experience of films that goes beyond image and sound to also include the haptic. Through an examination of the sharp intersections of movement and theatricality in the dance scenes of the Berlin School, this approach seeks to mobilize another dimension of this cinema's performance potential, namely, its outbursts of presence.

Solipsistic Dancing in Grisebach's Mein Stern *and* Sehnsucht

Valeska Grisebach's feature films *Mein Stern* and *Sehnsucht* both contain what appear to be altogether spontaneous and remarkably introverted dance scenes. Particular to Grisebach's films in this chapter on dance is her exclusive employment of nonprofessional actors, which, while not uncommon in Berlin School cinema (especially among the youth features),[10] is not necessarily the rule. In any case, Grisebach's "actors" and their documentary-style "acting" bring an additional dimension of contingency to the films, which, when read with Fischer-Lichte, might actually augment the quality of theatricality in these films. In Steven Shaviro's account of Warhol's choice of bad or inexperienced actors over professional ones, he suggests that nonacting or bad acting is doomed to an inescapable immediate presence, unable to get beyond exteriority (1993, 220). This aspect, coupled with Grisebach's intense interest in the body of the actor on-screen (for instance, there are rarely shots in her films, otherwise common in other Berlin School films, without the physical presence of an actor), lend a sharp, almost uncomfortably close connection to the body of the actor that subsequently shapes these dance scenes. The tension between the dancerly and the everyday, which finds reconciliation in Hollywood musicals and dance films, is brought to the fore in Grisebach's *Mein Stern* and *Sehnsucht*, as dance stunningly breaks out, spilling out over the realistic contexts and mise-en-scènes of quotidian banality as an alternative form of bodily movement. Dance becomes a kind of liberation from the everyday.

In her first film, *Mein Stern*, Grisebach captures the trivial, but never trivialized, ups and downs in the life of the Berlin teenager Nicole (Nicole Gläser) and her boyfriend Schöps (Christopher Schöps). Though the film is not conceived as a documentary, its characters maintain their real names and identities. In fact, most of the interpersonal relationships (romantic, platonic, and familial) and configurations of space are true to life as well. Leading up to the dance scene, Nicole has just been rather callously dumped by Schöps. Licking her wounds, she tags along to a dance club with a girlfriend and some neighborhood boys. At first, she stands around obstinately with a distracted and uninterested expression. A lengthy hug from her friend, however, provides precisely the necessary succor to get Nicole to join her on the dance floor. This dance sequence consists of three consecutive shots and is roughly three minutes long. The first image is a medium shot of the two friends grooving. Nicole's back is to the camera, and she partly blocks her friend, who faces her. The diegetic soundtrack gets rolling with the French Affairs' 2000 dance hit "My Heart Goes Boom." This song then crossfades into an earlier dance hit, "Electric Nature," from 1997. Music, and especially popular music, is an important agent in the film. Its sonic demand reaches beyond itself; it pokes and prods the bodies on- and off-screen, luring them into physical responsiveness. Indeed, Eugenie Brinkema astutely calls the sonic demand a "kinetic one" (2011, 223), whose direct relationship to the machinery of the body intensely avows corporeal vitality and presence. The German title of the film, *Mein Stern*, is actually borrowed from the name of another pop hit single, also from 2000, by the Tunisian German pop and soul singer Ayman; this is played later on in the film. The film could judiciously serve as a study on youth culture through music. Accompanying the diegetic score in this scene are ambient red-tinted disco lights. In the next shot, the viewer sees only Nicole. This is another medium shot that shows her upper body as she faces the camera. Her eyes are, however, turned downward or to the side, so that her face is often caught in profile. It is evident that her body has become less inhibited than it was in the first shot; her dance moves are more steady and continuous. In the third and final shot of this sequence, the wide angle confirms that Nicole is now alone on the dance floor.

Lasting more than a minute, this final shot is the longest in this sequence. While uninhibited, Nicole's body remains somewhat stiff; she moves within this fixed space of her own private dance floor and her movements are repetitive, almost robotic. Her frame simply shifts from side to side while her arms swing in nebulous vogue poses. Especially peculiar about this shot is that while it is not overtly voyeuristic or titillating, it is strongly exhibitionistic. While Nicole is not at all seductively dressed (her young body actually is drowning in layers of baggy clothing), her solo dance nonetheless draws attention to her body as spectacle. But the shot does not offer a reverse shot of a possible onlooker, which we would expect from classical narrative cinema. Grisebach eschews a point-of-view shot of a diegetic gaze that would invite a layer of distanced "narrative pleasure" (Mulvey[1975] 1990); instead, the viewer is uncomfortably cast as the direct spectator to this scene.

Within the context of the entire film, this dance sequence is particularly interesting. Much of the film is improvised; that is, while Grisebach had a prepared script, she also encouraged her actors to move and perform as they normally would in similar situations. Grisebach confesses, however, that in scenes that involved "corporeality" (*Körperlichkeit*), such as with the sex and kissing scenes, it was critical for her that everything was entirely choreographed, so as to not make the young lay actors too uncomfortable (2001). It is not altogether clear that the dance scene was considered of equal bodily intimacy such that it also needed to be choreographed; it seems unlikely, though. Yet the intimacy of this scene of a young woman dancing alone in a club is striking. Its pitch is so starkly private despite its publicness that the viewer is struck by a wave of uneasiness by the direct presence of this body. The intensity of the scene even eclipses the earlier sex scene between Nicole and Schöps, which appears to be choreographed and naively unrealistic in its execution. The breach between these two corporeal spectacles is for all intents and purposes spontaneity. On the dance floor, Nicole has simply been told to dance as she normally would in a club, and there is something unsettlingly tangible and direct about this performance of self, and specifically of the body, whose seemingly vacuous repetition of movement and gesture transfixingly draws attention to itself. A similar effect is produced in Grisebach's second feature film, *Sehnsucht*.

Thematically distinct from Grisebach's first feature film, *Sehnsucht* is notably more genre oriented, with its effectively formulaic plot of a man who has an affair and cannot choose between two women he appears to love equally. Further, an ethos of the German *Heimatfilm* of the postwar decades punctuates the mise-en-scène in its rural setting and its steadfast desire to hang on to tradition and the simplicity of village life.[11] Yet the dance scene in *Sehnsucht* yields another unsuturable gap that not only strikes the viewer as narratively out of place but also confronts us with the cinematic spectacle as such. In *Sehnsucht*, the main protagonist Markus (Andreas Müller) breaks into a solo dance at a village beer hall during a volunteer firefighter convention dinner. Whereas the viewer might be motivated to affectively contextualize this scene within the larger narrative of the film—that is, as the possible catalyst for Markus's extramarital affair—I read this scene beyond the pale of narrative significance. Apart from possible inebriation, there is no practical or cinematic force behind Markus's dancing. His demeanor throughout the film is otherwise rather painfully introverted. The director affirmed in an interview that "this man would never otherwise do such a thing as put himself on display [*sich hinstellen*] and dance" (quoted in Grundtner 2006).[12]

Once again, a prominent feature of this dance scene is the diegetic music. Comparable to that in *Mein Stern*, the choice of music for this scene pointedly frames the setting, in terms of both history and milieu. Despite the difficulty Grisebach encountered procuring the rights to use Robbie Williams's 2003 pop hit "Feel," she handpicked it as the perfect song for Markus's dance (Grundtner 2006). This song enjoyed such enormous success in continental Europe that by the mid-2000s it became something of a cliché in (and about) Germany, a nation renowned for its unparalleled penchant for English-language pop music.[13] In fact, the earnestness of the scene is troubled by the incredible cheesiness of the song, which dually serves to lighten the mood of the scene and to accentuate the backwardness of this small village in the former East German state of Brandenburg where Markus lives. Without downplaying the role of the song here or the seriousness with which several critics (even the filmmaker herself) read the effect/affect of this scene via the song's text—"I want to feel real life. . . ."—I am eager to underscore the ambiguity presented by a more nuanced reading of this scene, which I argue has more to offer through its materiality and kinetic capacity.

Markus performs an awkward solitary slow dance that lasts nearly the entire length of this Robbie Williams song. He twists his body in semicircles and languidly lets his arms sway around his upper body. The scene is composed of a single medium to medium close-up shot mostly of the back of Markus's head and his face in profile; the viewer is denied emotional disclosure of his face directly. Even when Markus briefly turns and faces the camera, his eyes remain closed throughout the scene. He moves as though in a trance. There is a discerning draw to Markus's body in this scene as it moves gawkily to the cadences of the music. It does not appear as though he is dancing for anyone in particular; as in *Mein Stern*, there is no reverse shot or visible diegetic audience. Even if there were onlookers, the shot scale minimizes the visual horizon around Markus's upper body, which in a larger-than-life manner consumes the frame. The scene nevertheless generates a kind of affect that engages the viewer and unfolds as a direct result of this head-on spectacle. In his reading of this dance scene, Marco Abel also underscores the affect engendered through Markus's dancing body. Offering an apt analysis, Abel suggests that watching this solitary dance elicits a sense of embarrassment in the viewer. He writes: "But before long *we* begin to feel slightly embarrassed, even awkward watching him give himself over so intensely to the moment" (2011, 216; 2013, 243, emphasis in original). Not unlike *Mein Stern*, the viewer is forced into a highly conscious position of direct spectatorship.

The diegetic solipsism of the solitary dancer in both of Grisebach's films offers a possible layer of interpretation. Despite their very public settings—a dance club and a beer hall—isolation appears to encapsulate these dancers. Through cinematography, they are presented as each film's only element of mise-en-scène, utterly alone. Reminiscent of the performance scholar André Lepecki's description of the solipsistic performances of the dancer Bruce Nauman, the actors/characters in Grisebach's films similarly seem to, in Lepecki's words, perform "explorations of [their] self-consciously isolated body's relation to motion, sound, anatomy, language, balance, space . . . and dance" (2006, 20). At the same time, the film viewer's seemingly uninhibited vista of these private scenes—that is, not "mediated" through the perspective of a visible spectator-other—offers an alternative mode of presence. One almost has the impression that these two dancers—both nonprofessional actors essentially portraying themselves—have been selected spontaneously from the audience to perform a dance during a musical interlude. Their dances are pedestrian but palpably real. Contrary to the musicals of an American Fred Astaire or a German Willy Fritsch, the improvisation and unprofessional quality of these two Berlin School dances impart a bodily candor more akin to the desultory, almost clumsy, exhibitionism of the "cinema of attractions" that the viewer can—and might be more inclined to—phenomenologically perceive. In other words, the viewer does not marvel at the dancer's techniques as much as at the simple presence of the actor's dancerly corporeality.

Letting Go in Schanelec's Plätze in Städten *and* Mein langsames Leben

As with Grisebach's two feature films, Angela Schanelec's films have their share of detached and even wistful dancers. Schanelec's dance scenes are similar to but at the same time discernible from those presented in Grisebach's films. Thematically well-aligned with *Mein Stern*, Schanelec's film *Plätze in Städten* (1998) is also about the trials and errors of a teenaged girl living in Berlin. This film has a tripartite of noteworthy dance scenes. The most striking of the three is a lengthy scene consisting of a mere three shots in which the main protagonist Mimmi (Sophie Aigner) and her friend (Katie Eckerfeld) dance alongside each other at a deserted indoor pool. The two dance to Joni Mitchell's 1971 folksy hit "California" on a diegetic track. In the song, which Mimmi's friend describes as *traurig* (sad), the singer's sensuous voice belts out her nostalgia for home in California.

Providing an uncanny setting for this dance scene, the pool is completely glassed in, and the dreary winter landscape outside seems a far cry from sunny California. The scene begins with a static long shot in which Mimmi can be seen doing laps in the pool. Mimmi's friend enters the shot and then joins her briefly in the pool. After a quick dip, the friend exits the pool, pulls on a bathrobe, and flips on a stereo that just happens to be on a table next to the pool. As though on command (indeed, sonic demand is kinetic), the friend's body immediately responds to the music and she begins to rhythmically move, slowly and carefully, on the slick surface of the poolside ledge. Mimmi climbs out of the pool and joins her. The two twist and dip to their own individual rhythms against this "sad" aural and visual backdrop.

Not overtly provocative, the scene is nevertheless more objectifying than the dance scene in *Mein Stern* in terms of its visual track and the bodies that make up its mise-en-scène. Mimmi's friend eventually sheds her robe and the two young women dance in their wet, body-clinging bathing suits. There is a vulnerability to these young pubescent bodies dancing for the camera in a transparent glassed-in structure. Similar to both of Grisebach's dance scenes, this extremely exposed scene does not appear to have any diegetic onlookers; instead, the dancers appear self-consumed, existing within their own fantasy world. Further, the architecture of this long shot is such that the space within which the young women dance (at the edge of the pool) consumes less than half of the entire space of the shot. The dancing figures are curiously sidelined by the pool, and as such they are not physically positioned as the main spectacle of the shot, which has a two-fold, contradictory effect. Their corporeal machinations are at once stifled and accentuated against the overwhelmingly monochrome opacity and stillness of the pool. Not only do these two young women create a visible contrast as they dance in their colored bathing suits against the gray winter landscape, but the almost split-screen effect in this first shot also emphasizes their lively moving bodies through a critical juxtaposition of still and mobile objects. In a second shot, Mimmi is shown in a medium-long view lying on her side, with her back to the viewer, on the pool's edge. The diegetic music continues in the background. Finally, there is a medium shot of Mimmi's friend, who is still dancing. Her eyes are now closed. The shot slightly resembles the one in *Sehnsucht*, in which Markus appears to be in a kind of trance. This medium shot turns long as Mimmi's friend dances away from the camera.

There is a melancholic playfulness and an innocence to this dance scene. Considered narratively, it precedes Mimmi's friend's loss of her virginity and Mimmi's own pregnancy and deliberation about an abortion. Indeed, Schanelec's use of music in *Plätze in Städten* seizes a teleological quality; the next dance scene in the film takes place in a Paris club and Mimmi sadly moves to the lyrics of Ben Folds Five's 1997 hit "Brick" (repeated twice in the film), a song about a teenage pregnancy and subsequent abortion. Yet this earlier dance scene at the pool seems to stick out as a narrative anomaly. The setting of this deserted indoor pool is a curious space that appears only once in the film. It is not clear if it is public or private, or why exactly the two young women are there. The provenance of the stereo and music is even more mysterious. Mimmi asks her friend what the song is called, and she does not know. Action and setting are perplexingly at odds in this scene. Two bodies appear awhirl at the slippery, possibly dangerous, edge of an indoor pool in nothing but their bathing suits against the backdrop of a dreary, suburban Berlin winter. The scene is almost oneiric in quality. Nessel even goes so far as to underscore the utter absurdity of this scene in her article "Ghost Dances: Tanzszenen im aktuellen europäischen Autorenkino" (2009b). To an even greater extent in Schanelec's *Plätze in Städten*, dance appears as an extranarrative spectacle of bodily movement that forsakes sense-making as well as linear progression and instead pushes the film sideways, not in a self-eclipsing slide but in a reverberating wiggle. It aims to explicitly *show* and *gesture* in an exhibition of the corporeal presence these young bodies engaged in motion for the sheer pleasure of motion.

The dance scene in the slightly later and better-known example of Schanelec's feature-length films, *Mein langsames Leben*, mentioned earlier in the chapter, follows a similar aesthetic principle of motion for motion's sake. Two hitherto estranged siblings, Valerie and Ben, have recently reunited following the (eventually fatal) stroke of their father. In spite of the mournful circumstances that have reunited them, their dance in a deserted nightclub, like that in *Plätze in Städten*, is wrought with a narrative framing of sadness, but it also exerts a playful air insofar as it resists the cumbersome sense of maladroitness and introversion that weigh so heavily on Grisebach's dance scenes. Schanelec's scenes are more about letting go. The bodies that inhabit her mise-en-scènes are much more extroverted and animated in their movements. They exude an overwhelming desire to break out of diurnal movement, of the body's disciplined motions. This emancipatory physicality propels a breaking away even at the formal film level, as bodies twist and turn in and out of the frame. Merten Worthmann has observed in his article about *Mein langsames Leben* in the German weekly newspaper *Die Zeit* (2001), "Whenever a character wants to let go [in Schanelec's films], then she or he dances. In this type of scene of Schanelec's films, the camera can look on for minutes at a time."[14] Such a kinetic manifestation of letting go can also be found in the films of the contemporary Austrian filmmaker Barbara Albert, whose work is often grouped with the films of the Berlin School. Examples include her films *Böse Zellen* (*Free Radicals*, 2003) and especially *Fallen* (*Falling*, 2006), which has been described as "a single dance scene" ("*eine einzige Tanzszene*") (Bradatsch 2006).

In my push to reflect on dance in the Berlin School as a spectacle of kinesthetics and gestures, I stress the immediacy of its presence as indelible. Thus, I resist the urge by some scholars to focus solely on the interiority of these dance scenes as psychological markers of loss among the characters (as in Nicole's breakup with her boyfriend in *Mein Stern*) or the anticipation of loss (of Mimmi's baby or in the present example of Valerie and Ben's father). This is the vein in which Sean Franzel examines dance and the space of what he suggestively calls the "Dorfdisko" ("village disco"), as a moment of shared nostalgia (2013, 93). Such a dubbing aptly underscores the strangeness and even backwardness at hand in many of these scenes, *Mein langsames Leben* being a prime example. Yet to suggest that this scene in the so-called Dorfdisko principally reveals the psychological state of these siblings does not account for the scene's explosion of movement and radical sense of presence. Juxtaposed against an earlier scene in the film, when a dance is performed entirely off-screen, the viewer is certainly struck by this shift from absence to presence.

But even in regard to this earlier scene of off-screen dancing, I argue for a more dialectical reading of presence and absence that flirts with Derridian notions of the same, where all presence is simply a trace of a trace of a trace (Derrida [1988] 1997). That is to say, the only thing present is the absence of the other. In another scene from *Mein langsames Leben*, a young girl, Klara (Chloé Hangard), commands her babysitter, Maria (also played by Sophie Aigner), to dance for her to Franz Schubert's famous rendering of Johann Wolfgang Goethe's poem *Erlkönig*. A number of scholars have cited this earlier scene as evidence of the film's overall eschewal of movement. The scene does appear to underscore an axiom of languidness, even stasis, that many critics uphold in their general reading of the film; it is a cinematic dance scene that is not even shown. But let us consider the scene further. How one might dance to such music in the first place remains a mystery unsolved. With only the diegetic music as evidence of this dance, the viewer looks on through a long take of Klara as she sits expressionlessly and appears to watch Maria. Characteristic of Schanelec's style and not uncommon to the Berlin School aesthetic, this reverse shot without the shot suggests not only, as Christian Metz has proposed in "Photography and Fetish" (1985), that the film's characters also act and live beyond the frame but, furthermore, that the viewers also are implicated in the actions of the film. For who is Klara actually watching? That is, who is really dancing? If the flow of the film seems to bend itself out of joint with Valerie's and Ben's later energetic moshing, then this earlier scene is an interesting antidote—a passing off of excessive action to the off. For the film image is more than what lies within its mobile frame. In "Theatre and Cinema," André Bazin writes: "A screen is not a frame like that of a picture but a mask which allows only a part of the action to be seen" ([1967] 2005, 105). This masking or passing off of action does not imply a lack of presence per se. In this, as in the following example, presence is produced not necessarily through absence but through viewer anticipation, which I argue can actually heighten in the absence of the spectacle. This is not dissimilar to Metz's formulation of the "wishful thinking" of the viewer outlined in the first chapter. More important, the scene in *Mein langsames Leben* critically throws into the question the strict dichotomy of presence and absence, and opens up the possibility of considering different kinds of presence effects that do not necessarily assert the directness of common time and space. Ultimately, Schanelec's own description of her general approach to filmmaking challenges the viewer to consider the contingency and theatricality of dance in her films that quite rigorously move beyond cognitive or teleological readings: "I am more interested in how people move, how things follow each other in succession, how unexpectedly and almost unforeseeably stories take turns (quoted in Suchsland 2005)."[15] It follows that many of Schanelec's films have a particularly fragmented and elliptical narrative. What one might call pinnacle scenes may be left out—for instance, the actual illness and death of Valerie and Ben's father in *Mein langsames Leben*—whereas scenes that seem unnecessary and disconnected from the plot, such as this later dance scene, are shown at length.

In both Grisebach's and Schanelec's films, emotional expression and disclosure are often relegated to bodily gesture through dance, possibly the most gestural and exhibitionistic of movements. Yet to propose that there is a semiotics at work in these films through gestural language would be an overstatement. What is being communicated is the presence and physicality of the body. This display of kinetic purposelessness in all four of these films—this movement for movement's sake—enunciates the physical presence of the dancer. Through dance there is a mobilization of bodily excess—what Brannigan calls "a corporeal mode growing out of everyday movements that accommodates the fact that we possess more vigour, more suppleness, more articular, and muscular possibilities than we need" (2011, 152). At its most mundane, the dancing in these scenes shifts away from mimetic movement of the everyday and becomes a site of performativity of bodily subjectivity through its repetition and flow of gestures, as it makes a spectacle of the body and subsequently brings it into a theatrical presence that confronts the viewer head-on (Lepecki 2004, 2).

Queer Performance Parody in Ade's Alle Anderen and Krüger's Unterwegs

Gesture and movement play out more categorically in the next two film examples as even more compelling spectacles of self-exhibition, where dance also becomes a mode of display as much as a mode of movement. The excess and playfulness of the following dance scenes are decidedly camp inspired, not necessarily for their triviality or tastelessness but primarily for their intentionally exaggerated style and heightened gesticulation that not only genderqueers but also directly refuses to take masculinity too seriously. As José Esteban Muñoz importantly notes, "Dance is an especially valuable site for ruminations on queerness and gesture" (2009, 65). The dancers' bodies in these scenes are amplified, sexualized, and queered. I refer here to the playfully ambiguous dance scenes in Maren Ade's *Alle Anderen* and Jan Krüger's *Unterwegs* as queer parody performances. Though aesthetically and affectively quite distinct from each other, these scenes have thematic parallels. They are framed by the male dancers' respective concerns about the efficacy of their masculinity as well as their heterosexuality. With these dance scenes both men seem to enact precisely that which "plagues" them, namely, a sensibility of sexual and gender nonnormativity. The consequences of their performances vary. For Chris (Lars Eidinger) in *Alle Anderen,* this dance performance simply elicits laughter from his girlfriend, Gitti (Birgit Minichmayr), but for Benni (Florian Panzner) in *Unterwegs,* his dance results in the awkward conclusion of the evening's party and the definitive end of his relationship with his girlfriend, Sandra (Anabelle Lachatte).

Commercially the most successful of the films examined here, *Alle Anderen* is the second feature by Maren Ade. Thematically compared to such classics as Michelangelo Antonioni's *La Notte* (*The Night*, 1961), Jean-Luc Godard's *Le Mépris* (*Contempt*, 1963), and Ingmar Bergman's *Scener ur ett äktenskapp* (*Scenes from a Marriage*, 1973), *Alle Anderen* is a dark portrayal of a young German couple in crisis while on vacation in Sardinia. Narratively not as elliptical as Schanelec's films, *Alle Anderen* does have a tendency to shift its mood quite rapidly from scene to scene (Nord 2009), which makes the legibility of the film and especially of its dance scene evocatively ambiguous. Yet the dance scene in *Alle Anderen* does exert more narrative and linear contiguity than we have seen thus far. The scene begins with Gitti's pleading for a night out at a local dance club, which Chris begrudges. As an alternative, he brings the disappointed Gitti to his mother's altogether kitschy private meditation room, adorned with ceramic birds and stacked with 1980s and '90s pop records, in the vacation house where they are staying and impishly proposes that this can be their club. The joke turns on Chris when Gitti randomly switches on the stereo and the 1984 country-pop hit "To All the Girls I've Loved Before" begins to play. Gitti pushes Chris into the center of the room—"the dance floor"—and demands that he dance for her. At first he resists and stands there reticently, but he eventually yields to her request. In a medium-long shot, we see Chris begin to shift from side to side to the rhythm of this decidedly undanceable tune. His eyes are averted downward, but he is ostensibly dancing for Gitti who is shown looking on in three brief reverse shots. The diegetic voyeurism of classical narrative cinema therefore plays a role here, but the gender reversal and the parodic nature of the scene throws the tradition of visual pleasure into turmoil.

Lasting on average twenty seconds, each of the four shots of Chris dancing is much longer than those of Gitti as diegetic spectator. In the third shot,

Figure 2.2. Dancerly exhibitionism in *Alle Anderen*, 2009. © Komplizen Film

the harmony of the music changes as the chorus begins and Chris's formerly lackadaisical swaying back and forth breaks into ballet-inspired gliding as his arms reach above his head in a pirouette gesture (see figure 2.2). He theatrically and acrobatically throws himself against a cabinet and slides down, then slowly and seductively pulls himself up. In the fourth shot he is framed against his mother's artificial tree, which is adorned with colored ceramic birds. His entire body swings as he prances with increasing vigor over to the window and violently throws himself into its frame, where he poses for a moment. From there, he again dramatically slides down the wall. His shirt is pulled up to reveal his midriff and his baggy jeans are edged down to display the low rim of his underwear. He rolls onto the floor and then seductively crawls towards Gitti. This exaggeratedly playful dance performance of self-subjugation and sexuality plays with and willfully recasts gender codes. Within the broader context of the film, this dance sequence, on the one hand, follows an earlier scene where Chris, wearing Gitti's makeup (which she has applied), asks Gitti if she actually finds him *männlich* (manly). On the other hand, the scene foreshadows Gitti's "real" subjugation later in the film, when she begs Chris on her knees not to leave her alone for the evening when he departs to visit a work acquaintance. This all prehensively and resultingly sets the stage, as it were, for this dance performance.

There is also a possibly rich intertext to this scene. Anyone familiar with the actor Lars Eidinger, who plays Chris, would recognize him as the *enfant terrible* of the Schaubühne Theater in Berlin whose 2006 performance in Thomas Ostermeier's radical adaptation of Shakespeare's *A Midsummer Night's Dream* raised quite a scandal. During performances, Eidinger regularly performed a complete striptease and declared to the audience, "The only goal is to obliterate your fun!" (Leinkauf and Pfaff 2011).[16] This declaration indirectly highlights the role of exhibitionism that evades the visual pleasure of classical narrative cinema. But even in a possible quasi reenactment of this uncomfortable striptease, the scene is both theatrical and cinematic. The intimacy of the film space in this dance scene of *Alle Anderen*, which has been called a *Kammerspiel* (an intimate play, or literally, a chamber play), represents on the one hand the most theatrical of film genres (del Río 2012, 90), and on the other is aesthetically indicative of Dogma cinema style in its spatial claustrophobia, the unsteady frame of the handheld camera, and the graininess caused by the lack of set lighting. For Dogma filmmakers Lars von Trier and Thomas Vinterberg, the "cosmeticization" of especially Hollywood cinema, with its "slick image" created by special lighting effects, polished photography, and complicated shot scales, "washes away the last grains of truth" from film (Geuens 2001, 192). By reintroducing a simpler (but not necessarily realist) aesthetics in this scene, *Alle Anderen*, like the Dogma films, re-creates a feeling of unmediated and unfiltered presence, intimacy, and spontaneity in this scene that likewise assaults the viewer's senses in its application of spectacle. Along these lines, the scene functions through a dense layering of the illusion of spontaneity and therefore presence and, at the same time, an almost theatrical staging through the intense spectacle of the (marked) body of the actor and his movement.

A dance scene found in Krüger's first feature-length film, *Unterwegs*, concludes this analysis. Bearing some thematic resemblance to *Alle Anderen*, Krüger's film tells the story of a young couple on a road trip that brings them to a small town on the coast of Poland. With its mildly fantastical and even vaudevillian aesthetics, the dance scene in *Unterwegs* contrasts significantly with the other examples considered in this chapter. Narratively responding to some extent to the sexual tension mounting between the two male protagonists, Benni (Florian Panzner) and Marco (Martin Kiefer), and possibly to the recently consummated sexual tension between Sandra (Anabelle Lachatte) and Marco, the dance's dramatic occurrence and mysterious quality are perplexing. Compared to the enigmatic figure of "the visitor" played by Terence Stamp in Pier Paolo Pasolini's film *Teorema* (1968), Marco's mysterious nature, including his rather ambiguous sexuality, seems to be central to the narrative and to the mystery of the film (Worschech 2004) and, I add, a motivation for Benni's queer dance performance.

As Sandra's young daughter's birthday party winds down and the adults enjoy some after-hours social drinking and dancing to generic country music on the porch of Marco's aunt's summer cabin in rural Poland, the music suddenly changes to a Polish folk song with sharp Romani elements, and Benni bursts through the front door with a transparent white lace shawl over his head. In contrast to Chris in his dance, Benni evidently prepared this performance. Under the shawl, which he seductively and dramatically lifts like a veil, he wears only a red-sequined skirt. His face is dramatically made up. His eyes are heavily accented with black eyeliner and his lips are partly painted geisha-style in black. His hair is gelled back to the crown of his head and his left nipple is covered in a black cross. Unlike in the dance scene in *Alle Anderen*, Benni's mere appearance accentuates his performance of gender and sexual ambiguity in this scene.

In the first shot of this sequence Benni is alone in the frame, and he performs flamenco-inspired movements, with sharp turns and dramatic flicks of the wrists. He gradually moves, hips swaying, toward his diegetic audience, and lifts the veil. The camera follows him in a tracking shot as he approaches one of the men at the party. He dances with him briefly and then shifts his attention to his girlfriend, Sandra, with whom he also dances briefly, dipping tango style and subsequently dropping to the ground. He repeats these actions with the other bystanders until there is a cut and he moves in on Marco. With Sandra as a dumbfounded viewer slightly out of focus in the background, he grabs Marco's head and in another shot pulls him in and aggressively kisses him on the lips, then violently pushes him away. The stunned bystanders, forced to play the audience, are implicated in the sociality of this queer burlesque-like performance, as though newcomers to a drag club. As Feuer writes of the musical, the film viewer may be encouraged to identify with the spontaneous audience (1993, 34). But again, this does not exactly follow the dynamic of identification of classical cinema. While Benni's dance is not performed for the sake of the film viewer alone, the unconventional nature of the scene, with its ambiguous narrative and absence of teleological motivation, troubles such classification.

Instead of engendering a kind of playful intimacy through a symbolic crossing of the fourth wall in this scene, the incensed audience (here especially Sandra) abruptly puts an end to the performance when Sandra destroys the party overhang, which was temporarily serving as a proscenium arch. The resulting spectacle is actually a shift in focus from Benni to Sandra in a performative transformation of roles. The audience, now including Benni, looks on disapprovingly as Sandra attempts leave the scene and drive away in her car. Benni's dance is transformative in a twofold sense: first, for its implication of its audience and second, because as the filmmaker himself points out, Benni is reticent throughout the film, and it is with the dance scene close to the end of the film that Benni finally extroverts himself to the extreme. That is not to say that Benni expresses his long-suppressed feelings through dance, as expressivity is not what is at stake here. Rather, as Krüger observes, Benni attempts to perform a comparably ambivalent and exciting sexuality (to that of Marco) through the corporeality of dance.[17] Similar to the other dance scenes considered in this chapter, the specific details of this scene were improvised by the actor playing the role.

The dance scenes in Grisebach's and Schanelec's films heed a heightened introspection, and even what sociologist Erving Goffman would call a "performance of the everyday" that nonetheless agitate habitual bodily movement, insofar as these dances "are not 'acted' or 'put on' in the sense that the performer knows in advance just what he is going to do, and does this solely because of the effect it is likely to have" (1959, 73). By contrast, an exaggerated self-display marks these latter two dance scenes from *Alle Anderen* and *Unterwegs*. The spectacles created by Chris and Benni are more representative of James Naremore's concept of layered acting, of "performance-within-performance" (126). Despite these differences, beginning with Nicole's demure disco dancing in *Mein Stern* and moving all the way to Benni's extravagant flamenco frolicking in *Unterwegs*, we can trace a pattern of intensified movement and gesture suffused with contingency and coincidence. It is clear that all of these dance spectacles are sophisticated examples of cinematic exhibitionism: they produce effects of theatrical presence that physically affect and even shock the viewer.

Just as the very early "cinema of attractions" had "its accent on direct stimulation" (Gunning 2006, 68), this recent German auteur cinema of the postclassical era embraces similar traditions of spectacle and exhibitionism that directly address the viewer through their presencing. Dance becomes a means of achieving a heightened sense of presence through its spontaneity and open presentation. With their particular dance scenes, Grisebach's *Mein Stern* and *Sehnsucht*, Schanelec's *Plätze in Städten* and *Mein langsames Leben*, Ade's *Alle Anderen*, and finally Krüger's *Unterwegs* all exert the qualities of theatricality and spectacle, which are not generally associated with the cinema of the Berlin School. Theatricality is engendered not only through dance's attributes of exaggerated self-display, gesture, and dramatic performance but also, following Fischer-Lichte, through its directness and contingency of action. Blending influences from early cinema to the musical, postclassical Hollywood cinema, and finally 1960s European art cinema, the Berlin School films' complex employment of dance scenes supports a significant dialogue with diverging film genres of spectacle. In my reading, these roots underscore the Berlin School's drive to create effects of theatrical presence. With careful examinations of a selection of scenes, I have sought to demonstrate the way in which the cinema of the Berlin School yields apertures for direct engagement between actor and viewer that challenge the conventions of both classical filmmaking and spectatorship.

This chapter pursues another dimension of Berlin School cinema that dovetails with but also diverges from more representational approaches. It especially urges a methodological move beyond this cinema's hitherto established aesthetic relationship to realist observation, reduction, and stasis (or at least slowness) to also consider its theatrical and even spectacular side that has the potential to phenomenologically engage the viewer through the movement of the dancerly body on-screen. The performance of movement for movement's sake through unchoreographed dance in these films is unhinging yet at the same time liberating in its undisciplined forms of embodiment. It confronts the viewer and offers a promise of presence. From screen to imaginary stage, the possibility for live performance and the engagement between the dancer on-screen and the viewer open up and offer a challenge to the conventions of classical filmmaking and spectatorship. Opening up these paths further, the following chapters will examine spectatorship of direct engagement also through the body in movement but along diverging courses.

Notes

An earlier and shorter version of this chapter appeared as an article in *The Germanic Review: Literature, Culture, Theory*. See Landry, "Dance and the Theatricality of the Berlin School" (2014).

1. A number of scholars have indicated this in their writing. See, for instance, Alasdair King's 2014 article "Still Lives in Transit: Movement and Inertia in Angela Schanelec's *Orly* (2010)" and Marco Abel's 2010 piece "Imaging Germany: The (Political) Cinema of Christian Petzold" in *The Collapse of the Conventional*. The description I cite directly here was part of the introduction to Berlin School cinema given by the German film scholar Gerd Gemunden at the Dartmouth Berlin School Symposium in May 2011: "The films adopt a minimalist approach as 'an aesthetic of reduction.' The films strive to achieve an objective depiction of reality by using long takes, opting for natural sound over a musical score and featuring unknown or amateur actors." (See Garczynski 2011).

2. A more interesting statistic, but only marginally relevant to this particular study, is that ten in twelve films made by women filmmakers (Angela Schanelec, Valeska Grisebach, Maria Speth, Sylke Enders [sometimes linked to the Berlin School], and Maren Ade) include dance scenes. This suggests that women filmmakers of the Berlin School tend to include dance scenes in their films nearly 90 percent of the time.

3. It should be noted that Jan Krüger's work has been only peripherally associated with the Berlin School. His film *Unterwegs*, however, is explicitly addressed by Rüdiger Suchsland in his important early article about the Berlin School "Langsames Leben, Schöne Tage: Annährung an die 'Berliner Schule'" (2005).

4. Rainer Werner Fassbinder famously began his career in the theater with the formation of his own Brechtian-influenced "Anti-Theater" troupe before he moved to cinema (see Barnett 2005).

5. It is notable that this was a more general remark about the Berlin School, and it was made in the discussion period of the GSA panel "Berlin School (2): Christian Petzold." Eric Rentschler also specifically describes the use of surveillance-camera footage in Christoph Hochhäusler's film *Eine Minute Dunkel* (*One Minute of Darkness*, 2010) as constituting a "cinema of attractions." (See Rentschler 2013.) Here he suggests that the employment of surveillance camera footage in Hochhäusler's film presents a nonnarrative assemblage of images that the viewer must then put into order and make sense of.

6. "Die Auseinandersetzung mit Filmen des frühen Kinos der Attraktionen öffnete den Blick für Formen, die nicht in erster Linie dem Erzählen zuzurechnen sind, sondern ereignisbezogene Operationen wie Zeigen, Performen, Präsentieren aufweisen."

7. "[Tanz] wird zum Symbol der Moderne und zum Schlüsselmedium aller Künste, die das neue technische Zeitalter als seine durch Bewegung definierte Epoche zu reflektieren suchen."

8. Nessel (2009b) explores the trajectory of dance from earlier European cinema to the Berlin School. She claims that dance scenes are not merely popular but almost obligatory in European cinema. Citing examples from Godard to Pasolini and Masson, Nessel suggests that the dance scenes in the Berlin School films are part of a continuing tradition of European art cinema. While instrumental in bringing attention to this tradition, Nessel's article, a mere six pages in length, does not leave room for an in-depth examination of the dance scenes or the development of a conceptual frame for understanding them. Further, she does not account for the differences between the dance scenes in, for instance, 1960s and '70s European art films and the Berlin School. Certainly, the films, such as those 1960s titles enumerated above, all have penetrating dance scenes. But whether it is the Madison in a café (Godard), the twist on an open country field (Risi) and in a ritzy evening club (Truffaut), or a new line dance at the bus stop (Pasolini), dance in these earlier European films shares one crucial component that seems to be lacking in the Berlin School films: the dancers are having fun. In other words, the explicit playfulness of dance in these 1960s spectacles seems to fall short of the complex ambiguity that affects the Berlin School films. That having been said, for the purposes of this study these earlier dance scenes are useful prototypes of (generally) unchoreographed dance in independent European cinema that very likely influenced Berlin School films, if only indirectly.

9. "Flüchtigkeit, Absichtslosigkeit, Genauigkeit, Erstauen."

10. Consider Thomas Arslan's *Mach die Musik Leiser* (*Turn Down the Music*, 1994), and Henner Winckler's *Klassenfahrt* (*School Trip*, 2002), all of which focus on young people and their stories. These use almost exclusively nonprofessional actors.

11. Both Bert Rebhandl (2006) and Catherine Wheatley (2011) have observed elements of the *Heimatfilm* in *Sehnsucht*. The *Heimatfilm* is a German and Austrian film genre that was especially popular in the late 1940s and '50s. It was considered a kind of escapist genre that characteristically featured idyllic country settings of German and Austrian landscapes and whose general (and questionable) aim was to reconcile German and Austrian heritage and traditions after their abuses under Nazism.

12. "Dieser Mann würde so etwas sonst ja nie machen—sich hinzustellen und vor anderen Leuten zu tanzen."

13. One of the most compelling examples of this is the Volkswagen Beetle commercial, in which a German man is singing this song on the street to earn some change to pay for his parking ticket. He not only sings terribly off key but also mixes up the lyrics. In a cameo, Robbie Williams appears, corrects him, and gives him some money.

14. "Wenn eine Figur aus sich herausgeht, dann am ehesten beim Tanzen. Da kann die Kamera minutenlang zuschauen."

15. "Mich interessiert es eher, wie sich die Personen bewegen, wie Dinge aufeinander folgen, wie unerwartet auch und wie wenig absehbar sich Geschichten wenden."

16. "Das ist das einzige Ziel: euch den Spaß auszumerzen!" While Eidinger did place a death mask over his genitals, he let his penis hang out through the mouth of the mask. For a glimpse of the theater play see http://www.youtube.com/watch?v=MkWjt2hXjTY.

17. Jan Krüger, email to the author, 14 Dec. 2011.

3 Between Movement and Affect
The Body's Shared Point of Sense

CINEMA'S ETYMOLOGICAL AND empirical inheritance as movement (derived from the Greek verb *kinema*, meaning movement, jolt, or change) is a historical fact familiar to most. The movement in question, certainly that which was brought into relief by early filmmakers, was of the human body. Corporeal locomotion lies at the heart of cinema. Nearly a century of cinema theory and scholarship has partaken of this kinesthetic tradition in various forms. In particular, since the early 1990s, film phenomenology has taken up the cinema's locomotive promise proliferated through vital on-screen bodies and recalibrated it with a turn to the spectator off-screen and the affect of reciprocity. But with the increasing ebb of traditional cinema in the wake of digital filmmaking, online streaming, and so forth, for some scholars the significance of the body in motion and its promissory on-screen/off-screen threshold have begun to recede into the background of film studies. Some have bemoaned this progression as a crisis of cinema; others have embraced it as a period of new possibility. Indeed, there have been few moments in film studies' scholarly history in which such tectonic shifts in theory and practice have been so visibly present.

I do not propose a candid return to rote theories of film phenomenology of the 1990s to early 2000s and what some detractors have criticized as its prolixity of the subject, its sentience, and its omphaloskeptic tendencies. Yet in many ways the present study is the scion of this tradition of cinematic corporeality. Thus, I begin this chapter with the Spinozian challenge about the possibilities of the body that continues to inspire thought: "For what the body can do no one has hitherto determined, that is to say, experience has taught no one hitherto what the body, without being determined by the mind, can do and what it cannot do from the laws of Nature alone, in so far as nature is considered merely as corporeal" ([1677] 1966, 133). If, as Linda Williams posits, "the desire to see and know more about the body . . . underlies the very invention of cinema" (1999, 36), what is the (cinematic) body still capable of? My response: a great deal. Even for film phenomenology's detractors, such as perhaps most recently Eugenie Brinkema, the body's place and function in film can be recast but certainly not elided. Phenomenological film theory continues to offer a tremendous point of departure and place for unfurling corporeal inquiry in new directions. The body, and the mobile body in particular, is, as I am eager to argue, the interstitial point where film and performance meet. To achieve this argument, I trace a theoretical line from phenomenology to affect studies in film. While this requires no theoretical sleight of hand, I make some unprecedented interdisciplinary twisting and turning between film and social theory. Ultimately, I seek openings for performance's sense of presence and relationality. I propose that the conjuncture of movement, embodiment, and affect in these films forms the chrysalis of performance more broadly.

Beginning with movement: As explored in the preceding chapter by way of the frequent occurrence of dance spectacles, the Berlin School films offer startling studies on movement. These films are startling because they otherwise elude, for instance, categories of action or dance film genres, in which heightened movement is anticipated. The films of the Berlin School are reputably slower paced in terms of narrative, devoid of heavy camera movement, and almost stiltedly unemotional à la Fassbinder. Yet they do not elude diegetic movement. Whether their motion is that of the ordinary everyday or explicitly travel adventure (which I explore in the following chapter), the Berlin School films share a penchant for characters on the go, through both familiar and foreign spaces. The general theme of movement in these films may stem from a postunification cinematic trend in German and European mainstream cinema. The film that most promptly comes to mind as a possible precursor to this inquiry is Tom Tykwer's 1998 internationally acclaimed hit *Lola rennt* (*Run Lola Run*). It is about a young woman who is in a race against time to save her boyfriend from the clutches of dangerous criminals after he neglectfully leaves behind a bag of their money on a subway train. Much of *Lola rennt* tracks its young female figure (Franka Potente) as she runs along geographically impossible routes across Berlin; the freedom of her movement in the streets of a barrier-free, newly unified Berlin is emphasized through Lola's dynamic urban dashing. Along similar lines, movement is thematized and politicized in 1990s cinema hailing from Germany and extending throughout much of continental Europe. Even (re)adopting the popular American road-movie genre (let us not forget Wim Wenders's earlier love affair with the road movie), European cinema disposed itself to movement and the freedom and expanse of the wide-open road in this post–Cold War period. Some of the prominent examples of this broader cinema trend included Aki Kaurismäki's *Leningrad Cowboys Go America!* (1989), Nanni Moretti's *Caro Diario* (*Dear Diary*, 1993), Wim Wenders's *Lisbon Story* (1994), and Fatih Akın's slightly later *Im Juli* (*In July*, 2000). This direction of filmmaking bore political undertones in its (generally positive) assessment of a unified and even postnational Europe. Movement and mobility became symbols of border crossing and borders collapsing. Just as Lola darts unhindered from (what was once) West to East Berlin, passing along and easily through areas where the ominous wall once stood, in Akın's romantic comedy *Im Juli*, Daniel (Moritz Bleibtreu) embarks on a fantastical journey through (formerly Soviet) Eastern Europe to the imagined romanticized and orientalized city of Istanbul in search of a woman he fell in love with at first sight. German unification (1990), the inception of the European Union (1993), and the subsequent development of postnational society and identity are all treated to varying degrees in much of the German cinema of this slightly earlier period. Without directly inheriting the selfsame historical and political currents of this pro-European cinema trend, the Berlin School films evoke a kindred kinesthetic energy. This kinesthetic inheritance is manifested through the diegetic body in movement. As this chapter aims to demonstrate, films by Thomas Arslan, Maria Speth, and Christoph Hochhäusler furnish remarkable evidence against the alleged quiescence of contemporary German cinema; instead, even in its apparent insignificance, pedestrian movement carries the viewer along new experiences of cinematic space and sensation. But first a few words on embodiment and film.

As it hurls the cinematic body into the viewer's field of vision, excessive movement yields embodiment and embodied viewing. The body in motion extends over space, makes the image mobile. This kinetically charged body on the screen alters the relationship of the objects in the frame. In cinema, the body in motion, orienting or disorienting itself over space, is critical to the concept of the frame. It effectively guides and shapes the viewer's perception and reception of the image, because he or she is perceptively drawn to that which is enfolded in movement. My methodological framework begins here with Maurice Merleau-Ponty. In a working note dated January 1960 in his final, unfinished manuscript *The Visible and the Invisible* ([1964] 1968), Merleau-Ponty underscores the importance of movement for perception. Not only are phenomena in motion more visibly perceptible, but it is also through movement that we are able to perceive the world around us—through a physical orientation toward objects and other bodies. Indelibly shaped by phenomenology's body-subject and intersubjective traditions, reading embodiment in film (or film as embodiment, if I may) inheres in what has been referred to as the performance turn in theater studies—namely, a turn to the audience. Body film theories similarly embraced a kind of turn to the audience inasmuch as they channeled the visceral responses and engagements of the *now* embodied film viewer over formal representation or symbolic projection. This theoretical turn to the body was ushered in with a germane shift in attention to the emotional and sensorial excess of body genre films, such as horror, melodrama, and pornography. At the forefront of this turn, the film scholars Linda Williams, Carol Clover, Vivian Sobchack, and Steven Shaviro initiated an exuberantly diverse archive of scholarship on both the embodied experience of cinema and spectatorship. They brought together thought inspired by feminism, queer studies, phenomenology, and Deleuzian philosophy. Sobchack's 1992 monograph *The Address of the Eye* and Shaviro's 1993 *The Cinematic Body* were most instrumental in film scholarship's subsequent turn to the body and went on to influence nearly two decades of film theory and scholarship.

Like Shaviro (generally recognized as more of a Deleuzian, but equally concerned with the body and sensation), film phenomenologists Sobchack, Laura Marks, Jennifer Barker, and Anne Rutherford (many others could be added to this list) sought to examine the body on the screen in excess of its representation. For these film scholars, filmic bodies were no longer reducible to a sign or symbol, as semiotic or hermeneutic, entangled in a burden of meaning. In this vein, Marks astutely remarks that the body on the screen "does not necessarily turn into a simulacrum, endlessly available for reinterpretation" (2000, 20). Instead, the body on-screen became a radical new subject of embodied affect. This lived body and its being in the film world became thick with what Rutherford refers to as "carnal density" (2003, 2). This flesh-and-blood being *really* cried and *really* bled. Even when this flesh-and-blood being was not a flesh-and-blood being but rather a ghost or a monster, as in Christian Petzold's film *Yella*, examined briefly in an earlier chapter, from a phenomenological point of view, if this being looks and talks like a flesh-and-blood human being, then we need to ascribe a human ontology, or better yet, a flesh ontology to it. For the viewer, vision thus literally becomes fleshed out; it adopts what Jonathan Crary might term a corporeal concept of vision, by way of which the "corporeal subjectivity of the observer . . . becomes a site on which an observer is possible" (1990, 69). Through movement the body on the screen becomes a living physical body, and the viewer's visual perception of this body becomes embodied. This phenomenon of intercorporeality forged a direct alliance between the body on-screen and the body in front of the screen that needed to be reckoned with.

By way of movement and especially embodiment, this chapter is directly concerned with the turns and developments of spectatorship and its intersections with phenomenological film theory, which unwittingly bid intersections with live performance's intersubjective, affective, and viscerally real qualities. Originally a critical component of psychoanalytic film inquiry, spectator studies had already begun to establish itself much earlier. By the 1990s, however, spectator studies were saturated with lively debates of previous decades that began the laborious process of chipping away at the paradigm of the hegemonic gaze of cinema. What about the female spectator, the LGBTQI spectator, and the spectator of color? Most famous among this initial wave of gaze theorists to argue for alternative viewing practices was Laura Mulvey, who in 1975 first demonstrated the profound extent to which the cinema was dominated by an embedded (white) male (and heterosexual) gaze. One way of reading the later phenomenological approach to cinema is as an alternative to the troubled paradigms of spectator studies hitherto mired in ideological and binary patterns of looking and looked-at-ness, subject and object. Phenomenological film theory wielded an embodied spectatorship that cultivated subjectivity instantiated not by the hegemonic politics of the *point of view* but instead by sensual experience, orientation, and physical attachments by means of what I refer to in this chapter as a *point of sense*. The viewer's relationship with the actor on-screen develops into a copresence of two or more embodied beings. Just as phenomenological inquiry fixes its attention on the way in which bodily perception directs our actions and interactions, phenomenological film theory holds that the viewer's engagement with what is on-screen is determined by the phenomenon of synesthesia. This means that the given visual and aural stimulation of film viewing becomes redirected through different senses, such as touch, smell, and taste. That is, I see a rose and can smell it, and so on. For some scholars, a phenomenological approach also relies on a noncognitive, somatic language that communicates embodied being by way of a principle of bodily empathy. Put simply, if the body on the screen is injured, the viewer feels the pain of this body. Sobchack's subjective (and utterly confessional) experience of watching the scene in Jane Champion's 1993 film *The Piano* when Alisdair Stewart chops off the finger of his wife, Ada, with an axe, as described in her phenomenological study *Carnal Thoughts*, is revealing here:

> It is a reflexive, protective action that attests to the literal body's reciprocal and reversible relation to the figures on the screen, to its sense of actual investment in a dense, albeit also diffuse, experience that is carnally as well as consciously meaningful. . . . Watching *The Piano*, for example, because I might feel it too intensely on both my body and hers (both bodies, to a degree, "mine"), I could not literally bear to see Stewart figurally chop off Ada's finger with an ax. I therefore not only cringed in my seat but also covered my eyes with fingers that again foresaw—in urgency rather than thought—the impending violation. (2004, 79)

Even if one has never lost a finger (in this way), the affect of violence becomes fleshed out on-screen and is experienced in a real way, triggering in any human being pain sensors that could allow the viewer to experience what it might be like to lose a finger to the axe.

For some phenomenological film scholars, embodied viewing may also be conditioned through the work of embodied memory. Because film, as Laura Marks suggests, "cannot technically represent" such senses as "touch, smell, and taste" the question arises of "how and why cinema might express the inexpressible" (2000, 129). What film does offer is the capacity to evoke memories of experiences that, as Marks avers further, point "beyond the limits of sight and sound" (ibid.). The crux of the matter is that cinema's phenomenological paradigm (of the mid-1990s to the early 2000s) celebrated film much the way that the early materialists did—as a somatic language of triggers. Béla Balázs was one of the first film theorists to laud cinema as the new universal language that marked the return of the sensual body over the mind and intellect. "Culture appears to be taking the road from the abstract mind to the visible body. . . . Conscious knowledge turns into instinctive sensibility: *it is materialized as culture in the body*" ([1924] 2010, 94, emphasis in original). Shared to some extent by his contemporaries Walter Benjamin and Siegfried Kracauer (whose work I explore in successive chapters), Balázs's "vitalist phenomenology" presents a phenomenological precursor in the film theory of the early materialists that not only introduces embodied specatorship but also makes a claim for the affective mood (*Stimmung*, to use Balázs's term) of film, which I will return to shortly. In *The Tactile Eye* (2009), Barker also engages with the notion of a cinematic *language* as "body language" at work between the screen and the body of the viewer. She describes this exchange in the following way: "If the film has a body, it must also have body language. The film's and viewer's relationship to each other is experienced and expressed not only on the surface of their skins but also through movement, comportment, and gesture, in the way they carry themselves through the world" (2009, 69). Barker's use of the panoptic term *film* instead of *filmic body* or body *on-screen* is notable. It implies the possibility of phenomenological engagement even in the absence of a human body on the screen, such, as for example, in the instance of point-of-view shots, which will be particularly important in the next chapter's discussion of the interactive gaze. But while Barker's comparatively late phenomenological study does open up new inquiries, many would contend that it is still anchored in its concern for the human subject as the sole bearer of meaning. Dylan Trigg, for instance, has drawn our attention to the deficiencies of the phenomenological film tradition to account for posthuman ontologies. Examining the nonhuman in science fiction and horror film in his slim monograph *The Thing*, Trigg argues that in phenomenology's failure "to think outside the subject," this "method purportedly reduces the world of things to an anthropomorphised world" (2014, 3). Certainly, posthumanist discourses, from Deleuze and Guattari's "body without organs" to Donna Haraway's "cyborg" and Rosi Braidotti's "nomadic subject," have called for the shift away from anthropomorphic and anthropocentric thought in pursuit of different types of empowerment and sustainability. Thus, I turn toward affect in this chapter as a means not only of rounding off this methodological triad (movement, embodiment, affect) but also of rounding out phenomenological inquiry. Tangential to the flexible vagueness and its "resistance to systematicity" (Brinkema 2014, xv), as that which privileges "those forces that cannot be fully socially determined and may be less prone to discipline regulation" (Hurley and Warner 2012, 99), affect has in the last decade been taken up by all manner of disciplines and theorists—these being the Deleuzians, the cognitivists, the social theorists, the phenomenologists, and most recently the formalists. For this study on movement, embodiment, and affect in the Berlin School films I attempt to piece together a model that not only fits the bill but also paves the way to performance.

Negotiating and extending the possibilities of the virtual dimension of film are some of the aims of this book. How can we imagine film as performance? How can we get beyond mediation, not to mention the deadness of the flat surface of the film screen? First, we must suspend our beliefs that film is just a matrix of codes, light, and shadows. Phenomenological film scholars have been perplexed by the virtual and the digital from the start. Sobchack (2004), for one, explicitly discounts "film" in her study of the exclusive embodied images of "cinema" as a digital agent of disembodiment. In her account, film and other electronic devices flout the possibility for the flow of sensation and affect between film and viewer. While compelling, Sobchack's argument is limiting. It pins us to a historical period of film viewing (in the cinema and on 35 mm) that is becoming more and more antiquated. A film theory that pertains exclusively to the cinematic experience no longer holds. For this reason, I propose that phenomenological film theory can take us quite far but affect theory can take us further. In his study *Post Cinematic Affect* (2010), Steven Shaviro picks up on the potential shortcomings of Sobchack's argument and explains in the spirit of Deleuze that in order to understand radical new forms of technology and mediatization we must also invent new methodological tools. He directs us toward a post-cinematic affect. Affect's unbounded (and boundary-dissolving) force of circulation and attachment makes it appealing to contemporary film studies and particularly to my pursuit of performance as liveness, movement, and sensation. In their introduction to their comprehensive volume to mark this contemporary turn to affect, *The Affect Theory Reader* (2010), Melissa Gregg and Gregory J. Seigworth invoke precisely this tone: "Affect is an impingement or extrusion of a momentary or sometimes more sustained state of relation *as well as* the passage (and the duration of passage) of forces or intensities. That is, affect is found in those intensities that pass from body to body (human, nonhuman, part-body, and otherwise), in those resonances that circulate about, between, and sometimes stick to bodies and worlds, *and* in the very passages or variations between these intensities and resonances themselves" (1, emphases in original). Affect as intensity and resonance becomes a lens through which to examine and understand the relationship between viewer and screen, or even actor/figure, as more than just a virtual one. It opens up and enriches the possibility of an embodied experience of film that moves beyond the parameters of genre and narrativization, not to mention the limits of the two-dimensional realm of cinema.

Affect is this extending hand that provides new depth and dimension—the other side of the screen's insufficient surface. It communicates something ostensibly not materially present. Much the same way that Balázs understood early film as a somatic language, so too is affect. This is what Ben Highmore, riffing on Eve Kosofsky Sedgwick (2003), calls that which "gives you away: the telltale heart; my clammy hands; the note of anger in your voice; the sparkle of glee in their eyes" (2010, 119). A phenomenologist might refer to this as the work of the senses making themselves perceptible—visible to the eye, tangible to the touch, audible to the ear. Indeed, if this is not an illumination of embodied perception, I don't know what is. A "transpersonal phenomenon," as the Deleuzians are wont to call it, affect is an uncodified form of communication between bodies. In his essay "Spinoza and the Three Ethics," Gilles Deleuze describes affect thus: "an effect [*affectio*] is first of all the trace of one body upon another, the state of a body insofar as it suffers the action of another body" (1997, 22). Yet others, and I would tend to agree, purport that affect extends not only from body to body but also from body to object and other material forces. Here it is helpful to consider the work of Sara Ahmed, who mobilizes affect as a means of conceiving our phenomenological (re)orientation toward objects perceived as positive. It is "an orientation toward something as being good . . . as *intentional* in the phenomenological sense (directed toward objects), as well as being *affective* (contact with objects)" (2010, 24, emphases in original). In Ahmed's reading of affect as a form of orientation, she remarks that we are oriented toward objects that make us happy and we move away from objects that invoke negative emotions, such as fear, anger, and sadness. This articulation, however, does not account for a general penchant for affective horror films or melodramatic weepies. Further, to say that we modulate our interaction and relationships with affects implies a structure of control and even ownership over affect with which I would tend to disagree. Affects do not emerge in isolation, but they are, to cite Deleuze's ever intoned albeit ambiguous claim, unintentional, autonomous forms.

Concretizing and ultimately exceeding Deleuze's claim for the autonomy of affect, Eugenie Brinkema's radical formalist study of affect, *The Forms of the Affects* (2014), is together with Shaviro's *Post Cinematic Affect* (2010) one of the few (but ever expanding)[1] comprehensive and explicit studies of affect and film that engages the affective turn in the humanities. She examines the way in which affects are the result of exteriority and film form, with an emphasis on mise-en-scène, or what she refers to as "mise-n'en-scène" (that which is physically absent but rendered formally possible in film). If affect may be constructed through the positioning of objects and bodies (as objects), lighting, and so forth on-screen, then affect is no stranger to mediation. The admittedly heavily mediated nature of Brinkema's approach to affect as that which can be configured through the careful visual pacing of a story, an elaborate and strategic deployment of color, or the simple placing of an enigmatic tear, displaces the central subjective role of the *feeling* viewer. Likewise concerned with how film formally creates affectscapes ostensibly devoid of "presence" and the potential of mediated affect, I am drawn to Brinkema's work. In terms of my own project on film and performance, however, her formalist pursuit of doing away with the (embodied) viewer completely goes too far afield. I must furthermore take into account the formal and genre disparities between the films taken up in Brinkema's monograph (mostly horror and avant-garde) and the Berlin School films, which are much subtler in their formation of affect and emotion. My pursuit of affect is premised on conditions of movement and embodiment, what Diana Taylor notably dubs "e-motion" (2016, 127), and the ways in which these shape affective filmscapes in which the viewer's sensorium is heightened rather than locating specific affects in the Berlin School films. Modulating the viewer's sensorium is nothing unusual in the context of multiple film genres, such as horror, action-adventure, melodrama, suspense, and even experimental; yet in their almost overwhelming ambivalence toward narrative teleology and generic sense-making, the Berlin School films do not (generally) follow the rules of the (genre) game. Notwithstanding their thematic borrowing of freedom of movement from post-1990s Europe and a flirtation with the road movie, which I explore in the following chapter, these films generally resist genre specification and systematization.

Lauren Berlant (2011) makes a convincing argument for the general ebb of genre. She proposes this in response to Fredric Jameson's notion of the "waning of affect," which Berlant corrects as actually a "waning of genre." In *Postmodernism, or, The Logic of Late Capitalism* (1991), Jameson infamously declares that postmodernism may be marked by the waning of affect, which he characterizes in rather bourgeois sentimental terms as feeling, emotion, and subjectivity. Berlant and others (including Lawrence Grossberg) have decried this declaration as misrepresentational because of Jameson's reductive reading of affect, which, with the dawn of affect studies, has vastly expanded its parameters. Berlant thus proposes instead the occurrence of a "waning of genre," which advances the argument that affect has not disappeared but that the rigid structures and expectations of specific feelings and affects of the modern period, such as for instance the melodrama, no longer hold and new types of worldings and attachments open up in its place. Affect offers an alternative to genre insofar as it supports the flow of attachment but does not attempt to systematize or normalize it. In *Cruel Optimism* (2011), Berlant articulates the complex concept of "affective atmospheres" or "affectspheres," which I propose gets me closer to my own theoretical pursuit of affect in the Berlin School films. A term borrowed from Brian Massumi and Teresa Brennan and premised on a discernment of affects as shared experience of time and space, "the material scenes of living on in the present" (15), affective atmospheres present occasions of intersubjective performances of being under an ever-emergent and ever-immanent historical condition of the present. Although not writing from a film studies perspective, Berlant provides the missing link and elaborates how film (which she deploys broadly) and other media do not pose a problem for the production of affective atmospheres. She explains that film and literature "not only archive what is being lost but track what happens in the time that we inhabit before new forms make it possible to relocate within conventions the fantasy of sovereign life unfolding from actions" (7). While Berlant is interested in the representational task of film as a tool of "archiving" and "tracking" affective atmospheres, she does not dismiss the possibility of film's productive power in also creating affective atmospheres. In her slightly earlier study on affect, *Ugly Feelings* (2005), Sianne Ngai likewise attests to the dint of the "affective atmospheres" conjured by literature and film. For both scholars, the affective atmosphere bears resemblance to Theodor W. Adorno's notion of the "atmosphere" (in an expansion of Walter Benjamin's notion of the aura of the artwork) of the artwork as that which actively extends art beyond itself to the observer and opens up the possibility not only of being tuned in to the artwork but also of attunement with the artwork (Adorno [1970] 1997, 354; Ngai, 274). In the spirit of this radical ambiguity (that the affective atmosphere is neither explicitly social nor aesthetic), I extrapolate on that which is left unsaid and return us both to Balázs's discussion of *Stimmung* as the vitalist capacity of film and to Brinkema's argument that film can structurally form affects. These two intrinsically subjective filmic modes inform my readings of the figure of the body in movement in these films.

In what follows, I examine this complex entanglement of movement, embodiment, and affect in five Berlin School films that provide countless images of bodies in motion over the exterior stages of the urban arteries featured in our everyday. Thomas Arslan's Berlin Trilogy begins this heady stroll with a focus on movement, rhythm, and the embodiment of translocality. A comparative look at movement, gender, and desire in Maria Speth's *In den Tag hinein* (*The Days Between*, 2001) and Christoph Hochhäusler's later *Unter dir die Stadt* (*The City Below*, 2010) ensues. Concerning all of these films is the question of how movement, embodiment, and affect work together, intersect, and coextend in these films. As an underpinning, I ask the reader to bear in mind throughout how these sites of entanglement open up possibilities to contemplate film as performance in its mediatized and digitally captured form in what is contemporary film. Is it even possible for digital technologies to manifest embodiment and transmit affect? My own concept of the film's point of sense develops in chorus with what Diana Taylor has broadly referred to as performance's "vital acts of transfer" (2003). For Taylor, performance is "a process, a praxis, an episteme, a mode of transmission, an accomplishment, a means of intervening in the world" (15). In a similar way, the point of sense is an epistemological, as well as phenomenological, mode that mediates experience and subsequently shapes the way in which the viewer perceives and responds to the film world. It performs a kind of "vital act of transfer" from film to viewer that disavows the hegemony and singularity of the gaze and its scopic regime. The point of sense is of course made possible and conditioned by a certain kinesthetic energy.

Taking the formal element of diegetic movement as a jumping off point, then, this chapter will consider the role of the walker or pedestrian and her embodied engagement with urban space as a performance of the everyday. Erving Goffman might aptly classify this genre of performance as "the activity of an individual which occurs during a period marked by his continuous presence before a particular set of observers and which has some influence on the observers" (1959, 22). Without suggesting that the figures in the Berlin School films are throwbacks to the flaneurs and flaneuses of the early part of the twentieth century, I do propose that they open up thresholds and orientations for new and different kinds of phenomenological, affective, and immersive experiences in the city that are largely affirmative and performative.

Arslan's Quotidian Performance and the Rhythm of the City

There is an abounding preoccupation with the quotidian in the films of the Berlin School. The film critic Rüdiger Suchsland has opportunely observed in the context of this cinema that "what we see on the screen is *'Alltagsgeschehen'* [literally: 'quotidian occurrences']. We watch a person as he or she lives. Mostly nothing special or unusual happens. What is more decisive is 'how' it happens" (2005, 7).[2] The Berlin School films yield a sensibility for the ebb and flow of daily life—not least for quotidian movement (*Alltagsbewegung*). Along these lines, Berlin School characters have frequently been compared to Benjaminian flaneurs (Peters 2005; Gallagher 2006; Abel 2008b; Mennel 2008). The classical concept of the flaneur (recall Baudelaire in the face of the Paris Haussmann project) as observer and pedestrian stroller is characterized by an aporia of dependency on and disdain for what Georg Simmel once decried as the "modern life flow" in his essay "The Metropolis and Mental Life" ([1903] 1998, 11). Such does not ring true for these contemporary urban figures in the Berlin School films. Rather, the figures in these films move with a purpose and general haste that often underscore an effortless mobility that actually seems to align itself with an unhindered embracing of urbanism. Neither expressly flanerie nor vagrancy, then, the quotidian movement in the Berlin School cinema pursues a bodily being-in-world that is shaped by keen spatial perception of the city. Against the cliché that the everyday is the place where nothing ever happens, and, furthermore, that *nothing ever happens in these films*,[3] movement instead presents itself as a performance of bodily assertion and phenomenological perception, which is heightened in these films. The actors' bodies in motion take on a more explicit role in orienting perception and shaping the film's capacity for affect. Quotidian movement becomes a kind of performance that affectively projects itself outward and connects with the viewer.

The cinema of Thomas Arslan is not about events that take place in space so much as it is about how urban movement is performed. For Arslan, cinema is about "people in movement, the haptic, the physical pursuit of conquering a stretch of space, that is cinema for me: it finds a rhythm and a form" (2013).[4] His

Berlin Trilogy (also referred to as his Migrant Trilogy [*Migrantentrilogie*]), which includes *Geschwister-Kardeşler* (*Siblings*, 1997), *Dealer* (1999), and *Der schöne Tag* (*A Fine Day*, 2001), offers a seemingly unremarkable glimpse into daily life on the go in Berlin. In his brief article "Bewegung durch Berlin" ("Movement through Berlin"), the film critic Ekkehard Knörer (2011) describes Arslan's films in the following way: "These are films which do something that seems simple but is certainly not. They show people in a specific place (Berlin) at a specific time (respectively: the present) in movement through their city."[5] That is not to suggest that Arslan's films are simply milieu films or social portraits, although this might be one possible reading. Rather, these films deploy movement as an intensification and thickening of space and body. Already a defining quality of cinema (compared to other media), movement highlights embodiment here. From three teenage siblings to a drug dealer and a young actress, these films' figures embody Arslan's commitment to movement and its performance on-screen. Arslan's films examine and ultimately enact what it means—paraphrasing Sobchack—to be embodied in the multiple and shifting spaces of the city (2004, 13). In Arslan's films in particular, the material body takes up an important authority of perspective as a mode and means of phenomenological perception, as his characters move through "spaces that seem of [their] own making" (ibid.).

Together with Arslan's films, a cadre of other Berlin School films similarly accentuate quotidian movement in the space of the city. Likewise set in Berlin, these films include Maria Speth's *In den Tag hinein* (*The Days Between*, 2001), Valeska Grisebach's *Mein Stern* (*Be My Star*, 2001), Angela Schanelec's *Mein langsames Leben* (*Passing Summer*, 2001), Sylke Enders's *Kroko* (2003), and Christian Petzold's *Gespenster* (*Ghosts*, 2005). Additionally, Christoph Hochhäusler's film *Unter dir die Stadt* (*The City Below*, 2010) explores this urban theme in the high-finance capital Frankfurt am Main. Examining a cross section, I connect these films, all remarkably distinct in terms of story and aesthetics, thematically and formally through their lively treatment of character mobility in urban space. These films' relationship to movement as an alternative language of affect of the everyday marks a phenomenological return to the subjectivity of the body as an agent of sensation and bodily expression, and even a medium of affective transmission.

With a focus on Turkish German figures, the films of the Berlin Trilogy have received much attention within cultural discourses on Turkish German and transnational cinema (Dehn 1999; Göktürk 1999, 2000; Gallagher 2006; Mennel 2008; Baer 2013). Mobility has also been taken up as a central theme in these films as a possible (re)defining "migrant" experience in German cinema. Generally celebrated for their circumvention of the threadbare cultural clichés of the films of the so-called Guest-Worker Cinema (*Gastarbeiterkino*) or what has also been dubbed "the cinema of duty" of the 1980s and 1990s,[6] Arslan's films avoid the narrative fixtures and themes of the lack of social mobility and the spatial marginalization of first-, second-, and third-generation Germans. By contrast, his films assert instead a heightened mobility of his subjects that aligns with what Deniz Göktürk calls "the modern metropolitan figure" (2000, 65). While this chapter is more concerned with a phenomenological than a sociopolitical approach to mobility in these films, I do not refute the critical intersectionality of the two. There is a pointed thematic comparison as well as a contrast to be drawn between physical and social mobility in these films.

The first installment of the Berlin Trilogy, *Geschwister-Kardeşler*, bears a doubled German and Turkish title; both words mean *siblings*. This earlier film explores the lives and movements of three young Turkish German siblings between the ages of seventeen and twenty-one: from eldest to youngest, Erol (Tamer Yigit), Ahmed (Savaş Yuderi), and Leyla (Serpil Turhan)—who live with their parents in Berlin's traditionally working-class immigrant district of Kreuzberg.[7] Frequently viewed as a milieu study of so-called second-generation (Turkish) Germans, this film should not to be read exclusively within these parameters. All three central figures in the film—albeit bound by familial ties—have markedly disparate life paths and goals. What they share, however, is their tireless movement through the exteriors of Kreuzberg. A possible study on urban movement in mobile images, *Geschwister-Kardeşler* tracks the youths on the move, on foot, through public spaces in their city. As Arslan said in an interview, the ways in which these young people orient themselves and move through space is a crucial part of the film (2011).[8] His characters are organically connected to the spaces through which they move.[9] In one of the few articles exclusively focused on Arslan's trilogy, Jessica Gallagher calls these urban spaces "autonomous zones" (2006, 340). She polemically limns these spaces as off the grid and under the radar, where the youths may go undetected. But Gallagher's reference to Gilles Deleuze and Félix Guattari's ([1972] 1983) notion of "autonomous zones" or what have also been translated as "zones of indiscernibility" ("zones d'indiscernibilités") demands further reading. These spaces are not simply about anonymity and escape. Beyond their veritable lines of flight, these liminal spaces of transition and transformation are also the sites where becoming and being converge. They are not unlike what Nigel Thrift has called "movement-spaces" (2004). Enfolded in movement, these spaces are formed by virtue of kinesthetic strivings. The peripatetic quality of the urban spaces of *Geschwister-Kardeşler* is not determined by the physical and social designs of a space itself—here the exteriors of Berlin-Kreuzberg—but rather, I propose, by the performance of movement in that space/of that space/through that space.

A paradigmatic instance of the quotidian performance of movement may be found in the second scene of the film, which contains almost no dialogue and offers no action that could in any way contribute to the film's already diluted plot. If titled, this scene would simply be called "Ahmed makes his way to school," because nothing happens on this way to school except movement. With a duration of more than three minutes (significant for a film that is only eighty-two minutes long), Ahmed's route to school is more illuminating than his actual presence at school, which the viewer does not see. Consisting of ten medium and long shots from a capacious range of angles, this montage of commute on foot is divided by a subway ride. A trip Ahmed makes every day is shown here with such precision and detail that it appears to embrace the verisimilitude of documentary film or cinema verité. While the camera is not entirely fly-on-the-wall static and unobtrusive, the film tends to avoid tracking shots and generally keeps its distance—correspondingly eschewing close-ups. Overall, the camera plays a more passive role in the film, counter to the intrusiveness of the probing camera of classical narrative cinema. The ascetic aesthetics of the cinematography here and elsewhere in the Berlin School films not only produce the observational-style images of a film such as *Geschwister-Kardeşler* but also refashion a dynamic of viewing that resembles the structuring of a staged performance—a kind of performance of bodily movement of the everyday as the figure moves across the stage frame, a kind of proscenium. I am struck here by what Lutz Koepnick refers to as the Berlin School's eagerness "to preserve the integrity of each cinematic frame and savor the continuity of represented action" (2014, 156). While Koepnick is intent on an emphasis of the languidness of movement captured through the Berlin School's frequent long takes, read against the grain his description of the cinematic frame astutely fits my own as a stage for movement. Ahmed's rhythmic, synchronous strides along the empty sidewalk sweep across the screen-cum-stage.

In a similar scene, Ahmed's elder brother, Erol, likewise leaves the familial apartment and hits the street in the same direction, toward the Kottbusser Tor subway station. But unlike that of his brother, Erol's destination is not only *not* shown, it is also never indicated to the viewer. Without a definitive destination, the film does not, however, seek to underscore Erol's "lack of place" (de Certeau quoted in Gallagher 2006, 339–40) so much as it accentuates Erol's performative movement through the streets. He not only walks with an air of arrogant confidence—his head held high as he shifts his body from side to side in a swagger, and occasionally spitting—that effectively undergirds his "macho" demeanor but also projects a corporeal knowledge of place. His bodily being-in-the-world is shaped by a phenomenological orientation that, while it does not always turn him toward positive objects, never causes him to lose his bearings. He habituates the streets the same way he does the hidden passageways and alleys, which he stealthily navigates. Despite the fact that Erol's movement is at times negotiated by an evasion of certain persons to whom he, for example, owes money, it is not outright compromised by these conflicts. Consistent with Erol's own aggressive and paranoid behavior, he is often the person that others—such as the two panicked neo-Nazis that he and his friends chase after and beat up—seek to avoid.[10]

Erol's mobile agility and constant (re)negotiation of his routes symbolically reflects the heterotopic experience of many modern urbanites whose movement within the city must remain flexible and contingent. The modern cityscape is constantly in flux; urbanism is equivalent to change. The city's inhabitants and participants must also be in flow with this change. That is not to say that the city's inhabitants are incapable of incurring change—quite the opposite, actually—but that this is an altogether phenomenological relationship, which in its course shapes both bodies and the worlds in which these bodies move, holds up.

Not seen on the first day as she makes her way to school, Leyla is nevertheless also seen on the go throughout the film. (Urban movement and embodiment are not just for men.) The film closes with a shot of the ambulatory Leyla. In this closing scene, there is a return to the extradiegetic music from the opening of the film (there is otherwise no extradiegetic music in the film), and in a medium-long shot Leyla walks along a crowded sidewalk. She walks toward her friend Sevim (Mariam El Awad), with whom she is often paired in the film—they attend the same vocational school, hang out together, talk on the phone, and dream of someday having their own place and being roommates. In this final scene, they meet and then continue on together. The music, which acoustically usurps the diegetic sound in this scene, is, as Göktürk points out in her 2000 article "Turkish Women on the Streets: Closure and Exposure in Transnational Cinema," "instrumental in configuring space and establishing a feel of urban circulation" (64). The rap song is actually performed by Savaş Yuderi, who plays Ahmed in the film but is better known for his music as the rapper Kool Savaş (formerly Juks). The song is titled "Hate" but, as Göktürk draws our attention to the lyrics, "I can't say fuck my place because I got better delay in other lands—I'm just passing" (2000, 64),[11] its relevance to the film's focus on movement rather than emotion, identity, or even space in the film is lucidly apparent. Representative of 1990s (African American–influenced) German Turkish rap, the song's *ostinato* bass and synthesizers in the background create an effect of steady flow.[12] Alignment with urban rhythm and flow in the exteriors of Berlin-Kreuzberg defines the corporeal subjectivity and orientation of all three siblings.

Of course, the character differences among these siblings—their individual performances, their attachments, their affective gestures—are loosely narratively structured, as well. Erol is a petty criminal who decides that completing his mandatory military service as a (male) Turkish passport holder is his opportunity for a new start, Ahmed is studious and seems to aim for university, and Leyla attends a vocational high school with the dream of moving out from under her father's controlling thumb as quickly as possible. But these differences are asserted more decidedly through movement and gesture than through dialogue. Utterly lacking in revelation, dialogue in the film is not only minimal but is also severe and occasionally stilted to the point of Brechtian. Typically alluding to the lack of emotion as well as the deployment of mimeticism though subtle gestures, this assertion also links to Arslan's unmistakable cinematic influences: French New Wave and the Post–New Wave (Arslan quoted in Seidel 2001).[13] Rüdiger Suchsland's formulation of language in Arslan's films as *bei-läufig* ("Sprache der Beiläufigkeit," or "random language") (2005, 7), which can appropriately be literally translated as "while walking/running," is, however, perhaps most elucidating in this context. The critic Anke Leweke remarks that "Thomas Arslan does not tell stories about the life of three figures, he displays their rhythm."[14] These actors do not simply portray locals, they perform an embodiment of the film space in its Kreuzberg setting. As I will continue to trace out in my investigation of Arslan's Berlin Trilogy, the intensity of these figures' spatial orientation within and the attachment to their city render both visceral and affective experience for the viewer. By dint of this experience, what happens here and in many of the Berlin School films is that the body on-screen becomes an engaging point of sensual orientation—a means through which the embodied viewer also lives the cinematic space as open and familiar. Anne Rutherford appropriately refers to this as "ambulatory vision, or the visual experience of a person walking or moving through space" (2003, 4). I extend this further with the concept of the point of sense. These filmic images produce a phenomenological as well as an affective proximity between actor/figure and viewer. The film transforms into an intersubjective space between the two sides where bodily perception and orientation become mutual and affective attachments are negotiated together. Seer and that which is seen become one and the same. This reversibility of subject and object, of viewer and viewed, has been formulated by Merleau-Ponty as follows: "The seeing that I am is for me really visible; for me the first time I appear to myself completely turned inside out under my own eyes" ([1964] 1968, 143). Indeed, the relationship between vision and embodiment has a long history that finds new models in Arslan's films in which bodies in motion (rather than the mobile movie camera) proffer perceptual cues of depth and sensation (Rutherford 2003, 4).

The second film of Arslan's Berlin Trilogy, *Dealer*, presents Can (also played by Tamer Yigit) as a drug dealer in Berlin whose job takes him daily into the streets. Despite its title and palpable genre leanings, the film is remarkably (or better, unremarkably) lacking in dramatic shoot-'em-up action. Expressly departing from the violence and drama of the "ghettocentric films" of the 1990s,[15] *Dealer* offers instead a strikingly calm and prosaic account of the life of a drug dealer on the streets of Berlin. A number of critics (Gallagher 2006; Burns 2007; Stehle 2012) have persuasively argued that Can is restricted by a psychological and even social passivity, but he is by no means static. His destination is often ambiguous, yet he walks with a purpose and haste reminiscent of Erol's streetwise performance in *Geschwister-Kardeşler*. Contrary to Erol's aggressive volatility, however, Can has an unmistakably ambivalent demeanor. Even his sporadic voice-over narration is painfully flat—offering mere performances in stoicism. The film has been aptly compared to Robert Bresson's *Pickpocket* (1959), which presents a kindred figuration of the banal day-to-day life of a pickpocket in Paris. Similarly bereft of dramatic action, Bresson's film even begins with the genre disclaimer: "Ce film n'est pas du style policier." ("This is not a detective-style film.") A cinematic precursor to Can, the main figure of *Pickpocket*, Michel (Martin LaSalle), is passive and introspective, and his monotone voice is more frequently heard in subjective voice-over narration than in dialogue.

The lack of explicit drama in *Dealer* is displaced by the affect produced by Can's body in motion. With scant impression or variation in his emotions, which might drive the plot or contribute to the development of his character in a traditional narrative sense, the exteriority of Can's kinetic body does register affective shifts. While Deleuze and Guattari have posited the imperceptibility of movement ([1980] 1987, 280–81), I argue that film presents a threshold for possible transformation and its attendant articulation. Indeed, as Deleuze said in *Cinema 1* ([1983] 1986), when actors move within a fixed-frame shot (which is quite often the case in *Dealer*), this changing in position provokes a "qualitative alternation" ("changement qualitative"). That is, when actors/figures move, they modify their positions in relation to one another other and to objects in the frame. These modifications can be minor but are nonetheless legible. Read phenomenologically, the movement of a body (in a fixed-frame shot) alters the physical relationship of the horizon of objects within the visual field. Inherently troubled by film because of its foreclosure (particularly in the case of the close-up shot) of the horizons vital to vision as a means of anchoring the object of the gaze (see *Phenomenology of Perception*), Merleau-Ponty would have conceivably been of the same mind as Deleuze that the perceived movement of the body on-screen would render a qualitative change, for a change of the horizon is equal to a change in being.

The open-image shot style of Arslan's films finds common ground with Angela Schanelec's films, which also unequivocally avoid heavy camera movement and are almost utterly devoid of continuity editing. Schanelec's description of her style of filming as setting a stage for action is particularly insightful here: "For example, when people move I always find it nice [*schön*] when the space remains the same and the people move within this space, out of the space and back into the space again, . . . I find it nice, to show the movement of a character and the possibility to perceive that character through movement, insofar as the shot remains. This is a matter of how to make movement visible" (Schanelec and Vorschneider 2005, 417).[16]

With her very subjective but also laconically generic language, Schanelec could easily stretch this description to apply to both of Arslan's films, *Geschwister-Kardeşler* and *Dealer*. Consonant with the cinematography of *Geschwister-Kardeşler*, there are few tracking shots in *Dealer*. The film's movement is almost entirely drawn from Can's visibly mobile body. His interactions within the diegesis are much more phenomenological than psychological. The film (like many Berlin School examples) stresses an immanence of inhabiting and navigating space, rather than enduring narrative states of mind. Read affectively, Can as the point of focus in many shots carries the viewer through these changing spaces (or horizons). Movement becomes vicarious. It is not through the camera's or even Can's point of view that the viewer experiences these different spaces in the city, but rather through Can's (body's) shared point of sense as it moves across the screen. The immobile camera establishes the visual frame of this point of sense, but it habitually circumvents the subjective gaze or viewpoint. Affect's language, conducted through the moving body—the steps on the sidewalk, the arms in a moderate swing, the back shifting slightly from side to side—mediates spatial sensation in a way that dialogue or even editing cannot. The viewer *feels* the movement, senses the space. As the intensity and resonance of embodied relatedness, affect fleshes out the gap between actor/figure and viewer. This relationship becomes more than just virtual, flat, two-dimensional, and distant. Similarly, Elena del Río lucidly writes that "the performance of movement . . . is not tied to the production of a visually coherent form; rather, movement is performed as an affective experience that touches and transforms the body" (2012, 171).

With a focus on Can and Erol, one might assume the trite convention that wandering the streets is tantamount to a marginalized identity of crime and an overall precarious existence. Such cannot be said of all of Arslan's characters. In the final installment of Arslan's Berlin Trilogy, all possible lingering clichés about the correlation between movement and unsettledness or lack of place (or even *Heimat*, supposedly belonging to neither Germany nor Turkey) fall. Certainly, from a narrative perspective, Arslan's *Der schöne Tag* is effectively distinct from the two earlier films. An aspiring young actress moves through her daily routine over one lovely summer day in Berlin. Played by a slightly older Serpil Turhan (from *Geschwister-Kardeşler*), the young woman in *Der schöne Tag*, Deniz, is independent, self-confident, and almost dizzyingly mobile. Like the other films, *Der schöne Tag* begins in the morning, here with an anonymous shot of a blue Berlin summer sky and the ambient sound of traffic. Deniz is in her soon-to-be ex-boyfriend's apartment. She looks on as he sleeps and then leaves. From this first movement on, as she descends the stairs of the apartment building and walks to the subway station, Deniz hardly stays still. *Der schöne Tag* not only compresses more than twenty-four hours of activity (Deniz is also shown the following day as she goes to and returns from work) into a mere seventy-four minutes but also imparts the impression of duration, because there is hardly any dead time between Deniz's various appointments. As Arslan himself explains: "It was clear that Deniz's routes through the city play an important role, that one accompanies her and that this would be pivotal for the rhythm of the film. I like to show how someone moves from one place to another. The routes are not dead time" (Arslan quoted in Seidel 2001).[17]

Nearly the entire film's trajectory is based around Deniz's movement through Berlin. Some critics have claimed that Arslan's choice to move the film away from central Kreuzberg, where *Geschwister-Kardeşler* and *Dealer* are set, further indicates a change in social milieu. That is a possible reading, but I resist the assertion that Deniz represents a more "integrated" figure because she lives closer to central Berlin and not definitively in the Turkish German neighborhoods of Kreuzberg, Neukölln, or Wedding, as some critics have suggested. What is instead highlighted in Arslan's film is that Deniz can physically access all the different points of Berlin, and her routes are still realistic in terms of the topography of the city (Arslan quoted in Seidel). It makes sense that Deniz's apartment, around which she orients herself, is on the western border of Kreuzberg (on Kochstraße), close to the more affluent and gentrified Berlin-Mitte. Sabine Nessel describes this matter-of-factly as the film's realism: "The proximity to the everyday in the cities, where one has to spend so much time to get from A to B, is obvious" (2008, 132).[18]

Even gendered norms do not seem to play a role or in any way limit Deniz's ease of movement or manifestation of urban embodiment. Her movement is faster paced and her body is slightly tauter than that of Ahmed, Erol, or Can, but this seems to underscore her corporeal assertiveness. Deniz knows where she is going and how she needs to get there quickly and efficiently. The adeptness with which she orients her body draws the viewer visually and aurally into her performance of movement—her back straight, her head held high, her arms rhythmically swinging from side to side. Always strident and purposeful, her walk occasionally slides into a kind of springy, rhythmic march (see figure 3.1). The film even amplifies the sounds of her movement—the slight abrasion of her jeans and the padding of her footsteps on the ground are curiously audible. Barthean acoustic close-ups of the body on the move fill the soundtrack (quoted in Peucker 2007, 117).[19] Finally, Deniz not only coolly rebuffs trivial harassment from neighborhood kids but also freely avails herself of the contingency of event and encounter on the street, including her spontaneous desire for intimacy and attachment most notably demonstrated through her quasi voyeuristic pursuit of men on the street and the subway, what Hester Baer astutely referred to, citing Manfred Hermes, as Deniz's "cruising gaze" (2003, 83).

Consistent with the style of acting in Arslan's two earlier films, Deniz's gestures and speech acts can be described as emotionally and dramatically restrained. Even her breakup with her boyfriend of two years elicits only a tear or two once she is alone in her apartment. If there are any ellipses in terms of the film's narrative of minor events, then these are precisely during the brief moments when Deniz is alone at home and physically static. It is never clear how long Deniz is home in each interval or what she actually does during these periods. The film, like Deniz, is simply not interested in stasis. In keeping with this

Figure 3.1. Deniz on the move in *Der schöne Tag*, 2001. © Pickpocket Filmproduktion

topos, she responds to her mother's inquiries about her breakup with her boyfriend: "Wenn es sich nichts mehr bewegt, dann ist es zu Ende" (literally: "When things cease to move, then it's over"). In many ways, this declaration resonates with the steadfast pacing of the film set to a rhythm of movement. *Der schöne Tag*'s narrative evidently does not fit into the mold of classical Hollywood cinema, which, according to David Bordwell in his definitively delineated teleological trajectory, as it "presents psychologically defined individuals who struggle to solve a clear-cut problem or to attain specific goals" (1985, 157). Deniz cannot be "psychologically defined," nor does the film offer a clear-cut struggle. There is a flatness to Deniz that precludes the possibility of psychologically defining her, insofar as she evokes neither sympathy nor antagonism from the viewer. Rather, in their depiction of the quotidian life in the city, these films (and their characters) are impelled by incidence and chance. Nodding to Siegfried Kracauer's classic thesis, one could aver that the street (re)asserts itself as a symbolic space of narrative film (especially these films) as the place of haphazard contingency, a stochastic world in which you never know what will happen next.

Sex and the City: Desire and Movement in Films by Speth and Hochhäusler

Shifting away from Arslan's decidedly emblematic trilogy of films about Berlin but continuing along the trajectory of mobile desire manifested in *Der schöne Tag* and aptly figured through Deniz's "cruising gaze," two other cinematic studies on urban movement and the quotidian may be considered. Maria Speth's *In den Tag hinein* and Christoph Hochhäusler's *Unter dir die Stadt* engage in dialogue with Arslan's Berlin Trilogy and expand the possibilities of movement, both geographically (from Berlin to Frankfurt) and temporally (to the nocturnal), as well as culturally, socially, and even sexually. Contrary to the figures featured in the Berlin Trilogy, neither of the main figures in these two latter films are Turkish German; one is from the upper middle class and in both cases the movement of these female figures is partially driven by desire and their visibly active sex lives, as both figures become involved in affairs. Tracing the steps of the savvy female urbanite is not entirely new to German cinema. But beyond the role of the sex worker, this archive becomes quite thin. That women would willfully and easily navigate urban space finds only minor exception (often) in more radical feminist films, such as Ulrike Ottinger's *Bildnis einer Trinkerin* (*Ticket of No Return*, 1979) about a rich alcoholic frolicking around Berlin in her final days. Nominally not a feminist film movement, the Berlin School nevertheless is abounding with female figures on the go. (Indeed, I dedicate an entire later chapter to the ambulatory performances of Nina Hoss in several more recent Berlin School films.) Motivated by desire and the thrill of contingency, the figures in *Der schöne Tag*, *In den Tag hinein*, and *Unter dir die Stadt* perform quotidian movement in the urban diegetic space that is remarkably witting.

Released the same year as Arslan's *Der schöne Tag* in 2001, *In den Tag hinein* is Speth's first feature-length film and notably, it is also about a young woman living and struggling to make ends meet in Berlin. The main female figure, Lynn (Sabine Timoteo), is, like Deniz, self-confident, independent, and capricious. Where Lynn parts from Deniz is in her excessive recklessness and lack of ambition. She anticipates Speth's more well-known figure of the negligent single mother of five, Rita (Sandra Hüller, in Speth's breakthrough film *Madonnen* [*Madonnas*, 2007]). Lynn likewise resembles the figure Mona Bergeron (Sandrine Bonnaire) in Agnès Varda's classic *Sans toit ni loi* (*Vagabond*, 1985); that is, she lives for the moment, as the film's German title proclaims: *In den Tag hinein* [*leben*] (properly translated as "to live for the moment"). More direct, however, are perhaps the film's references to Jim Jarmusch's debut film *Permanent Vacation* (1980), about a young man who wanders around a dingy New York. Speth apparently found inspiration in this earlier homage to urban wandering. In contrast to Arslan's films, *In den Tag hinein* is a nocturnal film. The setting of Berlin is steeped in murky hues of black, blue, and gray. Critics have called this diegesis a "topography of tristesse" (Buß and Glombitza 2004). The formal reading of color as a principal force in the production of a distinct affectsphere is certainly germane to this film, and visual studies more generally. But the film demands that we treat this almost "noirish" palette with equal doses of nuance and complexity. This coloration of melancholy easily gives way to desire. Night brings not simply despair or terror, but also amusement and adventure. During the day, Lynn sleeps and works; at night, Berlin becomes her playground.

What is materially singular about the diegetic movement in Speth's film is the consistent presence of Lynn's bicycle. The bicycle is a fixture of the film's mise-en-scène. Possibly invoking a slew of films from the archive of global art cinema, from Vittorio de Sica's classic *Ladri di biciclette* (*Bicycle Thieves*, 1948) to Evelyn Schmidt's *Das Fahrrad* (*The Bicycle*, 1982), Jean-Pierre and Luc Dardenne's *Le gamin au vélo* (*The Kid with a Bike*, 2011), and Haifaa al-Mansour's *Wadjda* (2012), the motif of the bicycle is frequently employed as a symbol of mobility, identity, and freedom. But in *In den Tag hinein*, the bicycle can be more compellingly read in literal terms as a phenomenological extension of Lynn's body. If she is not riding it, then she is lugging it up the apartment building stairs, walking it, or locking it up. In the opening scenes of the film, Lynn is on her way home from a nightclub where she occasionally dances for pay. Darkness gradually turns to bluish gray as dawn begins to break over the Berlin cityscape and Lynn wildly races barefoot through the streets on her bicycle. Crossing vast intersections, the camera follows Lynn in a fast-tracking shot that lasts nearly thirty seconds. *In den Tag hinein* does have more tracking shots than the films of Arslan's Berlin Trilogy. To a greater extent than in the films discussed so far, the camera in *In den Tag hinein* seems to share the mobility of its figures. Yet the point of sense generated through the body in movement is not rendered obsolete in this film so much as it is accelerated through the ancillary of the bicycle. In this early lengthy tracking shot, velocity transforms the body into an agent of speed and the diegetic space into a city unrecognizable: merely a backdrop of dark gray, traffic, and blurred pulsating lights.

Although the film opens with Lynn, *In den Tag hinein* is not exclusively her story. Following this opening scene, the film introduces Koji (Hiroki Mano), a Japanese student learning German in Berlin. Destined to become Lynn's lover, Koji is immediately presented as her kinetic kin. Independent and free-spirited, Koji is also frequently on route at night with his bicycle. In a striking backward tracking shot, Koji is shown cycling through the desolate Berlin Tiergarten tunnel as he practices newly learned German phrases aloud. In this resounding, cavernous passageway, the scene visually and acoustically articulates Koji's solitude, freedom, and even uncanniness (for instance, the German phrases he practices, which resound in the desolate traffic tunnel, are semantically odd). On their first night out, Koji cycles Lynn, who has been left to walk home after a ride with her brother in his taxi turns into a fight, around Berlin as though it were the most normal thing in the world. As the night rounds off and dawn begins to break, the two take the deserted Tiergarten tunnel again. This time, in a forward tracking shot, they advance easily atop one bicycle—two kindred bodies of mobility.

There is an indelible contrast drawn between Lynn and Koji, on the one hand, and, on the other, Lynn's boyfriend, David (Florian Müller-Mohrungen), who incidentally drives a car to get everywhere. Ironically, David is an athlete, a competitive swimmer constantly in intensive training. His movement, however, is restricted to the space of the pool and governed by a monotonous back-and-forth motion. While the cool blue of the pool in which David tirelessly practices aesthetically reflects Lynn's and Koji's nocturnal Berlin, there is a glaring distinction between the nature of their movements. In one brief but curiously revealing scene, David can be seen swimming in a three-meter-long tank. The first shot is from an overhead perspective: he dives into the tank and in what appears to be an expenditure of great force begins to vigorously swim in a front-crawl motion. For almost a minute, the viewer watches his body rhythmically push its way through the water only to later realize that he is not actually moving forward; rather, he is only moving against the water pressure in the tank, and he therefore remains in one spot. In another shot from the point of view of his trainer, we see his surging body submerged in the tank—in motion but not going anywhere. David's movement is not only spatially restricted but also under the constant surveillance and critique of his trainer. Mechanical and confined, his movement is disparate from the willful meandering of Lynn and Koji. Thus, I argue that movement in *In den Tag hinein* impresses on the viewer both a formal and an embodied method of reading for character differences and affective structures.

But again, I resist leaning on cognitive methods. Proposing an alternative to taxonomizing visual elements of film as a means of "guid[ing] a spectator comfortably through narrative straits," Eugenie Brinkema (2014, 36) broadly recommends reading such elements for affective forms. Reading for formal affectivity, then, it is David's repetitive, disciplined, and goal-oriented (for competition's sake) movement as so vividly presented in the tank scene which codes his figure as not only ambitious, apathetic, and boring but also replete with a clenching anxiety. Adventuresome, passionate, and emotional, Lynn and Koji are cut from a different cloth. Their nocturnal romps through the city connect their unpredictable movements with the colors, rhythms, and textures of a permeating topography of desire. Yet in its steely shades of blue, silver, and gray—not so chromatically materialized since Krzysztof Kiéslowski's *Trois couleurs: Bleu* (*Three Colors: Blue*, 1993) or to some extent Kathryn Bigelow's *Blue Steel* (1990)—the vivid fabric of *In den Tag hinein* is not only painterly but also kinetically alive with visceral experience. Already tinged with an affective atmosphere of ominous color, the accelerated movement featured in this film prods the viewer's sensorium and heeds her embodied attentiveness. To read with Jennifer Barker, in its explicit aesthetic draping the film deploys "a movement of the entire embodied being towards a corporeal appropriation of or immersion in a space, an experience, a moment." (2009, 13). The starkness of coloration in this film as both a performance and a condition for movement (so it seems) thus further expands the filmic space outward in its envelopment of the viewer.

In the final film of this chapter, light overtakes darkness in the unbearably overexposed realm of the ultramodern. Movement and desire become inextricably linked to the pursuit of something new, titillating, and ultimately consumable. Christoph Hochhäusler's feature *Unter dir die Stadt* (2010) thematically diverges further from Arslan's Berlin Trilogy. Alone its geography and social milieu mark a change in register: Frankfurt am Main in the upper echelons of society during the economic crisis. Svenja Steve (Nicolette Krebitz) is the central figure in this film. Like Lynn, Svenja is carefree and sexually promiscuous. In contrast to the native Berliners in the other films, however, Svenja has just recently arrived in Frankfurt, having followed her husband to his new job in high-finance investment banking. But her self-confidence, style, and wealth (she is always stylishly and expensively dressed) seem to trump any indication of spatial ineptness or lack of mobility in her unfamiliar surroundings. On the one hand, Svenja is the typical bored (desperate!) housewife who fills her time with shopping, jogging, and eventually romantic escapades with her husband's boss. On the other hand, she is anything but housebound. The opening scene of the film effectively introduces and highlights Svenja as an impulsive woman looking for adventure in the everyday.

Unter dir die Stadt begins with a close-up of a woman's back, which gradually becomes a medium and then a long shot as the woman walks away from the camera, a possible homage to the emblematic establishing shot in Hitchcock's *Marnie* (1964). In Hochhäusler's film, however, there is less of a focus on the woman's purse, as in *Marnie* (containing the stolen money, symbolically vaginalized), than on her shirt. The reverse shot reveals another woman (Svenja) in the exact same shirt sitting in a street café. Svenja not only keenly eyes the other woman as she passes by but also gets up and follows her. An oddly fashioned "fashion" pursuit scene ensues and Svenja is shown in various shots on her doppelganger's trail through the street. The woman enters a decadent pastry shop and Svenja follows her inside. Hardly noticing Svenja, the woman nonchalantly orders a pastry and then exits the shop. Curiously watching the woman disappear, Svenja orders what appears to be the same pastry (the shot is taken from the street through the shop window out of acoustic range). In the final shot of this sequence, walking casually along the street again Svenja takes a bite of the pastry she has just purchased and then spits it back into its paper bag. This peculiar scene introduces the viewer to Svenja, who evidently has too much free time and money. Beyond that, though, the scene establishes Svenja's penchant for movement and the contingency of the quotidian on the street, even if it is disappointing—as in the case of the pastry.

In a film about the perfunctory yet wavering life of the investment-banking world with its habitual business meetings, cocktail parties, and clandestine hotel room visits, Svenja's freedom of movement and regular strolling along the streets of downtown Frankfurt provide a contraposition. Svenja is the only figure

Figure 3.2. The "vitrification" of the gaze in *Unter dir die Stadt*, 2010. © Heimatfilm

in the film to experience the city *down below* in the film's symbolic Fritz Lang *Metropolis*-style layering class juxtaposition of above and below or possible reference to Wim Wenders's division of the metaphysical and the physical in *Der Himmel über Berlin* (*Wings of Desire*, 1987): *Unter dir die Stadt* literally means "under you the city." She is the only character in the film who spends any amount of time on the street, or in exterior spaces altogether. The others (mostly men) are almost exclusively *above the city*—haunting high-rise office buildings, chic restaurants, hotels, mansions, penthouse condominiums, or in luxury cars. This loaded juxtaposition of above and below is critical to discourse on urban space. In the chapter "Walking in the City" of his study, *The Practice of Everyday Life* ([1980] 1984), Michel de Certeau discusses the literal and figurative *leverage* of being above and beneath a cityscape. He writes: "When he goes up there, he leaves behind the mass that carries off and mixes up in itself an identity of authors or spectators. . . . His elevation transfigures him into a voyeur" (92). With the vast transformations of our neoliberal societies and the increase in urban living, Lauren Berlant and others have proposed that everyday life theory no longer corresponds to present day realities; de Certeau's writing on the pedestrian is still compelling in the context of Hochhäusler's film, however, not to mention the broader theme of this section. De Certeau's linking of elevation and voyeurism is pronounced in a shot near the end of the film in which Svenja's bank manager paramour, Roland Cordes (Robert Hunger-Bühler), stalks her in his car as she walks along the street. Recalling an almost hackneyed figuration of cinematic voyeurism—man in car watching woman on street—the shot chiefly underscores Svenja's mobility as she experiences the city through walking in it. De Certeau opportunely refers to this as the division between "voyeurs and walkers." Indeed, Roland's gaze is so often mediated through glass—the window from the back seat of his luxury car or the glass window of his high-rise office (see figure 3.2). One could even take this to the postmodern summation of what Sulgi Lie has referred to as the "vitrification of affects and things" (2016, 52).

Engaging de Certeau's thesis, Roland's distance and, in many cases, elevation transforms him into a "voyeur" ([1980] 1984, 92), as he is frequently seen in his ominous, hypermodern, completely glassed-in high-rise office building. Svenja, by contrast, is more explicitly a "walker" in the sense that her body can more easily "follow the thicks and thins of an urban 'text'" (93). While de Certeau postulates the lack of agency of the walker, who, as he avers, "[is] unable to read the [urban text]" (ibid.), I argue that the walker in her performance of and access to bodily experience actually has more freedom and flexibility than the voyeur, who from his Archimedean point is physically restrained to a totalizing visibility. This is even alluded to in this same scene of *Unter dir die Stadt* when Roland stalks Svenja in his car. Svenja easily eludes Roland when he finally exits his car to follow her into a construction site. After assuming that she is close by, he catches a glimpse of her from an upper story window as she (now on the street again) jumps into a taxi on the street below and he is left alone. If Hochhäusler provides a metacommentary on the fluctuating role of the film viewer with this set distinction, the embodied walker, Svenja, offers this source of intersubjectivity. It is through her point of sense that the viewer experiences the fabric and textures of the city, and not through the voyeuristic point of view of Roland.

In contradistinction to de Certeau, Franz Hessel has conceived of the city as a text exclusively decipherable to the flaneur or flaneuse (1929; see also Gleber 1997 65–69). A vestige of modernist Europe, if any Berlin School character can be called a flaneur or a flaneuse, then perhaps it is Svenja with her quite literal pedestrian subversion of the top-down order of the city. Not only does her money and privilege as an investment banker's wife allow her the freedom to stroll and shop all day long, but it also offers her confident indifference. Whereas for Deniz, who tirelessly commutes from place to place, the street serves more "as a space of transition en route to functional purposes" (Gleber 1997, 60), Svenja seems to merely idly stroll along the streets of Frankfurt. For example, I argue that Svenja is more representative of the flaneuse than Angela Schanelec's character Sophie in the film *Marseille* (2004). Sophie might easily paint the picture of the flaneuse for twenty-first-century Europe by means of her placid strolling, discovering, and photographing of Marseille. Sophie remains a tourist in this French city, however, and while she is not a typical tourist—that is, she is not overly visible—her position is still loaded with a sense of unawareness and naïveté, palpably exemplified by the occasion of her assault at the end of *Marseille*. Svenja, although new to the city, is not a tourist in Frankfurt; she simply lives out her everyday. In other words, despite her free-floating consumerist existence, Svenja's relationship to the city is underscored by a certain commitment, awareness, and identity. She and her husband actually laugh about this at one point in the film: What does it mean to be from Frankfurt? She jokes, "Goethe and such." Svenja claims to miss her former hometown of Hamburg, but her reluctance to leave Frankfurt when her husband is offered a new position in Jakarta suggests a connectedness to this new urban setting. By contrast, the tourist generally has a noncommittal and often othering relationship to the space in which she or he moves. By way of her flanerie, Svenja instead tries to access and "befriend the new city" ("versucht, sich mit der neuen Stadt anzufreunden") as Carolin Ströbele writes in the German weekly *Die Zeit* (2011), even though it may, as both she and Roland bemoan, appear like every other major Western city. Thus, if Svenja is what one interviewer calls a "foreign body" ("Fremdkörper")[20] in this overwhelmingly male world of high finance, it is not simply because of her gender but also because of her mobility and real access to the *city below*, which no other figure in the film seems to share. She easily accesses any space. Effectively rendered the object of Roland's gaze in several scenes, Svenja's presence does present a host of gender issues. Yet to respond to Anke Gleber's ever-pertinent question, "to whom do the streets belong?" (1997, 60), in this case, it is Svenja.[21] The embodied impact of her physical access to the streets and her practices of wandering position Svenja as a compass for phenomenological and affective viewing.

All of these films demonstrate new ways of considering a nongenre of street films, which reconfigure the street as *the* stage for filmic performances of being through movement. Framed against the momentum of urban rhythm and flow, the actors'/figures' bodies on the go engender highly phenomenological perception of motion and space. The impact of these embodied experiences is (inter)subjective; the viewer is not disembodied, but reembodied (or "resensualized," to borrow Berlant's term). This is possible because movement and sensation are, as Brian Massumi (2002) has noted, inextricably linked. Through movement, the body manifests itself as a living, kinesthetic, and oriented being; it articulates its embodiedness. My intervention here is to propose that for the film viewer (not unlike the theater spectator) the presence of the embodied consciousness of the actor/figure can be so physically unsettling that the viewer may be unable to forge a distance between her own body and that of the actor/figure. Hence, the phenomenon of the embodied actor/figure on-screen has a particular and powerful relationship to the similarly embodied viewer. This critically direct relationship between actor/figure and viewer becomes negotiated and reciprocated through a type of bodily affect. Massumi describes this process more generally as the autonomy of affect. Affect possesses the power "to escape confinement in the particular body" (1995, 96; 2002, 35) in order to circulate to other bodies with which it interacts. Some affect theorists have gone so far as to diagnose the circulation of affect as contagion, what Anne Gibbs describes as a "leap[ing] from one body to another" (quoted in Ahmed 2010, 39). In terms of these films, I suggest that the body of the actor/figure in motion—the vital and kinesthetic body—is a catalyst of affect and a locus for affective, even possibly contagious, interaction between actor and viewer.

Even in the case of *Unter dir die Stadt*, which is loosely based on the biblical (moral) tale of David and Bathsheba and employs a more explicit dramatic narrative framework compared to many of the other Berlin School films, the potential for phenomenological engagement is still rich. That is not to say that the film necessarily forecloses the possibility of a teleological approach to the figures and their acts. Hochhäusler himself has been quick to observe, perhaps unlike most other Berlin School directors, his films do not always focus on the quotidian, and plot is an important element of his filmmaking reference. Still, affect in these films does not emerge as a result of emotional or psychological proximity (or even antagonism) to these characters and their predicaments, so much as through a somatic engagement with their physical positioning and movement. Of course, highly psychological films can also engender strong affects, such as suspense or horror. Take for example, the auteur cinema of contemporary Austrian filmmakers Ulrich Seidl (*Hundstage* [*Dog Days*, 2001]; *Import/Export* [2007]; and *Paradies: Liebe*; *Paradies: Glaube*; *Paradies: Hoffnung* [*Paradise: Love*; *Paradise: Faith*; *Paradise: Hope*, 2012]; and Michael Haneke (especially his earlier so-called glaciation trilogy in which the bourgeois family comes under attack: *Der siebente Kontinent* ([*The Seventh Continent*, 1989], *Benny's Video* [1992], and *71 Fragmente einer Chronologie des Zufalls* [*71 Fragments of a Chronology of Chance*, 1994]). Often viewed as more psychological than phenomenological (or artistically formal in the work of Brigitte Peucker and Eugenie Brinkema) and with no accent on movement to speak of, their films are still highly affective, and have appropriately been dubbed the "feel-bad cinema" or the "cinema of revulsion" (D. Lim 2006). The effect of the Berlin School films is instead not necessarily about making the viewer feel a certain way or enter into a particular emotional state. In this sense, the work of affect explored here aligns most fully with what affect theorists call the force of what makes us feel, as opposed to the state of emotion that develops as a result of this force (Shaviro 2016, 2). The process of feeling through heightened experiences of embodiment via these films makes the viewer feel neither good nor bad. Shedding pathos, then, the film examples explored in this chapter focus on the possibility for the impression of physical proximity and intensity in these films, which forges an awareness of embodied potential and vulnerability through a sensual intersubjectivity, or a point of sense. These are essentially moments defined by affect—"moments of *intensity*, a reaction in/on the body at the level of matter" (O'Sullivan 2001, 126, emphasis in original). Such moments arise in various forms in the Berlin School films.

More broadly, this chapter examines the crucial role of diegetic movement and its extensive yet ordinary everyday manifestations in many of the Berlin School films as a form of performance. If the performative acts of flanerie historically responded to the shocks of rapid urbanization during the early part of the last century by deliberately attempting to decelerate the pace of urban life, then the ambulatory movement in the Berlin School, by contrast, corresponds to a bodily embracing of more contemporary urban flows. It is a performance that affirmatively bends and extends the possibilities for embodied experience, immediacy, and intimate encounters on the site of the urban. Central to this examination is the performance of urban movement in its drawing power to urge the viewer into a sensory experience of this rhythmic film world. In these innervating mise-en-scènes, a point of sense guides and expands the viewer's mimetic experience of new resonances and sensoria. These are the startling dramas of affect that emerge as a result of the films' "affectspheres" and continue to occasion "moments of intensity" and performance through movement.

Notes

1. The interest in affect in film studies continues to expand. In 2016, Anne Rutherford edited a special issue of *The Cine-Files* titled "Dossier on Cinematic Affect" that included contributions from Jennifer Barker, Eugenie Brinkema, Elena del Río, Gertrud Koch, Laura Marks, Steven Shaviro, and others.

2. "Was man auf der Leinwand sieht, ist Alltagsgeschehen. Man schaut den Menschen beim Leben zu. Es ist zumeist nichts Besonderes oder Ungewöhnliches, was da passiert. Entscheidender als das, was passiert, ist, 'wie' es passiert."

3. The oft-cited, extremely reductive description of the Berlin School by the German filmmaker Oskar Roehler has had considerable influence on the reception of the Berlin School: "They are refractory, always austere. In the films, nothing really happens. They are slow, sad, dismal, and nothing is ever said—that is the 'Berlin School'" (quoted in Suchsland 2005, 6).

4. "Menschen in Bewegung, das Haptische, Physische beim Versuch, eine Strecke zu bewältigen, das ist für mich Kino: dafür einen Rhythmus und eine Form zu finden."

5. "Es sind Filme, die etwas tun, das einfach klingt, aber sicher nicht ist. Sie zeigen Menschen an einem spezifischen Ort (Berlin) zu einer spezifischen Zeit (jeweils: der Gegenwart) in der Bewegung durch ihre Stadt."

6. Prominent examples of this film movement include Tefik Başer's *40 qm Meter Deutschland* (*40 Square Meters of Germany*, 1986), Hark Bohm's *Yasemin* (1988), and Yüksel Yavuz's *Aprilkinder* (*April's Children*, 1998). Hamid Naficy (2001) has written extensively on the trope of spatial confinement and claustrophobia in this earlier Turkish German cinema. For an important exploration of the phases of Turkish German Cinema and its grounding influence in Black British Cinema, see Göktürk (2000).

7. It should be noted that Berlin-Kreuzberg has increasingly become the destination of students, artists, and young professionals. While still heavily populated with Turkish Germans and influenced by Turkish German culture, gentrification has significantly altered the neighborhood in the decades following German unification and has resulted in a significant rise in living costs for its long-time inhabitants.

8. See "Extras" in the DVD *Geschwister*: "Thomas Arslan über GESCHWISTER" (2011).
9. Ibid.
10. The film takes place in a period shortly after the gang wars in Kreuzberg of the 1980s and early 1990s, when young Turkish German men (known as the "36 Boys") successfully fought back against neo-Nazi groups when the police neglected to protect their community. Al Jazeera World Online has produced a very informative video about the "36 Boys." See http://www.aljazeera.com/programmes/aljazeeraworld/2012/12/2012122411620527434.html.
11. Göktürk actually appears to misquote this line of the song as "I can't say what my place was . . . because I'm just passing. . . ." (2000, 64).
12. There is also something to be said about the importance of Turkish German rap as a critical hybrid and politicized music scene in Germany, which has had a similar cultural/social development (albeit slightly later) in Germany as (predominantly) African American rap in the United States. For a wonderfully erudite study on the similarities between the sonic cultures African American and Turkish German rap, see Weheliye (2005).
13. These include Jean Eustache, Maurice Pialat, Éric Rohmer, and Abbas Kiarostami (Arslan quoted in Seidel 2001).
14. "Thomas Arslan erzählt nicht über das Leben der drei Protagonisten, er bildet dessen Rhythmus ab." This is a commentary located on the film's DVD cover.
15. For a comprehensive study on the genre of so-called ghettocentric films, see Stehle (2012).
16. "Zum Beispiel, wenn sich Leute bewegen, finde ich immer schön, wenn der Raum bleibt und die Leute sich im Raum, aus dem Raum raus- und wieder reinbewegen, . . . Ich finde schön, die Bewegung einer Figur zu zeigen und die Möglichkeit durch die Bewegung eine Figur wahrzunehmen, indem die Einstellung bleibt. Das ist eine Frage, wie man Bewegung sichtbar machen will."
17. "Es war klar, daß man sie dabei begleiten und daß dies für den Rhythmus des Films ausschlaggebend sein würde. Mir gefällt es zu seigen, wie sich jemand von einem Ort zum anderen bewegt. Die Wege sind keine tot Zeit."
18. "Die Nähe zum Alltag in den Städten, wo man viel Zeit aufwenden muß, um von A nach B zu kommen, ist offensichtlich." Nessel also remarks that one viewer suggested that film could potentially serve as a "Werbefilm für den städtischen Nahverkehr" ("Advertisement film for municipal transportation") (2008, 132).
19. I am indebted to Nora Alter for pointing out this concept by Roland Barthes in the context of Arslan's films during the seminar "The Berlin School and Its Global Contexts" at the 2015 Germans Studies Association Meeting in Washington, DC.
20. See the main webpage for film ("interviews"): http://www.unter-dir-die-stadt.de/
21. With protest movements such as Slut Walks and Take Back the Night, this question remains relevant and critical.

4 Accelerating Performance
From Car Travel to Car Crash

From the city streets to the highways and byways, furthermore, from Berlin and Frankfurt to beyond Germany's borders, this chapter considers automobility in its important relationship to orientation and disorientation through familiar and unfamiliar spaces. Despite its label, a vast number of the Berlin School films are not actually set in Berlin; many are set in other cities in Germany and in other (mostly European) countries. Angela Schanelec's *Marseille* (2004) and *Orly* (2010), and Jan Krüger's *Auf der Suche* (*Looking for Simon*, 2011) are set entirely in France. Henner Winckler's *Klassenfahrt* (*School Trip*, 2002), Christoph Hochhäusler's *Milchwald* (*This Very Moment*, 2003), and Jan Krüger's *Unterwegs* (*On the Road*, 2004) are partially set in Poland. Thomas Arslan's *Aus der Ferne* (*From Afar*, 2006) is a cinematic travel diary through Turkey, and his film *Gold* (2013) is a historical account of a German gold expedition to the Klondike River through Western Canada. Maren Ade's *Alle Anderen* (*Everyone Else*, 2009) is set entirely on the island of Sardinia and, finally, Ulrich Köhler's film, *Schlafkrankheit* (*Sleeping Sickness*, 2011), takes place in France and Cameroon. Geographical location aside, Berlin School films readily assert a regard for overland travel, at times on a bicycle (Jan Krüger's *Rückenwind* [*Light Gradient*, 2009]) or on horseback (Arslan's *Gold*), but mostly by automobile. Proudly home to so many automobile manufacturers and, of course, to the infamous autobahn, Germany is a fitting provenance for films about car travel. A prominent earlier cinematic meditation on German cinema's penchant for automobility is Harmut Bitomsky's documentary about the German autobahn, *Reichsautobahn* (1984–86), which, as Volker Pantenburg observes, explores and celebrates (beyond the autobahn's Nazi trappings) the visual pleasure of driving on the autobahn: "How nice it is to drive on the autobahn! Gazes chase down images. The street seems made for seeing, a medium. A medium, which simultaneously produces images and blind winks of the eye (2005, 23)."[1] This citation attests to the intrinsic relationship not only between automobile travel and movement but also between automobile travel and the act of film viewing itself. The distinctiveness of automobile travel (compared to, for instance, walking) is that it simultaneously articulates the paradox of movement and stasis. In other words, we can sit immobile in a car and still be moving through space. The driver/passenger peers out the window of the car and sees the landscape change, sometimes so quickly that it is not visually possible to perceive this change. Some suggest that this view out the window of the passing landscape is reminiscent of film viewing. What Pantenburg has termed the "automobilization of the gaze" ("Automobilisierung des Blicks," 2010) suggestively evokes this analogous perceptual experience of automobile travel and film viewing. To paraphrase Pantenburg, in this context the automobile is like an interface between the actor and the documentary reality of the landscape. It is a "perception chamber" ("Wahrnehmungskapsel") that permits a flexible gaze out over the landscape (98). More provocatively, it invites the viewer to participate in the vital and mobile citation of how we so often perceive our surroundings—through the windshield or side window of an automobile. As a film movement keen on moving into new and unexplored spaces, the Berlin School is appropriately replete with this gaze.

In this chapter, I accelerate my focus on movement examined at length in the proceeding chapters to consider car travel. Deploying and expanding on Pantenburg's "automobilization of the gaze," the first half of this chapter investigates how viewers become drivers and passengers in participatory filmscapes of performance. In concretizing this pursuit, the Berlin School flirts with the genre of the road movie as a means of expanding its geographical and narrative horizons, but this flirtation is just that, and these films often go in their own directions. Yet travel and the exploration of uncharted landscapes also play with dimensions of disorientation and its attendant affects. Returning to ordinary automobility, in the last section of this first half of the chapter I take stock of driving more generally in the Berlin School films. An act of the everyday, and indeed a mode by which we so often experience and explore the world, driving is brought into stark relief in all manner of Berlin School films as a parallel to film viewing. As such, it becomes an important idiom for mobile, embodied, and affective interaction within the entangled network of film-actor-figure-viewer.

Automobile travel is also notably problematized in Berlin School films as the cause of many accidents and often even death, however. As I will examine at length in the latter sections of this chapter, examples abound of this destructive narrative variant of car travel. For instance, nearly half of Christian Petzold's films end in a car crash. Pursuing automobility further, then, this chapter maintains its focus on the space of the street and the road but also ultimately breaks away from these spaces—that is, it slides from the road to the shoulder, the field, the ditch, the river. I probe the off-the-(beaten)-path movement, not unlike that which brings us to Brian Massumi's "off-the-grid" or "no-body's land" space (2002, 4). Such movement tricks our sense of perception as it extends itself to the unconventional and nonnormative. In this context, I turn to the myriad car crashes in the Berlin School films, which I propose not only thematically but also quite literally epitomize this notion of an off-the-road movement that leads to disruption and, as we will see, remarkable change.

Ordinary or thrilling, automobility in its myriad directions and manifestations presents an undeniably phenomenological mode of orientation through changing landscapes and foreign (or simply unfamiliar) spaces. This phenomenon of being on the road as a self-reflexive manifestation of worldliness and subjective processing is readily one of the tasks of the road movie genre that, according to Wendy Everett, offers "a self-conscious exploration of the relationship between spatial and temporal displacement of [not only] the journey [but] also of the discourse of the film itself" (2009, 167). Skeptical of genre specificity tout court, I should note that there are only a few Berlin School films that might fall under the genre category of road movie in the conventional sense. Taking this one step further, Randall Halle resists the label "road movie" altogether and applies the more neutral title of "travel movies" to Berlin School films such as *Milchwald* and *Klassenfahrt* (2014, 117). Indeed, these films are a far cry from the classic road movies of the 1960s with their escapist narratives that are occupied by figures on the margins of society in search of freedom and transcendence. But some elements of the road movie have left their mark on a number of Berlin School films, particularly the discursive and formal preoccupation with road travel.

The journey as a metaphor for the trajectory of the story in the road movie is a successful claim and can be explored in the context of some Berlin School films: most recognizably, Christoph Hochhäusler's *Milchwald* and Jan Krüger's *Unterwegs* and *Rückenwind*. For the Deleuzians, the road movie can also offer a reflection of cinema as such, whose moving images are tantamount to all means of locomotion. As Gilles Deleuze states in *Cinema 1*, "The essence of the cinematographic movement-image lies in extracting from vehicles or moving bodies the movement which is their common substance, or extracting from movements the mobility which is their essence" ([1983] 1986, 23). Not coincidentally, Deleuze refers here to Wim Wenders's prominent road movies, *Alice in den Städten* (*Alice in the Cities*, 1974) and *Im Lauf der Zeit* (*Kings of the Road*, 1976), as effective illustrations "of concrete reflections on the cinema" (22–23). Wenders's *Im Lauf der Zeit* even appropriately traces the story of a traveling cinema projection-equipment repair mechanic, who goes from town to town to visit old movie theaters.

If there are moments in Berlin School films that resonate with Marco Abel's conceptualization of the "sensation of movement" as the replacement for actual movement (2013, 21), then it is in a contemplation of automobilization. As driver or passenger, the perspective from a moving vehicle yields both a sense of movement and a sense of stasis for the actor/figure in the film; this must also be the case for the viewer watching the film. The sensation and affect of movement are engendered through this shared point of view, which not only visually but also corporeally registers the displacement through space and time. While a point-of-view shot from a character running or even cycling along a road might produce a similar affect visually (shaky frame and all), such as Anne Rutherford's concept of "ambulatory vision" (2003, 4), this perspective may not be as easily shared or even embodied by the viewer, who in all likelihood is sitting rather sedentarily in a cinema or at home on the couch. That is not to say that the body of the viewer is completely incapacitated or immobilized as such, as it certainly maintains the ability to assimilate motion. In the case of the automobilization of the gaze, this is an especially simple task. Just as the viewer's gaze is framed and focalized by the screen, so too is the character's gaze framed by the window of the car, bus, train, and so forth.

Thus, I begin with a set of Berlin School films that engage aspects of the genre of the road movie and the cinematic possibilities this exploration opens up as it is spatially and temporally reconsidered in Germany (and Europe) of the early 2000s. From there, I turn to the more sweeping aesthetic trend of Pantenburg's "automobilization of the gaze" in Berlin School films and examine how it operates in and outside of film. The phenomenon of this gaze presents a concept through which we may effectively compare the act of film viewing and driving. The work set out in the first half of the chapter is to investigate how to conceive of viewer engagement and interaction with the film on a participatory level through affective anticipation. Such an interaction is possible through affect insofar as it occasions body-to-body transmission through the mutual acts of viewing and driving. The sense of reversibility made possible by the automobilization of the gaze is taken to a wildly dangerous level as this chapter finally extends to the phenomenon of the car crash in several films by Petzold, as well as Valeska Grisebach's *Sehnsucht* (*Longing*, 2006) and Christoph Hochhäusler's *Falscher Bekenner* (*I Am Guilty*, 2005). Without bringing movement to an abrupt halt, the car crash wields a politics of performance that once more throws into question the ontology of film. The car crash literally and proverbially smashes through the disciplinary and discursive potholes and even culs-de-sac that appear to divide film and performance. Walter Benjamin's ([1936] 1968) appeal to the shock effects of cinema and its unexpectedly performance-oriented evocation of proximity leads off this pursuit of the cinematic car crash. Finally, José Esteban Muñoz's (1999) reparative call for worldmaking in the midst of ruin pushes it to new dimensions.

Disorientations: The Berlin School Road Movie?

As a genre often associated with 1960s American cinema, the road movie found its influence in the tenets of the literature of the radically free-spirited Beat Generation (Cohan and Hark 1997, 7–8). American cult film classics such as Dennis Hopper's *Easy Rider* (1969) established the cinematic genre tradition as a masculine escapist narrative essentially about freedom, drugs, and wide-open spaces where anything seemed (and was) possible. While 1990s American mainstream cinema witnessed a reconfiguration of this narrative with such films as Ridley

Scott's *Thelma & Louise* (1991) and Gus Van Sant's *My Own Private Idaho* (1991), the European road movie had already taken the genre in its own direction.

There were rumblings of the road movie in European cinema as early as the 1950s with Roberto Rossellini's *Viaggio in Italia* (*Journey to Italy*, 1954); the 1960s with films such as Dino Rissi's *Il sorpasso* (*The Easy Life*, 1962), Jean-Luc Godard's *Pierrot le fou* (*Pierrot the Madman*, 1965), and *Weekend* (1967); and then in the 1970s with Wim Wenders's Road Movie Trilogy, which included *Alice in den Städten* (*Alice the Cities*, 1974), *Falsche Bewegung* (*The Wrong Move*, 1975), and *Im Lauf der Zeit* (*Kings of the Road*, 1976), but the road movie as a genre made its mark more prominently in European cinema in just the last couple of decades. Tracking this development, Ewa Mazierska and Laura Rascaroli's study *Crossing New Europe* (2006) provides a comprehensive look at the new European road movie. As mentioned in the previous chapter, films such as Aki Kaurismäki's *Leningrad Cowboys Go America!* (1989), Nanni Moretti's *Caro Diario (Dear Diary*, 1993), Wim Wenders's *Lisbon Story* (1994), and Fatih Akın's *Im Juli* (*In July*, 2000) have become the prototypes of a new and more explicitly "European" road-movie genre that celebrates the opening of borders and the newfound freedom of movement celebrated by the average European citizen in the wake of the collapse of the Iron Curtain, the advent of the European Union, and the establishment of the Schengen zone.

My skepticism about the role of genre and its pointed narrative teleology aside, the treatment of elements of the road movie in films such as Henner Winckler's *Klassenfahrt*, Christoph Hochhäusler's *Milchwald*, and Jan Krüger's *Unterwegs* cannot be disregarded. All set in the border regions of Germany and Poland, these titles are furthermore part of a panoply of recent films hailing from Europe that, as Halle posits in *The Europeanization of Cinema* (2014), rather suddenly became interested in the German-Polish border as a critical European interzone. A more expansive examination of these films concretizes this claim. These Berlin School films are not only studies on movement but also expeditions in (dis)orientation through and along the ideological nonplace of the liminal border zone. A space of transit, here the border zone is at once anonymous and marked in the vein of Marc Augé's nonplace and a fantasized rural Poland, which Kristin Kopp investigates at length in her article "Christoph Hochhäusler's *This Very Moment*: The Berlin School and the Politics of Spatial Aesthetics in the German-Polish Borderlands" (2010, 302–303). Straying from the manifestly xenophobic representations of Poland prevalent in 1990s German cinema, as a country allegedly steeped in crime, corruption, and prostitution (299),[2] these Berlin School films still (at times questionably) mark Poland as a space of indeterminacy and difference, where language, cultural, and social barriers inhibit and ultimately shape the (German) characters' experiences and (dis)orientations. Without willfully disclaiming that these films, especially *Milchwald*, are at times dubious in their othering and even racializing representations of Poland, the more concerted aim of this study is to examine how the encounter with difference becomes a phenomenological experience of navigating and ultimately getting lost in "foreign" spaces. In effect, I propose that these road movies further yield what Lauren Berlant (2011) referred to as "affective atmospheres," discussed in chapter 3. Affective atmospheres are the charged phenomenological spaces through which we move and must constantly (re)orient ourselves, that is, spaces in which "bodies are continuously busy judging their environments and responding to the atmosphere in which they find themselves" (15).

Winckler's *Klassenfahrt* chronologically introduces this trio of Berlin School films, which revisit and reenvision the Polish space through an ambiguous approach to the road movie genre. The film is about a high school group of sixteen-year-olds from Berlin that takes a bus trip to Poland's Baltic Sea coast to a small resort town, Miedzyzdroje, just over the border from Germany. With a striking opening shot of the passing Polish landscape from the perspective of the moving bus, *Klassenfahrt* immediately establishes a sense of disorientation, transitoriness, and a lack of spatial definition. The gaze from the moving bus is revealed in a reverse shot as that of Ronny (Steven Sperling), the film's main figure. Together with Ronny, the viewer experiences this strange new landscape in its disorienting, headlong images through the window as it flashes by. Though the school group does reach its destination already within the first five minutes of the film, there is a lingering sense of unsettledness, of *never quite arriving* (at one's anticipated or desired destination)—a generic trait of the road movie. This deferral can be ascribed in particular to the dreary destination, which is a far cry from any envisioned beach vacation. In this deserted seaside town, summer is long over and the tourists have returned home. Further, the shabby hotel, which resembles a Soviet-style precast concrete apartment building (*Plattenbau*), is anything but inviting. The suggestively labeled *Sonnenschein* ("Sunshine") tour bus in which the group arrives almost mockingly underscores this temporal and spatial disorientation.

As the detached and fearless outsider, Ronny fits the archetype of the road-movie figure well. Only a few days into the group's stay, he has had enough of his classmates' inane banter, drinking, and philandering, and restlessly breaks away. He literally packs his bag and hits the road. He hitches a ride with two middle-aged Polish men who do not understand his question, repeated twice (in German): "Wohin fahren Sie?" ("Where are you going?") He nevertheless continues on with them until they finally drop him off on the side of a deserted wooded road. The two men bid Ronny farewell and explain something in Polish: he is evidently both linguistically and spatially confused and disoriented. The viewer, who like Ronny is not meant to understand the men or recognize the unmarked geography, shares his confusion and disorientation. Winckler explains that he has intentionally avoided subtitles in these scenes, so that the (German-speaking) viewer can understand only as much as Ronny does (Lünstedt and Vogt 2002).³ The sense of confusion heightens when in an attempt to hitch another ride Ronny is passed by a speeding car that drives right off the road and up a grassy hill. Unscathed but visibly angry, the driver exits the car and yells to himself with excited gestures. Ronny rushes to the scene and inquires (in German) if everything is all right. The driver angrily points away and yells something in Polish. Comically absurd, both Ronny and the viewer are completely perplexed as to what has happened and unable to comprehend the man's angry words.⁴

After Ronny makes his way on foot to a village, drinks coffee, and tries to call one of his classmates, Isa (Sophie Kempe), he attempts to hitch another ride. To his disappointment, Marek (played by the Silesian musician Bartek Błaszczyk), an acquaintance from Miedzyzdroje and his romantic competitor for Isa's attention, pulls up and offers to bring him back to his hotel. Ronny is not only annoyed at seeing Marek but also struck with a sense of defeat when he discovers that his travels so far have failed to get him anywhere, as Marek's familiar face indicates that Ronny has not actually traveled very far. His potentially great adventure has turned into a short outing and a circular (mis/re)-orientation back to the place from which he was trying to escape. The drive back to the hotel in Marek's van is curiously reminiscent of the drive into Miedzyzdroje at the beginning of the film. There is a sequence of six point-of-view shots from out the window of the moving van. These landscape images are again disorienting not only in their depiction of a foreign space (from the perspective of Ronny)—countless Polish villages flash by—but also, more specifically, because the view of this space is presented in individual shots, like snapshots, rather than in one continuous shot. The suturing of these incongruent shots (much like the effect of jump cuts) renders a lack of continuity in the landscape and a bursting sense of not getting anywhere.⁵ Such a sensation prevails to the end of the film.

Myriad parallels can be drawn between Winckler's *Klassenfahrt* and Hochhäusler's film *Milchwald*, which was released just one year later. In lieu of a class trip, two children travel with their stepmother to Poland to go shopping. An altercation arises between the impatient stepmother, Sylvia (Judith Engel), and the insolent children, Lea (Sophie Charlotte Conrad) and Konstantin (Leonard Bruckmann). Sylvia consequently leaves them on the side of the road for a time out and drives off. On returning, however, Sylvia cannot find the children. Rather apathetically assuming that they have been abandoned by their "wicked stepmother," the children appear to have embraced the opportunity to embark on an adventure and start walking in another direction. For the rest of the film the children wander through rural Poland and haphazardly attempt in vain to return home to Germany; their effort is not dissimilar to Ronny's futile endeavor to (presumably) return home to Berlin. Also not a conventional road movie, *Milchwald* nonetheless similarly contains rumblings of the genre. The opening image of the film, which Kopp describes as an evocation of the "Western" (2010, 292), could just as well typify that of a road movie with its extreme long shot of a desolate, arid highway. In fact, it almost directly cites the opening shot of Fatih Akın's previously mentioned *Im Juli*. But the juxtapositional abstraction of the extradiegetic music in these scenes perceptibly sets up two diverging stories and two very different relationships to the road. In *Milchwald*, Hochhäusler's signature minimalistic discordant music sets a tone of dissonance and ambiguous foreboding, whereas the soundtrack in the opening scene of *Im Juli* is much more innocuous—light and melodious. Further, the odd appearance of two children walking alongside this deserted highway at the opening of *Milchwald*, instead of the arrival of a car, which the viewer almost expects and which is given in *Im Juli*, is disorienting. The viewer is promptly perplexed by this space, which offers no means of geographical orientation. Kopp's description of this scene is illuminating: "In this desolate environment, [the children] seem out of place; they have appeared out of nowhere, and we see no buildings nor other infrastructural elements to indicate where they might be headed" (292). The opening shot of *Milchwald* thus sets up the entire film as a road movie not about freedom and adventure but about an utter loss of orientation. This of course does not inhibit the production of affect. As Sara Ahmed vividly intones throughout her study *The Cultural Politics of Emotion* ([2004] 2015), affect comes into play and shapes the body not only through its orientation but also through its lack thereof. While not an affect per se, disorientation is certainly capable of forming (often negative) affects that elicit an emotive sensational response in the viewer, such as fear, distress, and anxiety. I will consider this further in my investigation of the film.

Once Sylvia crosses the border to Poland with the children, there is a medium shot of Lea peering out the car window, and then a sequence of point-of-view shots (see figure 4.1 and figure 4.2). Similar to *Klassenfahrt*, early on in *Milchwald* the viewer becomes implicated in the moving gaze through the car window at a passing (literally) foreign landscape. There are numerous shots—some blurred by velocity and others slowed down through a sense of focalization. The speed of shots and their varying impressions in what appears to be an ever-changing yet repetitive landscape of sky, woods, and fields give the impression not only that the stepmother and children have covered a great distance but also that they have been driving for a long time. Spatial and temporal displacement confounds any sense of direction, and it becomes impossible to orient oneself in relationship to these shots. Poland promptly—indeed, immediately after crossing the border—transforms into a space of disorientation of rural, unmarked wilderness. A whole host of issues arise here, as Poland expressly becomes a projection that is not produced from knowledge, but fantasy (Halle 2014, 115). Yet insofar as

116 | *Movement and Performance in Berlin School Cinema*

Figures 4.1 and 4.2. Lea's affective landscapes in *Milchwald*, 2003. Courtesy of Christoph Hochhäusler

landscape is primarily conceived through the gaze of the observer, as Barbara Pichler and Andrea Pollach posit (2006, 16), and here from the fantastical and impatient perspective of children, Hochhäusler creates phenomenologically affective landscapes. According to the filmmaker, children have an infinite capacity for feeling. Through their perspective, he seeks to emulate what he calls "infinite or boundless feeling spaces," ("unbegrenzte Gefühlsräume"). As a result, Poland's landscape takes shape (also for the viewer) through the perspective of Lea as a space of mystery, adventure, and danger. In an interview with Hochhäusler,

Abel refers to this perspective as the film's "psycho-geography" (2007). Such a claim can discerningly be made, especially with regard to this initial scene in Poland; however, the sensation of this geographical disorientation—of being lost in space—ultimately shifts to a much more embodied experience as the film progresses. The film's germane allusion to the Grimms' fairy-tale *Hansel and Gretel*, what Vivian Sobchack calls the classic Western paradigm of being lost in space, directly engages precisely this sense of phenomenological disorientation (2004, 13). In these initial scenes, the element of fantasy in *Milchwald* works to displace (or at least defer) negative affects and nurtures instead possibilities for excitement and curiosity. But fear and distress seem to bubble just below the surface and finally do latch to forms of physical and sexual assault, both imagined and real. The children never find their way home; they never reorient themselves out of this geography; they live it; they are part of this landscape of affect. At no moment in the film is this as evident as in its final image.

Milchwald ends with a long shot of a desolate road that is reminiscent of the film's opening shot. Instead of walking toward the camera, however, Lea and Konstantin walk away from it and away from their Polish acquaintance Kuba (Miroslaw Baka) who, in a gesture similar to that of the frustrated stepmother at the beginning of the film, has kicked them out of his van after Lea attempts to poison him. The children do not glance back as they walk away, nor does the shot shift to a frontal view of their faces. All that is visible are the backs of their bodies as they move forward. The vast open road quickly dwarfs their miniature silhouettes as they eventually reach the film image's vanishing point and morph into dark specks on the landscape before finally disappearing. Painstakingly long in duration, the shot lasts a full two and a half minutes. The soundtrack reprises the dissonant music also heard on the opening track of the film. This never-ending shot of a barren highway landscape engenders both contingency and possibility. Yet the film's ending is much more ambiguous than liberating and hopeful. Lea and Konstantin's movement continues without a destination in sight. Here, too, there is a circular quality to both the children's movement and to the film's narrative that further underscores the sense of disorientation that is never shed.

Of the three films I consider under the rubric of the road movie, the last one, Jan Krüger's *Unterwegs* (*On the Road*), is perhaps most true to the genre. The film's title alone immediately invites such interpretive inclinations. As Rudolf Worschech observes, "[t]here is a lot of traveling in the new German cinema. People are searching for orientation, meaning, safety, and security. Krüger's first feature-length film is something of a road movie" (2004).[6] For Benni (Florian Panzner), Sandra (Anabella Lachatte), and her daughter Jule (Lena Beyerling), a road trip to Poland signals precisely the desire for disorientation, contingency, and adventure. What begins as an uneventful family camping trip somewhere in the eastern state of Brandenburg turns into a road trip to the Baltic Sea coast in Poland and beyond after the young family meets up with the mysterious and adventuresome Marco (Martin Kiefer). Unlike in *Klassenfahrt* and *Milchwald*, an excursion across the border in *Unterwegs* evokes excitement and diversion for the protagonists, who joke among themselves that this will be a "Bonnie, Benni, and Clyde" trip.

In a spontaneous burst of wanderlust, the four travel overnight to reach their destination. Once more the first perspective of Poland is through the window of the moving car—through the automobilized gaze. The film viewer glimpses a nightscape of darkness punctured with streetlights, headlights, and a large billboard featuring a bikini-clad woman. An upbeat new age music track accompanies these moving shots, pushing the scene rhythmically forward. This time the view appears to be through the front windshield from the perspective of the driver, as the other passengers are presumed to be asleep. At first there is no reverse shot, and there is a moment of suspense and excitement. What is the provenance of the gaze through which the viewer is taking in these images of the road? These shots vaguely echo the phantom rides of early cinema, which were images often shot from the front exterior of a moving train (in the days before dollies) and offered the exciting sensation of travelling while sitting still. "With a very slight stretch of imagination he [the viewer] can fancy himself tearing along at great speed on a cow-catcher, with the landscape simply leaping towards him. . . . A more exciting and sensational piece of realism has never been presented to the audience" (quoted in Barnes 1996, 145). These words aptly describe this anonymous gaze from the automobile and its capacity to engender the sense of movement that is imparted on the viewer. The main difference lies in editing. Phantom rides offered no reverse shot and furthermore no visible means of movement. Thus, the shots from the moving car in *Unterwegs* are not true phantom rides as the camera is from the perspective of the driver through the front windshield, which contextualizes the image and in some ways reveals the provenance of the gaze.

Poland appears far less strange and desolate in the moving perspective visualized by *Unterwegs*. But here as well, travel to a foreign place is marked by a sense of disorientation and an affective sensorium of excitement and curiosity. As the sun begins to rise, there is finally a reverse shot of the inside of the car and the travelers drowsily taking in their new surroundings. In another shot it is morning in a small town, and there is activity in the streets as the travelers swiftly pass through to get to their desired seaside destination. While the overcast and rainy Poland in *Unterwegs* is not exactly the sun-drenched paradise advertised on the billboard along the way, it is by no means the dismal and deserted space presented in *Klassenfahrt* nor the wildly desolate and menacing hinterland of *Milchwald*. What connects these three films in their portrayals of the Polish landscape is a pursuit of a vividly transitory space that ultimately disorients and redirects. Even for the optimistic and seemingly happy couple Sandra and Benni, their adventures in Poland lead to betrayal and breakup.

Phenomenologically speaking, disorientation—that is, getting lost—is of course not necessarily a bad thing. "Getting lost," Sara Ahmed asserts, "still takes us somewhere; and being lost is a way of inhabiting space by registering what is not familiar: being lost can in its turn become a familiar feeling" (2006, 7). In *Unterwegs*, getting lost has a potentially affirmative outcome insofar as a willful reorientation takes shape. This is exemplified most directly in what appears to be an allusion to *Milchwald*. Marco brings Sandra's daughter, Jule, into the woods and leaves her there on the premise of enacting her own real-life fairy tale. As Kopp astutely observes, "the scene is rich with ambiguity" (2010, 302). Unlike in *Milchwald*, however, Sandra and Benni quickly find Jule. Finally, in the closing scene of *Unterwegs* Sandra and Jule drop Benni off at a rest stop from where he will presumably find his way back to Germany, and mother and daughter appear to head off in another direction to continue their adventure. The final shot of the film is a forward tracking of their car on its way. Even with the return of the same extradiegetic music that accompanied the travelers in the earlier scene on their arrival in Poland, this final shot on the road diverges from the previous ones. Distinct from the gaze *from* the car (the automobilization of the gaze), the car itself orients the camera and the viewer's gaze through space as the camera moves with it (behind it). By contrast, the final shot in *Milchwald* of Lea and Konstantin as they walk forward into the distance remains static. There is a continued sense of disorientation and even stasis in *Milchwald*, as the viewer not only does not know where the children are headed but also is not invited to follow—curiously abandoned and static.

If the Berlin School films follow narratives occupied by restless figures in search of identity in the globalized world, as suggested by Sabine Wolf (2009, 42), and as Abel posits, "these narratives . . . ultimately render these German places and characters as being out of place, out of sorts, oddly unhinged, askew, in a word: lost" (2013, 72), then these three films are most in accord. Tracing movement as an impacting experience of a number of Berlin School films, from a genre perspective *Klassenfahrt*, *Milchwald*, and *Unterwegs* articulate what has become the commonplace condition of continuous movement and lack of permanency of the European lifestyle in the twenty-first century (Mazierska and Rascaroli 1). Still, labeling these films as road movies is not my main objective. My claim is rather that these films' subtle turn to the road movie genre gives license for an uninhibited exploration of movement and (dis)orientation into parts unknown. The strikingly literal *traveling* shots in these Berlin School films present an operative point of view that phenomenologically and affectively engages the viewer's sense of shared voyage and adventure in all of their exciting and daunting actualizations. The viewer experiences both movement and getting lost, fortified of course by the affects they mobilize.

The "Automobilized Gaze" and Participatory Landscapes of Affect

Beyond the films that play with the road movie genre and take the viewer into unfamiliar spaces, a whole host of Berlin School films employ the automobilized gaze (my own slight adjustment of the "automobilization of the gaze"), touched on throughout the previous section. Introduced to film studies by Volker Pantenburg (2010), this is hardly a phenomenon exclusive to film. In his study *Driving Germany: The Landscape of the German Autobahn 1930-1970* (2010), Thomas Zeller thoroughly explores the increased interest in the relationship between technology, movement, and landscape via the sociological concept of the automobilized gaze. In this context, it may be useful to recall myriad highway and road beautification projects, such as the Highway Beautification Act in the United States (1965), or other minor endeavors aimed at keeping drivers entertained without distracting them too much, such as the placement of large pastel-colored geometric shapes along the major A4 route in France. On average, Germans spend about thirty minutes each day commuting (see OECD 2016). The windshield (or passenger window) has literally become our mobile window to the world.

It is not surprising then that cinema would *mobilize* this automobilization of the gaze as a citation of our habitual mode of seeing the world. In cinema's analogous drive to show us how to see things and to transport us into other worlds, it demonstrates a significant phenomenological relationship to the automobile. Pantenburg astutely draws a parallel between the two screens: "Windshield and silver screen: Two screens, which frame our gaze of the landscape, two visual membranes that mediate between different spaces" (2010, 94).[7] Just as the Panavision-shaped windshield of the automobile represents the movie screen, like cinema the automobile symbolizes a journey through both movement and stasis. As Paul Virilo likewise claims: "What goes on in the windshield is the cinema in a strict sense" (Virilo quoted in Beckman 2010, 5). If sitting in the car looking out through the windshield at the passing landscape is comparable to watching a film, then the presence of the automobilized gaze in cinema self-reflexively wields a doubled screen. Rather than distancing viewers from the action through the effect of the doubled screen qua doubled mediation, however, the automobilized gaze in cinema actually brings them into proximity with the action and the movement on the screen through its citation of everyday experience of mobility and a vision of reality. This perspective duly fits Christian Metz's postulation that "films release a mechanism of affective and perceptual *participation* in the spectator" (1974, 4, emphasis added). In this sense, the automobilized gaze in cinema is phenomenologically akin to something like interactive car video games.[8]

This takes a different approach to what Adam Lowenstein (2015, 45) called "interactive art cinema" to refer to surrealist-influenced films that draw the viewer in through self-reflective video game play, as exemplified for instance by David Cronenberg's *eXistenZ* (1999). In the Berlin School films, participation is rendered possible through the shared gaze between driver-viewer and viewer-driver. Or, as Christoph Hochhäusler puts it: "A film should make a world visible that can only be told when one completes it with one's own life and takes it along in life" (quoted in Zinsmaier 2009).[9] Films such as Christian Petzold's *Gespenster* (*Ghosts*, 2005), *Yella* (2007), and *Jerichow* (2008); Angela Schanelec's *Mein langsames Leben* (*Passing Summer*, 2001) and *Marseille* (2004); and Ulrich Köhler's *Montag kommen die Fenster* (*Windows on Monday*, 2006) are just some of the many examples found in the Berlin School that present this participatory automobilized gaze in compelling ways. Perhaps more than any other effect explored throughout this study, the automobilized gaze engenders affect directly through its extension of sensation via mediation. In this shared gaze, the body is signaled (even forced) to respond to the mediated images of the road through the sensation of *really* driving. The effect of this pull, this orientation to look out through numerous layers forges a structure of affect that is formal yet also phenomenological in its demand. This structure of looking does not ask us to feel a certain way; rather, it forces us to position ourselves with the driver (or the passenger, as the case may be). Thus, I must disagree with Lutz Koepnick's argument in his brief article on "Cars" in Berlin School films, in which he asserts that it would be a mistake to perceive the shots of the road and/or the driver as a space for empathetic or even interactive viewing (2013, 77-78). Quite on the contrary, I propose that the automobilized gaze in the Berlin School films does offer a tremendous sense of visual and phenomenological reciprocity. The automobile and its attendant automobilized gaze quite convincingly become the chassis of Berlantian "affective atmospheres," by way of which we as viewers must endlessly (re)orient ourselves. Thomas Arslan succinctly articulates this phenomenon of filmmaking in the following way: "You have to leave the viewer some leeway to participate [*Spielraum*]" (quoted in Baer 2013, 79).[10]

Petzold's employment of the automobilized gaze in his films is significant both in occurrence and impression. In all three instances considered in the following (*Gespenster, Yella*, and *Jerichow*), this gaze is set up like a phantom ride, as discussed previously. The source of the point of view through the windshield is never immediately revealed, but often uncannily delayed. Not only does Petzold effectively establish a sense of mystery through these shots, which ultimately introduce new characters to each film respectively, he also sets up the possibility for (inter)active spectatorship. With no driver in sight, there is an unwieldy impression of being behind the wheel and driving oneself. In Petzold's film *Gespenster*, the opening shot offers the perspective through the windshield of a vehicle driving along a three-lane highway. For the first twenty-five seconds of the film, the viewer is the driver. This shot, like the film itself, is acoustically ushered in by Bach's haunting first cantata *Ich hatte viel Bekümmernis*, the film's musical motif. Highway signs might indicate to the more familiar viewer that the car is entering the German capital, Berlin, but there are no discernible landmarks in sight. In these first twenty-five seconds, there is no sign of a driver, no voice, not even a hand gesture; he (in this case) is entirely off-screen. The gaze is rigidly directed forward at the approaching cityscape. One cannot help but consider this opening citation of the phantom ride in the context of the film, which is appropriately titled *Gespenster*. Already in this first shot, a disembodied gaze enters the setting of the film, propelled forward by an unknown source.[11]

Petzold has a tendency of introducing his (male) figures as mysterious drivers. Jumping ahead chronologically to his film *Jerichow*, the abstractness of the phantom ride is accentuated in a shot that evokes the emblematic image of the ghostly nocturnal highway from David Lynch's cult classic *Lost Highway* (1997). In *Jerichow* this is a night shot; the only visually legible objects are those mistily illumined by the headlights of the automobile: an unpaved country road, the outline of a white picket fence, and blurred road signs. Similar to the automobilized gaze in the opening scene of *Gespenster*, this is a point-of-view shot of a (male) character the viewer has not yet encountered. Again, there is no visible sign of the driver. A lively Turkish pop song, *Karar Verdim* (*I Decided*) by the 1980s artist Nilüfer, emanates diegetically from the car radio. Although this music is not exactly a motif in the film, it does return and is associated with the driver, Ali (Hilmi Sözer), who we learn later is Turkish German. The combination of the upbeat Turkish pop music and the tenebrous dark (German) country road is at first confounding; somehow the visual (albeit meager) and aural tracks do not seem to match up. This contradiction disconnects the shot further. The sense of disorientation and displacement is nevertheless dissipated by a clear sense of direction and forward-moving propulsion that the shared gaze of driver-viewer/viewer-driver engenders.

Bearing a quality of contingency, the automobilized gaze still effectuates an acute layer of control and power. In his film *Yella*, Petzold deploys this strategy yet again. This example of the automobilized gaze is, however, explicitly scopophilic, as it is less focused on the passing landscape than on a passing female pedestrian. Rather than on a highway approaching Berlin, this scene in *Yella* is set in the small town of Wittenberge on the Elbe.[12] An automobile appears to be stopped at a traffic light. Framed by the distended front windshield is the image of a traffic intersection through which the female figure, Yella (Nina Hoss), walks (see figure 4.3). The automobile then becomes mobile and turns right, in the same direction as the woman. What appears to be the handheld camera's attendant flexible gaze remains fixed on the woman—panning from the front

Figure 4.3. The "automobilized gaze" as the privileged male gaze in *Yella*, 2007. © Schramm Film Koerner & Weber

windshield, to the driver's side window, the backseat window, and finally in an over-the-shoulder shot out the rear window—as the automobile passes Yella. In his study on the horror-genre elements in this film, Jaimey Fisher refers to this shot as "a deliberate point-of-view shot from a male predator's perspective" (2011a, 193). While the source of the gaze is cursorily revealed through this pan in its passing glance at the rearview mirror and a close-up of the back of the driver's head, the viewer is disconcertingly positioned, not only as driver, but also as voyeuristic predator. The automobilized gaze functions affectively not only through its ability to create an identificatory sense of perception but, moreover, due to its structure of interactivity that positions (and embodies) the viewer in the same physical and sensational space and activity as the male driver/actor. Affect emerges through encounter; the proximity of the viewer to the film by dint of the interactive or even participatory gaze readily provides such an encounter. It galvanizes the body of the viewer as it positions her in line with that of the actor/figure. Finally, it phenomenologically transmutes the viewing experience into an affective experience of driving/stalking that produces potential feelings of excitement and possibly even distress.

What is perhaps most interesting about the automobilized gaze in this scene from *Yella* is its distinct manner of seeing things—of seeing the world. Fisher remarks that from the driver's (to whom the viewer is shortly thereafter introduced as Yella's ex-husband, Ben) point of view in this over-the-shoulder shot, the town of Wittenberge appears lively and teeming: "full of traffic and shoppers, bustling as one would expect in a small city on a summer afternoon" (2011b, 447). However, as soon as the driver exits his vehicle to speak to (or better: to harass)

Yella, the perspective changes: "the town appears empty, devoid of both street traffic and pedestrians" (ibid.).[13] This seems to imply that the automobilized gaze is sanguine, like putting on a pair of rose-colored glasses. Similar to *Gespenster* and *Jerichow*, this gaze in *Yella* is also accompanied by diegetic music. The score is Julie Tippetts's (formerly Driscoll) 1960s jazz hit "Road to Cairo." This song is definitively a motif in the film and returns on two other occasions throughout the film. To an even greater extent than the Turkish pop music in *Jerichow*, this lounge-style tune seems ill matched to this (albeit banally) eerie scene of stalking. It may be possible to conclude that the music undergirds a certain fantasy perspective from the point of view of the driver that is intentionally matched with the privileged automobilized gaze.

Does the world appear better from an automobile? Certainly, the automobile opens up the possibility of unrestricted and accelerated looking. As a moving box with many windows and mirrors for convenient multidirectional glancing and gazing, the automobile is what Jean-Luc Nancy called a *boîte à regarder* (literally "a gazing box") (2001, 15), or what Ian Balfour refers to as a *camera non obscura* (2010, 36). More generally, of course, the automobile signifies power and security. Hence, the automobilized gaze is a privileged gaze. It offers experience, access, and mobility without physical exertion and potential danger of exposure. (Just consider the popularity of, for example, tinted—or even bulletproof—windows.) There are unequivocal parallels to the cinematic gaze, which Anke Gleber fittingly describes in the following way: "The darkened space of the cinema removes her from the gaze of others and at the same time allows her own gaze unrestricted and accelerated access to all the shocks and impressions of modernity, approximating and even exceeding the experience of the street" (1997, 77).

Here Gleber explores early cinema as an alternative for women, who were often not at liberty to engage in the pleasures of flanerie, or automobility for that matter, the same way that men could in the early part of the last century. This description of the cinema experience sounds undeniably analogous to the automobilized gaze. Ironically, in Petzold's films it is, however, the male figure who (almost exclusively) has the privilege to enjoy this gaze. The few times we see women driving in his films it is generally with a borrowed (man's) car, or in the case of a more recent film, *Phoenix*, the woman driving (Lene) is decidedly genderqueer. Yet despite the lingering clichéd association of "masculinity and technology," inherent in the early road movie (Corrigan 1991, 143), men are not the only bearers of the automobilized gaze in Berlin School films.

Angela Schanelec's films *Mein langsames Leben* and *Marseille*, as well as Ulrich Köhler's *Montag kommen die Fenster*, for example, offer instances of women also in possession of the automobilized gaze. In *Mein langsames Leben* there is a peculiarly brief shot through the front windshield of a car being driven along a rural German road. Within seconds the car stops at a railroad crossing and there is a cut to a completely different scene. The viewer can only assume, based on the following scene, that the driver is Valerie (Ursina Lardi), who has returned to her hometown of Ludwigshafen to visit her ailing father; like so many other shots in this film, however, there is no reverse shot. Only the visible right hand on the steering wheel in this shot divulges possible identity markers, such as the gender of the driver. In contrast to the other scenes examined in this section, there is no music. Instead, the shot's acoustic consort comprises merely the sound of the automobile's trembling motor. The use of original sound is typical of Schanelec's films. As she herself claims, "I can't imagine working with anything but original sound" (2001).[14] The realistic representation of this shot again signals the plausibility of the viewer to position herself as viewer-driver. Simple and seemingly irrelevant to the film, this scene—consisting of a brief single point-of-view shot—not only is characteristic of Schanelec's elliptical style of filmmaking and general eschewal of reverse shots[15] but also enunciates the shared position of the off-screen of actor and viewer. With the absence of the reverse shot, this particular scene opens up the possibility of considering the interchange of on- and off-screen positions in its capacity to engage the viewer's participation in a spatial, phenomenological way through the potential encounter of bodies.

By placing the actor (with the exception of a hand) in the viewer's potential off-screen space—out of view—the shot throws into question the divide between on-screen and off-screen positions, usually occupied by actor/figure and viewer, respectively. Read phenomenologically, this shot may be contemplated with Vivian Sobchack, who avers that the experience of a film does not simply mean to *see* it (as the viewer never sees the driver here); instead, the "lived body" of the viewer enacts perception. Sobchack calls this "the flesh's reversibility." In this reversibility, the abiding notions of on- and off-screen as "mutually exclusive sites or subject positions" begin to collapse (2004, 66–67). If reversibility of on- and off-screen positions inheres in the automobilized gaze, then speaking of a participatory structure at work here is by no means a stretch. The viewer does not merely watch and observe from a third position but finds herself, if not at the wheel, then, like a loathed backseat driver, eager to take over.

In an opening shot that is thematically and affectively reminiscent of Petzold's *Gespenster*, Schanelec's film *Marseille* begins with an arrival—this time not in Berlin but in Marseille. A young woman is driving. Distinct from that in the other examples, the perspective of the opening shot, directly over the right shoulder of the young woman, reveals the driver in a dark silhouette. Shallow focus hinders a clear view of the street ahead; nonetheless, it is apparent that the scene is in an urban setting due to the activity in streets—the stop-and-go movement of the automobile in traffic and the driver's constant shifting of gears. There is again no music in this scene, but the driver converses with a passenger off-screen. Yet the sententious conversation offers scant information about these two figures. Rather than a beginning, this arrival seems to exhibit an in medias res of a narrative—who are these women and how do they know each other? This is never fully revealed in the film.

Maintaining her signature style, Schanelec does not provide a reverse shot of the driver; instead, in the same shot the viewer sees the driver pull over to the curve, exit the car, purchase a city map, and then return to the car. On her return, a frontal view of the driver is revealed. While the viewer's spatial positioning in this shot is more as backseat passenger, the shot's explicit focus on the driver and her almost overly active gestures—she is perceptibly driving through busy city streets with a standard (versus an automatic) car—is so startlingly embodied that it spurns the viewer's everyday corporeal and affective participation in the act of backseat driving. Indeed, the driver overzealously yanks the stick shift, gives gas, breaks, and yanks the stick shift again, and so forth. The irritating grating sound of the clutch is omnipresent. She is evidently a rather bad driver; we are eager to relieve her and take over. Consequently, the viewer's body and senses are immediately situated in the film experience, which so closely mimics that of the quotidian experience of being behind the wheel. In this case, the viewer does not *fill in* the position of the absent driver, as in the Petzold scenes; rather, the viewer participates in this active automobilized gaze via bodily responsiveness to the driver's actions directly. In other cinematic contexts, Sobchack refers to this type of responsiveness as "prereflective." As she explains, its function is to pique the "carnal knowledge of our acculturated sensorium" (2004, 63). The viewer's own embodied familiarity with driving, the movements and actions required, engenders a phenomenological as well as an affective relationship to the driver in this scene.

The final film I examine in this section, Köhler's *Montag kommen die Fenster*, features a nocturnal drive on the highway, through a small town, and over an isolated wooded road, which evokes the impression of the phantom ride anew. Bored with her daily existence and languishing from bourgeois anomie, the film's female lead, Nina (Isabelle Menke), takes off in the family car on the premise of picking up her daughter from her parents' house. On a busy highway she pulls over to a rest stop to answer her cell phone. After a heated conversation with her husband during which she tells him she will not be returning home, the scene and point of view changes. A cut to a gaze through a car (it is not immediately evident from whose point of view) reveals a group of what appear to be Dungeons and Dragons LARPers performing in semi-darkness on the side of this busy highway. Rather randomly sutured into this scene, the shot is disorienting; the spectacle is unexpected and appears at first like a real battle scene. A glance at this strange scene becomes the literal point of departure of this rolling field of vision through the perspective of the windshield of a car on the move. While the viewer might assume that the point of view belongs to Nina, there is no reverse shot or indication of her presence in these subsequent shots. From the time the automobile begins to move, and for an entire one minute and thirty seconds the scene proceeds like a phantom ride, during which the viewer shares the gaze of an anonymous driver.

The scene unfolds so realistically and meticulously that the gaze follows that of the driver through the winding street of a small German town almost exactly. The gaze is mobile even within its automobilization. For instance, as the automobile approaches the building of a bank, the camera gaze seems to follow that of the driver in an upward cant to peer at the bank's looming overhead sign. An affective relationship of intercorporeality and intersubjectivity with this performative scene develops through what Megan Watkins refers to as "the corporeal instantiation of recognition" (2010, 273). In actualizing this notion, it may be argued that the viewer aligns herself not only with the actor's point of view but also with the actor's point of sense and course of action through the bodily (even somatic) recognition of the act of driving, which in this scene comes forth so congenitally that the viewer cannot help but feel affectively engaged to participate in this scene.

The interplay of fixity and motion integral to both driving and to the film experience critically links the two activities. As a result, the road movie and its potential offshoots present a self-reflexive genre of the ontology of film viewing. Succinctly put, it offers an explicit engagement with moving pictures and landscapes created through the double mediation of the automobilized gaze. As I have sought to show, these Berlin School films embrace (auto)mobility as a crucial mode of (visual and sensual) experience of the everyday in Germany and beyond its borders. Because driving has become a condition of the everyday in the Western world, the automobilized gaze presents a lens (in more ways than one) to explore this cinema's affinity to a mode of movement that affects the average person on a regular basis. Driving as not only a habitual act but also one with which the viewer is physically and phenomenologically intimate, effectively and affectively translates through film. Film and film viewing thus *mobilize* a direct application to movement through a literal and ideational semblance to driving. Yet as an action of chiefly bodily stasis, driving (like film viewing) nevertheless offers a transitory experience of spatial and temporal transportation in its vehicular quest for new sensoria, movement and space that directs us back to an epistemology of live performance. The body of the film viewer should therefore not merely be rendered useless, because it always exerts a degree of kinesthetic energy. Sobchack explicitly argued the same in her earlier *The Address of the Eye*; that is, that the viewer is not "motionless" or "vacant," as some earlier scholars have asserted (1992, 273). That experience, sensation, and even knowledge may be transmitted through bodies is paramount to the way in which the automobilized gaze works in my readings of these films. In the proceeding sections, automobile travel and its attendant gaze shifts affective registers to the physically thrilling and dangerously accelerated that results in splash and ash.

Proximity, Benjamin, and the Car Crash

Walter Benjamin was perhaps the first performance studies scholar. Indeed, many of the debates about performance and liveness were already encapsulated in Benjamin's famous essay on film, "The Work of Art in the Age of Mechanical Reproduction" ([1936] 1968). In his typically nostalgic approach, Benjamin describes the decay of the aura of the artwork in a period of increasing reproduction, including the advent of the art of film. The aura is the artwork's unique presence in the time and space where it was rendered (220). This uniqueness proffers a quality of distance, aloofness, and inapproachability also connected to the aura, which contrasts with the "closeness" of reproduced art— something that can be had and handled by all. Writing in 1993, Peggy Phelan indirectly offers a response to Benjamin in the final chapter of her book *Unmarked*. Performance, whose "only life is in the present," according to Phelan, may just be art's saving grace in the age of reproduction. Although Phelan later opens up her definition of performance to create a bit more wiggle room,[16] in *Unmarked* she steadfastly asserts that "Performance cannot be saved, recorded, documented, or otherwise participate in the circulation of representations *of* representations: once it does it becomes something other than performance" (146, emphasis in the original). In the decades to follow, many scholars have both praised and criticized this rigorously constrictive ontology of performance, but what impresses me is how Phelan actually charts us back to Benjamin, and ultimately (albeit unwittingly) to the question of film.

As much as it might seem as though Benjamin (and Phelan, for that matter) portrays film as the epitome of not only the absolute inversion of auratic art but also a medium of complete commodity alienation, this is simply not the case. While Benjamin does employ a lamenting tone of pretension in his discussion of film— this medium of the masses—he also underscores the potential of film's spatial and human closeness ([1936] 1968, 223). Whereas a Marxian reading of Benjamin would assert "proximity" as the capitalist desire for possession and therefore the resulting alienation between possessor and the original product (its material history: its traces of blood, sweat, and tears), anthropology and performance studies view proximity as the means of overcoming objectivity. Proximity implicates direct engagement. Closeness or proximity on both fronts, however, creates an automated relationship—one that often inhibits the capacity for reflective thought. Indeed, proximity is diametrically opposed to Brechtian distanciation, which encourages critical reflection and dispenses with a too-close emotional connection. But for Benjamin, the proximity ushered in by film (and certainly early film) is not one of pathos; we are not drawn in by overwrought sympathies with the characters on the screen in the scene of melodrama. Instead, this proximity is determined by unreflected and unconscious, even embodied, acts of reception and perception. Benjamin writes: "The camera introduces us to unconscious optics as does psychoanalysis to unconscious impulses" (237). As Steven Shaviro (and others) pointed out, already in the mid-1930s Benjamin recognized film's "capacity for freeing perception from the norms of human agency and cognition" (1993, 30). This automatism of film viewing that freed perception from cognition has become the hinge between early materialist film theory and phenomenological film theory.

Benjamin's unspoken but axiomatic turn to immanence and embodied experience inheres in his theory of film reception. For the film viewer who must abandon all ability to contemplate and evaluate and instead is rocked into the throes of thrill and automatic sensation, film constitutes a shock effect. By means of speed and movement, film assails the viewer's senses and evokes an indelibly physical reaction. The blinking of the eyes, the raising of the eyebrows, the opening of the mouth, the tightening of the neck, the twitching of the shoulders and back: these are all classic motor reflexes and kinesthetic reactions that the film experience induces in the viewer. Taking "the physical shock effect out of the wrappers" ([1936]1968, 238), film, like no other medium, has the capacity to make both our ears and our retinas ring. Like performance, then, film relies on the presence of living bodies, certainly in the form of the gazing—and even trembling—viewer. The adventure and exploration of the uncharted territory of film proffers new experiences. Film at once mirrors and heightens the experience of everyday reality. In his final and unfinished manuscript, *The Arcades Project*, Benjamin briefly returns to film and its effects. In a broader meditation on the city and city life, he ruminates on the possibilities of film as an unfolding "of all the forms of perception, the tempos and rhythms, which lie performed in today's machines" ([1940] 1999, 394), such that it prepares us for the shock factor of the physical reality and technology of modernity. Benjamin's contemporary, Siegfried Kracauer, who wrote extensively on film, drew out this materialist approach and extended it further. He viewed film as the articulation of the textures of everyday life—its physical reality and material existence—which in turn ramifies its impact to a direct engagement of the reality of the viewer. In her astute introduction to Kracauer's *Theory on Film*, Miriam Bratu Hansen emphatically underscores his concern for what she calls "the physiological impact of film, including moments of shock, panic, and suspense and kinesthetically induced reflexes" (1995, xxviii). Such corporeal impacts of film were for Kracauer, as for Benjamin, a kind of (re)performance of the effects and affects of modern technology on human experience (xi).

No filmic trope more accurately and thrillingly exploits Benjamin's and Kracauer's material theories of film and their corollary critiques of modernity as the cinematic car crash. Karen Beckman elucidates this in her monograph *Crash* (2010). In the hope of reevaluating film studies in all of its transmutations and bastardizations, Beckman intentionally signals the messiness of the ontology of film through the lens of its history of wreckage. She declares that the cinematic car crash is "one of film's earliest and most persistent self-reflexive tropes" (1). Beginning with the inception of film, Beckman chronologically maps out the presence of the cinematic crash and especially its formative role in early cinema. Very early film, what Tom Gunning has famously referred to as "cinema of attractions" (considered at length in chapter 2), had a penchant for collisions both locomotive and automobile. As Beckman also points out, Gunning's reading of early silent film's "aesthetics of attractions" as an experience of shock but "also a kind of thrill previously found in an amusement park" (9) overlaps directly with Benjamin (and, I would add, Kracauer).

But whether the ends of the cinematic car crash were in the vein of Benjamin and Kracauer, a response to the velocity of modern urban culture or a manifestation of cinema's own self-experimentation, I would agree with Beckman that the crash embodies cinema's own dialectical tensions. Between "stasis and motion, body and image, proximity and distance, self and other, inside and outside" the film experience is one of flux and encounter (Beckman 2010, 1). With the addition of two more sets of tensions—presence and absence, and visibility and invisibility—this list of dialectically opposed elements equally speaks to performance. If we consider the politics of the cinematic car crash beyond its eschatological telos of death and destruction and instead regard it as something that also yields difference and change through the transgression and even explosion of both discursive and physical boundaries as well as modes of representation, as Beckman suggests (24), then the transformative politics of performance begins to come into view.

The car crash is nothing less than the result of a dangerous excess of movement and a break with usual flow. But what is it doing in the Berlin School films in particular? It cannot be a coincidence that nearly all of Christian Petzold's features have a car crash and Valeska Grisebach's *Sehnsucht* (*Longing*, 2006) and Christopher Hochhäusler's *Falscher Bekenner* (*I Am Guilty*, 2005) are essentially about the aftermath of a car crash.[17] On the one hand, the car crash presents a site of terrible violence and even death that hardly seems to nurture a space of possibility; on the other hand, however, it does open up a space of excess and difference through a very real enactment of failing to go in the proper direction at the proper speed, which in turn can cause an important disruption of order and a leveling of current conditions as a means of making way for something new and different. Notwithstanding the horrific and traumatic reality of car crashes, my claim is that the Berlin School films are preoccupied with the acutely physical nonnormative flow of movement—too fast, too dangerous, too out of control—of the car that crashes and its site of wreckage. The crash site becomes a liminal space—an undetermined threshold, unsanctioned, and unmarked.

Not surprisingly, Koepnick reads the car crash in Berlin School films as utterly incapable of disrupting, or in his words, of "derailing the dull automatisms of the day" (2013, 81). Further, he indicates that in the car crashes' tendency toward circularity they only reinforce hegemony of everyday monotony. While he is correct in his observation that in many of Petzold's films there is a circularity to the car crash, his reading only offers an interpretative impasse. Fisher by contrast avows Petzold's habitual employment of the car crash as a direct commentary on the conditions of existence under neoliberal capitalism. He writes that "[t]he car wreck as narrative culmination underscores Petzold's indictment but also his serious engagement with global capital's constant creative destruction of space and, apparently, individuals" (2011b, 461). Along similar lines, Shaviro has made a convincing plea for precisely the possibilities of what he refers to as the movement of "accelerationism"—"the going through" at full speed. Shaviro does not explicitly treat the phenomenon of car crashes in his brief study *No Speed Limit* (2015), or film for that matter, but the germ of his critique is vividly fitting. He argues that accelerationism "exacerbates our current conditions of existence," causing them to finally explode, so that we may "move beyond them" (2). Indicative of the role of car crashes in the Berlin School films, the need for speed of the overdrive approach proffers an alternative reading of crashes as more than just a derailing of minor consequence. I view the car crash in these films (even in their circularity) as always potentially transformative. The following will examine both the act of destruction and the literal off-the-road spaces of the car crash. These are not so much sites of carnage and annihilation as they are radical spaces of change and opportunity, though at times ambiguous. This section thus examines how the Berlin School's new directions and the deterritorialization of the car crash may have bearing on perception and interaction, as they challenge the viewer to experience and participate in extreme modes of being-as-movement and relating to the world through image and sensation.

Performance Worlds Found/ed on a Scrapheap

To approach the cinematic car crash and its force of deterritorialization as a political performance, queer performance theory offers a productive trajectory for getting us from the destructive, disorienting site of the crash to the productive site of social change, redirection, and new worlds. Performance may be read as the transformative event that makes new worlds of social and political understanding. José Esteban Muñoz's *Disidentifications* (1999) dedicates a chapter to the conceptualization of worldmaking as a critical and reparative course through which it becomes possible to understand the political and philosophical weight of disidentifactory (and I suggest even deterritorializing) practices, which according to Muñoz "deform and re-form the world" through the disavowal of majoritarian culture (1999, 196). The concept of worldmaking is much in vogue these days as a more expansive alternative to teleological sensemaking or narrativizing. The former can be loosely understood as an ongoing process of creation and formation, often used to pertain to nonhegemonic worlds. In his work, Muñoz harks back to one of the founding conceptualizations of worldmaking as presented by Nelson Goodman. Goodman's study *Ways of Worldmaking* (1978) delineates worldmaking as essentially the *re*making of worlds (6). According to Goodman, new worlds are formed from preexisting worlds. Muñoz calls this a revisionary "weighing" and "ordering" (196). While Goodman's rather staunchly systemic approach directly disregards the sociopolitical aspects of worldmaking, Muñoz draws a parallel between disidentifactory performance and worldmaking. He makes the bold claim that both are acts of transformation that "effect a change through the performative act" (ibid.). As such, the performative act has an imprint on the real world. In order to assert that performance has the power to endure, I take up the persisting debate in performance studies about the potential of performance as a phenomenon that produces traces and residue that may spark social and political change. This well-trodden tangle in performance studies has given rise to a number of dated but still active binaries: presence versus absence, liveness versus mediation, disappearance versus endurance/repetition. Performance scholars such as Joseph Roach, José Esteban Muñoz, Philip Auslander, and Rebecca Schneider have been vociferous champions of a more fluid and capacious approach of performance. They have tirelessly stretched the boundaries of performance as more than an act of "disappearance," as upheld by the performance and theater scholars Herbert Blau, Peggy Phelan, Erika Fischer-Lichte, and Hans-Thies Lehmann.[18] This enduring, some might argue stale, debate remains a convention of the discipline. According to the first group, the temporality of performance must neither be immediate nor linear. Performance can endure and return. Further, even if its act is ephemeral, performance has the power to issue ripple effects that can manifest a social and even political afterlife, for as Muñoz claims in *Cruising Utopia* (2009): "Something is embedded within those [performance] acts, traces that have an indelible materiality" (71). That performance may not only reckon with a material way of being in the world but also leave traces attests to its force of transmission and transformation. In this specific context, Muñoz refers to the act of writing, the commitment of the ephemera to language, that "indelible materiality." But he includes the affective traces of live performance as an equally viable means of "transmutation of performance energy" (274). These lingering gestures function "as a beacon for queer possibility and survival" (ibid.). According to Muñoz, even live performance leaves its residue, a remnant and a marker of a site not just where something has happened but also an interstice where new worlds may be mapped. The utopian overtones of Muñoz's work may seem infelicitous to a study on cinematic car crashes, but sometimes it takes acceleration and destruction to create apertures of possibility in the glossy surfaces (or better: shiny wrappers) of the present.

The loaded phenomenological and formal event of the careening car that eventually crashes confronts the cinema viewer with images and experiences *out of line* with a normative cadency of narrative cause and effect, and the here and now. They engender, instead, new and alternative, even gnarled, perspectives of the world—perspectives that may be borne of violence and trauma but that also epistemologically question or even throw into crisis normative and hegemonic views. This is akin, at least theoretically, to what Muñoz has referred to as "queer worldmaking"—here the space of social crisis offers a locus for transformation (through disidentification or deterritorialization) that displaces the prerogative of conventional life, orientation, and modes of perception, and makes room for something new. Unlike Muñoz's empirical envisioning for this something new, this possible futurity, explicitly of sexual liberation and a utopian paradise of polymorphous identities and sexualities (to also paraphrase Lauren Berlant and Lee Edelman [2014, xiv]), this "something new" is never made glaringly distinct in the Berlin School films. Rather, it becomes a subtle provocation to the viewer that remains even after the end credits roll. What is stunningly apparent is that the Berlin School films duly engage formal and thematic figurations of the car crash as a disruptive force that inflicts both destruction and a leveling of prevailing conditions, which in turn opens up a liminal space for difference. Every figuration is an opening, is a promise. Herein lies the crux of the Berlin School's worldmaking quality, which I propose is not the construction of a brave new world, or worlds, but rather the creation of a physical and phenomenological space of experience.

Cinema Found/ed on a Scrapheap

Cinema certainly has its share of car crashes. The Berlin School is no exception. The most celebrated example to be found in European cinema is irrefutably Jean-Luc Godard's *Weekend* (1967). An orgy of smashups, *Weekend* is quite literally littered with brutally fatal car crashes. Dubbed as a film "found on a scrapheap" ("trouvé à la ferraille"), Godard's masterpiece is exemplary of Petzold's description of the car crash as a site of film's birth. While the influence of the European art cinema movements on the Berlin School is ineluctable, it would be undiscerning to suggest that it has simply adapted a Godardian repertoire of symbols and themes. When asked about the Berlin School's more general relationship to French New Wave cinema, Petzold actually distances his work: "With the Nouvelle Vague they set out to destroy what came before; in our case, we thought we just had to reinvent something" (quoted in D. Lim 2012, 3). The element of reinvention is no stranger to the Berlin School films; this process of reinvention likewise bears out over an initial path of velocity and destruction, as the ubiquity of car crashes in these films will demonstrate. To this end, echoes of Godard's infamous call for the "end of cinema," as symbolically stated at the end of

Weekend, reverberate throughout the Berlin School. The same might be said of New German Cinema's allied declaration of the "death of *Papas Kino*" with the Oberhausen Manifesto of 1962.

To begin, I turn my attention to four films by Petzold: *Die innere Sicherheit* (*The State I Am In*, 2000), *Wolfsburg* (2003), *Yella* (2007), and *Jerichow* (2008). These films go out with a bang—that is, they literally end with a crash. Petzold indicates the prevalence and importance of car crashes in his films as precisely the locus of the birth of film (Suchsland 2007). For Petzold, film is meant to offer a new register of experience: "cinema is about the extraordinary, about the breakdown of fate in the daily grind" (ibid.).[19] If we agree that cinema is a medium of the extraordinary and the breakdown of fate, such as Petzold contends, then the occurrence of the car crash in film imparts an ontological order in its performance as a self-reflexive trope; that is, it is also performative. Petzold's employment of the car crash stands out. His crashes are irrevocably dialectical—always in tension with and working in response to something, even if that something is simply their own self-contained repetition. A number of his features begin and end with car crashes. On the one hand, Petzold's choice to open and close his films with the car crash serves the very conventional effects of narrative (en)closure, traumatic recurrence, and even symbolic transcendence. On the other hand, the nature of these crashes—their performance of sheer excess and violence—takes us beyond narrative finitude and steers us quite literally off course in the direction of a nonlinear, potentially extranarrative experience that is perhaps less interested in *Weekend*'s metaphor of the car crash, as "the end of the story" ("le fin du conte") than it is in film's hypostasis of the car crash as material spectacle. Enacting nonnarrative moments of cinema, epitomized in the vaudevillian images of the "cinema of attractions," the car crash in Petzold's films is unsettlingly and spectacularly appealing.

In one of Petzold's earlier films, *Die innere Sicherheit*, there is only one crash scene. Let us begin at the end of the crash. Consider the close-up image of the teenage Jeanne (Julia Hummer) postcrash, with her lower lip bloody and a dirt-smudged visage (see figure 4.4). This image closes the film. More than one critic has agreed with the assertion that this was "the symbol for a younger German cinema, for the Berlin School and beyond" (O. Möller 2007, 40). Although this film's crash scene comes at the end, it has been read as marking the beginning of something beyond its diegetic capacity. Not only does it usher in an uncanny terminus of the film and the end of the first installment of Petzold's Ghost Trilogy, but as the first (relatively) commercially successful film of the Berlin School, *Die innere Sicherheit* has also become a sign of the movement itself.

Possibly the most spectacular of Petzold's crash scenes, the accident in *Die innere Sicherheit* is strikingly action packed and violent. It is morning; the fugitive former Red Army Faction family—mother, father, daughter—attempts to

Figure 4.4. After the crash: The face of the Berlin School in *Die innere Sicherheit*, 2000. © Schramm Film Koerner & Weber

escape Hamburg in their old white Volkswagen station wagon after a failed bank robbery (during which the parents kill a bank employee and the father is shot in the leg). The scene begins with a pleasant sequence of shots of the family in the car. Jeanne lays her head on her mother's lap as she drives, a sign of reconciliation after their fight over Jeanne's new boyfriend. The injured father appears to doze peacefully in the back seat. Light streams in as dawn breaks. The sense of a new start for the family lingers with aspiring intensity. Petzold composes a brief but impressively idyllic family scene, considering the circumstances of their flight. But the hope of escape and a return to normalcy, back on the path to "the good life," is quickly quelled when there is a sudden cut to a high-angle long shot from outside the car whose architecture is immediately reminiscent of a high-speed car-chase scene, employed in so many action films. Considered in the German context, the image may also eerily return the viewer to the establishing shot of Michael Haneke's horror-thriller *Funny Games* (1997), released just three years earlier. A chase ensues and immediately turns into a collision when three apparently anonymous black BMWs advance on the white station wagon and strategically and brutally force it off the road. The precision and execution of this action bear no other explanation than pure intention—as a means of swiftly and efficiently disposing of these alleged terrorists. An earlier scene reveals Jeanne's boyfriend, Heinrich (Bilge Bingül), as he surreptitiously places a call after Jeanne reveals her family's true identity to him. The direct causal agent of the car chase and crash is thus evident. But the sheer violence and spectacle of this rapid sequence of events are still shocking to the viewer. Alluded to by many critics as Petzold's denunciation of the (West) German government's legacy of authoritarian treatment of RAF members in the period of urban terrorism and "Germany in Autumn" and for decades to follow, the scene reveals how the family is arbitrarily disposed of by what appear to be three state cars (identically black with tinted windows).

The abruptness and violence of the deliberate attempted assassination of the family in this final scene—an altogether visual escapade of unexpected cinematographic maneuvering and rapid editing—are just added details to the experience that emanates from this cinematic event. Throughout much of the crash, the viewer's perspective is positioned with the family in the car through the automobilized gaze as it loses control, violently flips off the road in a sailing catapult and somersaults onto a dewy field of mud and grass. Deliberately taking the viewer out of the experience of the everyday, as Suchsland (2007) has suggested, the point-of-view shot through the windshield from within the rolling car displaces any typical visual field and gives way to an altogether overwhelmingly visceral and spatially disorienting experience. Shaviro might call this the tactile image par excellence: where "film hyperbolically aggravates vision, pushing it to an extreme point of implosion and self-annihilation" (1993, 54). Complete darkness is punctured by patches of light. The windshield is shattered and fogged, hindering our view of what appears to be mostly grass and dirt. There is no screaming from the victims inside the car (perhaps the screams are caught in our own throats; perhaps crash victims don't scream); there is only the sound of crashing metal and shattering glass. The embedded cinematic screen of the car windshield in this scene forcefully pulls the viewer in to experience the bodily traumatic—but possibly also liberating—sensation of losing control of one's movement. An unlikely pairing, trauma and liberation acutely illustrate the otherwise emotionless expression on Jeanne's face postaccident in the previously mentioned closing image of the film. The sole survivor of the crash, Jeanne regains consciousness and proceeds to pick herself up. Her body is at a remove, displaced several meters away from the car wreck, which is now a mere blot of heaped metal on the periphery. The sounds of screeching tires, scraping metal, and broken glass are replaced by the almost cheerfully benign distant chirping of birds. The sun now fully rises to illuminate Jeanne's face and golden hair. The visual and aural tracks suggest something of a rebirth, albeit an ambiguous one. Gradually, Tim Hardin's 1966 melancholic "How Can We Hang on to a Dream?" symbolically opens in the final few seconds of this last shot of Jeanne to introduce the credits.

If the car crash represents a new beginning or a rebirth of cinema, as Petzold has remarked, then it also indicates a break and spilling over into something new—into an unmarked space of possibility and difference. The car crash is a displacement and a deterritorialization, which articulates the new as an unsettled, possibly even hybrid space. Beckman remarks that filmmakers often turn to car crashes as a means of wrestling with political, ethical, sexual, and aesthetic issues (2010, 7). The cinematic crash, she asserts, "frequently leads us into spaces of hybrid identity and nonnormative sexuality, that demand exchange across disciplines and media" (ibid.). Physical and symbolic derailments, crashes are what Beckman calls "radical projects of destabilizing discourses" (19). They are modes of transition to alternative perspectives of the world—perspectives that question and even throw into crisis normative and hegemonic views. The traumatic personal experience of the car crash translates into a social aim in the context of Muñoz's worldmaking. Developed further in later sections, I propose that the destruction wrought by the crash yields an unsettled space where transformation begins to become possible. Processes of deterritorializing and reterritorializing inhere in worldmaking, whose objective is to garner new forms of identity and community which displace the prerogative of conventional life, orientation, and modes of perception. Such articulates the projection for the end of *Die innere Sicherheit*, what René Thoreau Bruckner broadly refers to as the not-quite-fatal accident that "leads to radical novelty" (2008, 376). This propels us to another set of Petzold films featuring automobile crashes that follow a circular pattern. This circularity does not unfold in a systematic open-and-shut way but rather along an unpredictable trajectory of repeated disruption.

Petzold's Circular Crashes

Although the circular phenomenon of the car crash prominent in a number of Petzold's films potentially underscores the work of narrative through the repetition of an important event, the nature of the car crash as accident—that is, as something aleatory and unexpected—problematizes such a straightforward reading. The car crash, even when it is repeated and foreseeable, resonates with the accidental and tends to overwhelm and disorient us with its burden of unpredictability and out-of-placeness. A lucidly apt description of the repetition of the car crash is formulated in Katherine Hayles's commentary on the accidental: "The 'accidental' happens where waves break on the beach of knowledge. Before a wave breaks, it is part of the undifferentiated mass of things about which we have no knowledge; as it breaks, it comes within the horizon of our experience but has not yet solidified into *terra cognita*" (quoted in Bruckner 2008, 378). Hayles avers that even an epistemological basis for the accident cannot physically and emotionally prepare us for its occurrence. In other words, the car crash always arrives as a syncopated shock and a disturbance to the expected flow of things.

Petzold's films *Wolfsburg*, *Yella*, and *Jerichow* heave with examples of car crashes that set up as well as disrupt film narratives. In these films, car crashes are not dissimilar to what Donald Crafton has referred to as "the potholes, detours and flat tires of narrative" (1995, 121), which may be intrinsic to a given story, but still "misdirect the viewer's attention, and obfuscate the linearity of cause-effect relations" (119). Whether working within or against the narrative, the frequent car crashes in the Berlin School films trouble conventional modes of cinematic perception and spectatorship. The three films I consider here literally begin and end with car accidents. Already the hinted circularity of their stories through the repeated event of the car crash may be viewed as a subversion of narrative convention. Most serendipitous is Petzold's film *Yella*, whose circular car crash works on a principle of regress insofar as the second crash cancels out the first and thereby casts a shadow of doubt on the reality of the events between the two crashes as nothing more than an oneiric interlude, ultimately external to the "real" plot. No film performs this more wittingly than David Lynch's psychological thriller *Mulholland Drive* (2001), whose second crash scene proffers a rerendering of the first and forces the viewer into a reevaluation of the events and characters. Beyond narrative codes, however, the repetition of the car crash also creates a double rupture in these films that opens up the cinema space to other dimensions—not once but twice. The doubling of the car crash thus underscores to the extreme the fluidity and futurity of the cinematic as something that is constantly unfolding.

The qualities of fluidity and futurity of cinema have been effusively underscored in Rick Altman's work. Championing a performance-oriented approach to film (as opposed to a text-oriented one), he has conceived of cinema as a "macro-event," which he describes with almost science fictional verve as "floating in a gravity-free world like doughnut-shaped spaceships." He clarifies that "cinema events offer no clean-cut or stable separation between inside and outside or top and bottom" (1992, 2–3). Arguing for an open—even Möbius-strip-like—concept of cinema as an event characterized by not only performance but also instability and multiplicity, he asserts a reading of film as an object always in flux. Caught in metastasis, then, film's *moving* images are certainly not fixed objects; our experience of film is likewise equivocal and subject to change. Each time we view a film, we are viscerally interacting with its images in new and different ways; we perceive things we have not seen before—a subtle movement of a hand, a twitch of the mouth, faint music in the background. This process of endless unveiling becomes exemplified by the event of the (repeated) cinematic car crash. In *Cinema 1*, Gilles Deleuze describes film as a continuous movement within an open frame. For Deleuze, the film image (here as the "movement-image") is always oriented towards something else, towards another ([1983] 1986, 55). Proceeding from this line of thought, film is positioned in a protracted state of becoming, and therefore also in a state of exhilarating possibility. Cinema is a kind of ontological practice for Deleuze, something fundamentally unfinished and fragmented. Inasmuch as cinema cannot contain the world—it can only show parts of it, for its parts are ultimately greater than its whole—it is perpetually signaling to a beyond, both temporally and spatially. In a similar vein, Stanley Cavell calls on the urgency to recognize cinema as the phenomenon of the not-yet-there, as "neither a world just past nor a world of make-believe. It is instead a world in the immediate future" (1979, 82).

The futurity of film lies in its perpetual state of becoming, its incompletion, and perhaps even its ontological deferral, as Abel (2013, 5) has illustrated for the Berlin School via Deleuze and Guattari's concept of the "minor". Along similar lines, my reading of these films points to an organic capacity that is pronounced by the presence of the (double) car crash and its relationship to the contingency of the accidental. The double car crash invites us to consider the possibility of alternative spaces and directionality already on the level of film form. Set in and named after Germany's Volkswagen capital, Petzold's first double-crash film, *Wolfsburg*, turns the automobile into a critical agent as an instrument of destruction, an object of knowledge, and a self-reflexive cinematic motif. Maria Vinogradova cannily writes: "In Christian Petzold's film *Wolfsburg* (2003) it is hard to say whether the main characters are people or cars" (2010, 160). *Wolfsburg* begins with a landscape image of a country road flanked by green fields. This image could almost set a bucolic scene save for the distant pillars of multiple smokestacks of the Volkswagen factory in the background and the cluttering of cumulonimbi overhead. This establishing shot calls attention to the important layered setting of the film: Germany, Wolfsburg as the city of cars, and the road. The stasis of the shot is abruptly disturbed with the entrance of a red sports car crossing the frame at high speed. The driver, we later discover, is, fittingly, a car salesman, Phillip (Benno Fürmann). The film cuts from exterior landscape to a medium close-up of the man in the car. In this first scene Phillip gets into an argument on the phone with someone who turns out to be his fiancée. She hangs up on him, and he attempts to call her back. In his attempt to redial the number, his cell phone drops to the floor of the car. Dangerously reaching for it, Phillip briefly averts his eyes from the road and at that moment seems to accidentally hit something. We do not see the accident, but like Phillip we hear the bang and smash of something hitting the car and *feel* the bump of the car driving over something. Phillip stops to see what it is, but instead of getting out of his car, he simply glances through his rear window in a double-take gesture. From his mediated perspective, the viewer eyes the image of a young boy lying on the road immobilized next to his bicycle. This is *Wolfsburg* crash #1.

In contrast to what appears to be a purely accidental collision in *Wolfsburg*, in Petzold's two later films, *Yella* and *Jerichow*, the first accident is not only withheld for roughly the first ten minutes but also appears to occur more explicitly within a cause-and-effect structure of the film. In *Yella*, the eponymous protagonist (Nina Hoss) accepts a fateful ride with her ex-husband, Ben (Hinnerk Schönemann), to the train station that ends in a (attempted) murder-suicide. As a prelude to this crash, the film evinces Yella's desire to escape both Ben's persisting abuse and the dire socioeconomic situation of her small town of Wittenberge in former East Germany and to start a new and hopefully better life in Hanover. In an extreme culmination of Ben's brutality and abuse, he tries to hinder Yella's escape by madly racing them both over the side of the Elbe River bridge. This is *Yella* car crash #1. In Petzold's *Jerichow*, a minor car crash is committed out of drunkenness and, as we learn later, a possible death wish, as the driver, Ali (Hilmi Sözer), precipitously whirls his SUV off a country road and down a river embankment. This is *Jerichow* car crash #1. More than simply an instrument of death and disaster in these three opening crash scenes, the automobile and the site of the crash are actually both introduced as an instrument of narrative disturbance and an ambiguous aperture of possibility. While the violence of the car crash always evokes dimensions of unease and foreboding, in these initial scenes, we are presented with brief moments of trauma, uncertainty, and inertia that actually instate breakers that temporarily quell excessive energy. Arresting the films' ethos of movement and speed, these brief standstills at the beginning of *Wolfsburg*, *Yella*, and *Jerichow* interpolate minor shifts.

On Phillip's returning to the scene of the crime in *Wolfsburg*, his sudden and short brake to peer through his rear window at his accidental victim is immediately followed by an accelerated flight. Phillip speeds away again from the scene of his recklessness and leaves the boy lying paralyzed on the road. But more than depicting just a hit-and-run scenario, this scene offers a filmic reflexivity. Phillip looks through his window but does not exit the car. He sees but does not *perceive*. It is as though he is looking at a film screen and witnessing an accident that is present but also absent. The expedience of this metaphor is its dimension of embedded liveness and its urgency to not dismiss the objects on the screen as the shadows of irreality. According to Petzold, *Wolfsburg* is "about a man who must open his car door and realize that the windshield is not a screen and the soundtrack from the CD is not real" (Petzold quoted in Reinecke 2003). In this moment the "reality" of the viewer's experience of this scene is underscored through Phillip's own wishful negation thereof, for it is ultimately from the perspective of the still conscious (but paralyzed) victim that the viewer witnesses Phillip's fast getaway, and from a third perspective that she perceives the final shot of this scene, which offers a return to the landscape shot of the Volkswagen factory (as in the establishing shot of the film), except now it is marked as the site of a crime with the abandoned, immobile body of a child lying on the road in the foreground. The mise-en-scène of the first shot appears now as a *tableau vivant* turned *tableau mort* of a three-part narrative: car, road, death.

In spite of the magnitude of the initial car crash in the film *Yella*—a stories-high plunge into the river—it pans out as an apparent brush with death that seems to serve more as a Craftonian pothole than a major catastrophe. Shortly after

Ben's Range Rover submerges, Yella can be seen pulling herself up onto shore, sprung from the river as though reborn and still somehow not too late to catch her train to Hanover. This miraculous and enigmatic scene of survival initially evokes suspicion in the viewer but is ultimately played out in a way that appears realistic enough to subdue earlier bouts of skepticism. Contrary to its cinematic predecessor, Herk Harvey's horror film *Carnival of Souls* (1962), *Yella* gives way only to minor slippages and cracks in the verisimilitude of its representation. Enigma turns to near farce in *Jerichow*, where the first car crash hinges on the ridiculous, what Petzold himself describes in the DVD's voiceover commentary as resembling a slapstick sketch. On hearing the squealing of wheels, a passerby, Thomas (also played by Benno Fürmann), rushes to the site of the crash on foot with two grocery bags swinging in his hands. He finds the inebriated Ali staggering around and cursing his luck. After helping Ali by single-handedly towing his automobile out of the ditch, Thomas even voluntarily eludes the busybody local policeman who happens on the scene and correctly suspects that Ali has been driving drunk—again. Aside from inebriation, neither driver nor SUV are too worse for the wear after this minor brush with fate, and with Thomas's help both man and car casually head homeward as though nothing has happened.[20]

Such attempts at teleological readings of these introductory crash scenes, however, can only take us so far. Are car crashes in the Berlin School films in fact "failed derailments of the dull automatisms of the day" without real consequence, as Koepnick claims, or perhaps even Hitchcockian MacGuffins that simply distract us from the plot? Whether banality or gimmick, the performance of the car crash nonetheless elicits spectacular and phenomenological shock that physically and affectively agitates and excites. Hands down the most viscerally assailing of the three scenes, the first car crash in *Yella* has been aptly described in the following way: "The spectacular move effectively breaks the narrative trajectory of the film after barely ten minutes and throws the viewer into speculative turmoil about the continuation of the story line" (Biendarra 2011, 467). Yet the temporary paralysis invoked by the shock and sheer spectacle of the crash halts but does not hinder the worldmaking potential of the car crash. This is especially true of Petzold's films, which present car crashes just as Godard's *Weekend* did, "not simply as nihilistic spectacles of disaster, but . . . rather as sites for exploring the condition of living on after 'the end'" (Beckman 2010, 205). In myriad ways, the Berlin School examples here exist in extended time and space—on the physical and allegorical "scrapheap" of the car crash. Even Petzold's return to the scrapheap at the close of each film does not necessarily neatly (or better: messily) conclude matters and place things into a methodical narrative package of circumscription; instead, the car crash maintains this emphatic sense of open-endedness.

In *Wolfsburg*, the young hit-and-run victim dies in the hospital some days later but not before he reveals the color and possible make of the car that hit

Figure 4.5. The flying instrument of death in *Wolfsburg*, 2003. © ZDF

him: a red Ford. We learn only later that the prostrate child had misread the FO-RD on the car's license plate (the FO actually short for Forchheim, a city in northern Bavaria where Phillip had previously worked) for the make of the car, consequently stalling the police's search for the killer. Phillip's own guilty conscience draws him to the child's mourning mother, Laura (also played by Nina Hoss), however, and eventually the truth is exposed, not by Phillip but by his car. Although Phillip personally repaired the dinged panel of the car after the first accident, it still becomes the incriminating clue that leads Laura to suspect him of the murder of her son. She subsequently seeks her revenge through the destruction of both the driver and his instrument of death—the red sports car. In what could be read as a possible murder-suicide, Laura tearfully stabs Phillip from the passenger's seat, causing him to lose control and flip the car onto the side of the road (see figure 4.5). Miraculously surviving the crash intact, Laura pulls herself up from the wreck apparently unscathed and walks away from the scene, not dissimilar to Yella after the first crash scene or to Jeanne at the close of *Die innere Sicherheit*. But before abandoning the gravely injured Phillip, who lies paralyzed under the wreck of his belly-up car splayed over an open field, Laura calls for the help that Phillip should have requested for her son at the beginning of the film. Yet Petzold denies the viewer narrative closure (as he himself states in the audio commentary to the film) insofar as he does not show the arrival of an ambulance. Instead, he concludes the film with his characteristic ambiguous shot from behind as Laura walks away from the crash. While *Wolfsburg* certainly has much more narrative transitivity and consistency than Godard's *Weekend*, or even Petzold's *Yella*, the double auto collision underscores the film's transgression rather than compression of spatial and narrative boundaries. Its elliptical story line and lack of closure at the end propound its break with an overly conventional film narrative. The final crash scene with its powerfully violent long shot of Phillip's red sports car flying through the air aggressively gestures toward this shocking transgression: with its excessive thrust of movement and technology, the car crash is the epitome of speed and the frightening suddenness with which things can happen—expected or not.

This transgression of spatial and narrative boundaries returns with a jolt in the double car crash in *Yella*. Instead of landing in a heap, Ben's black Range Rover quickly disappears into the murky waters of the Elbe River. An important landmark in German geography and history, the Elbe River once divided a portion of East and West Germany in the area of the North German Plain, not too far from Wittenberge where part of the film is set. The river's role as a metonymic border is emphasized in the film by the appearance of its still untouched and undeveloped riverbanks. In contrast to the *dividing* river, then, the bridge over which Ben and Yella plunge, physically and symbolically, connects the two sides. The Elbe, once having served as a border between East and West, already represents a kind of transitory no-man's-land between two different worlds. The site of the crash in this literal and figurative border zone constitutes a multilayered transgression of spatial boundaries. *Yella*'s crash site is thus already framed as a historical, geographical, and political boundary that drives the basic structure of this filmic narrative, essentially about a young woman from the former Eastern state of Brandenburg who seeks wealth, success, and happiness in the West in vain (Abel 2010, Biendarra 2011; Fisher 2011; Nessel 2011; Miller 2012). The border zone as a kind of performative space also literally becomes the overextension of physical limits and its resulting surplus. It is the space of the breaking of the bridge barrier and the violent splash from the Range Rover's displacement of the river's surface. Further, it is the floating debris and the unknown space lurking beneath the opaque water, which hungrily swallows Yella and Ben, and his massive instrument of speed, technology, and death.

Blending trauma with thrills not unlike that in *Die innere Sicherheit*, *Yella*'s crash scene involves a powerful point-of-view shot from the perspective of the passengers. There is something thrillingly visceral in this twice-occurring shot (in both crash scenes of the film) that resembles the sensation of a rising and dipping roller coaster ride. As Beckman also claims, "the cinematic crash seems to offer viewers thrills, views, and transcendence of bodily and subjective limits as the careening car itself" (2010, 115). The view through the windshield of the plunging automobile forces the viewer's participatory attention, clearly citing the automobilized gaze, and an even more phenomenological experience of the crash, of its physically puncturing and squealing explosiveness, and jettisoned debris. In the final scene of *Yella*, following the second crash scene, which deviates in formal detail only in subtle ways from the first, the police have arrived on the scene and a large crane lifts the wrecked Range Rover out of the water. The bodies of Yella and Ben are also retrieved from the river and laid out on the shore, only to be conclusively covered up with a space blanket. In this final scene, the two are dead but death does not feel like a permanent state, especially if we consider that according to the film's end Yella has been dead nearly the entire time. The film concludes not with the image of the corpse of Yella but with the return of the earlier overhead perspective of the rustling trees and blue sky. This identical shot is presented as the point of view of Yella when she awakens after the first episode of the accident. If Yella is now dead, with whose point of view could the viewer be aligned in this last shot? Contrary to Roger Cook's reading of this final shot, which forecloses the possibility of Yella's lingering subjective gaze (2013, 31), I suggest that Petzold inserts this final point-of-view shot as a means of leaving the film and the fate of Yella in a quagmire. Certainly, the film's compulsion to repeat, its circular narrative, would suggest a preclusion of closure itself.

Whereas Abel posits that death in Petzold's films is the result of failure, that is, "the characters' failed attempt to escape the transitional zones that hold them captive" (2010, 276), I take this one step further and propose that death itself is precisely this transitional zone of the nonplace. There is nothing definitive about the state of death in these films. Notwithstanding the ethical chasm of pain and fatality that threatens to rend this frame, this horizontal zone, at every turn, the cinematic car crash does become a critical site of transgression and interrogation, even if it is through death and failure, as Abel likewise proposes. Judith [Jack] Halberstam's treatment of failure in *The Queer Art of Failure* (2011) assures us that failure is not "mired in nihilistic critical dead ends" but instead wrenches pathways to "alternative ways of knowing and being" (24). The possibility promised by the cinematic car crash lies in what Muñoz would call "the 'excessive' final act," as a performance act that leaves traces—that is, "different lines of thought, aesthetics, and political reverberations" (2009, 148). In the case of *Yella*, this excessive final act cuts through and damages the symbolic bridge from former East Germany to the former West and vice versa, cutting off normal flow and literally effecting the way in which mobility from east to west occurs.

The final car crash in Petzold's film *Jerichow* bears out this logic of the excessive final act *mutatis mutandis*. In keeping with its narrative precursor, namely, James M. Cain's novel *The Postman Always Rings Twice* (1934) and its classic film noir adaptation by Tay Garnett (1946), in the final scene of *Jerichow* a plot by the lovers—Ali's wife, Laura (again played by Nina Hoss), and Thomas—attempt to incite a car crash to murder Ali backfires. In Petzold's version, however, Ali ends up committing suicide out of rage and wrath when he discovers their plot against him.[21] Ali drives himself off a cliff that scales the Baltic Sea. The crash as the SUV hits the embankment below and the subsequent explosion of the engine are heard but not seen by Laura and Thomas as they retreat from the scene. Once the two turn around and Laura rushes to the edge of the cliff, the viewer watches from Thomas's distanced perspective as the beautiful seascape is quickly and menacingly consumed by an enormous plume of black smoke. While there is a dark and apocalyptic aesthetic to this final tableau of Laura's silhouette dwarfed against the rush of black smoke on the edge of the cliff,[22] this final shot is not entirely and bitterly fatalistic. Too many questions are left unanswered and problems are left unsolved in terms of both the film's narrative and the themes it treats and tracks, such as neoliberal capitalism, domestic and sexual violence, and racism. Although Ali is an alcoholic and an abusive husband, his death through the suicidal car crash is not portrayed as a final occasion of justice served. In *Jerichow*'s grim post-Fordist noir tale, all three protagonists are presented as guilty and victimized at the same time. Unlike in Caine's novel and Garnett's film, which I propose even more problematically and less self-reflexively explore the same themes, Petzold's version ends abruptly with the car crash and Ali's death, and not with the typical noir turn to so-called narrative justice, that is, to Laura's and Thomas's punishment for adultery and (at least attempted) murder of Ali. Further, to propose that justice is served by Ali's death ignores the critical ambiguity of the car crash. What is to become of Laura and Thomas is a question that remains an open wound. Here, as with *Wolfsburg* and *Yella*, the viewer is again thrown into turmoil and left to work through this film and its final car crash on her own. With all three of these films, there is a need to reconsider the work of the cinematic car crash that takes us beyond narrative categories and forces us away, in the case of *Jerichow*, from the ideological framing of the film noir genre and its offshoots and brings us closer to experience and embodiment.

Embodiment does not necessarily exclude narrative, but it does not hold to the heady promise of teleological sensemaking so inherent in the latter. Narrative and genre often work to cognitively (re)insert the viewer into a space within the boundaries of the given world. By contrast, in its destructive and negating jolt, the car crash in the Berlin School films tests and ultimately exceeds those boundaries. Petzold ends *Jerichow* with a confounding car crash that does not discipline or smooth over the bumps and fault lines, but rather yields a (literal) descent into violence and destruction. This explosive descent eludes our cognitive reflection and instead occasions the imperative force of the violence enacted both on and by Ali. The viewer is drawn in through a powerful embodied imaginary that first and foremost mobilizes phenomenological engagement. Whether we choose to read the close of the film narratively as Ali's act of sacrifice to or resistance against Laura and Thomas, what is resonant in this act is the residue of violence and pain that lingers and sticks like the black smoke in the atmosphere. It is in these traces that an interstice appears. This aperture is not a narrative cliffhanger (pardon the pun), but an important place of rift and detour.

The car crash, as a death scene in so many Berlin School films, can ironically often be counted among the most alarmingly animate—and most *alive*. It is this occasional slippage into speed, a loss of control, and a general breaching of limits, lines, and roads that not only make these Berlin School films interesting and exciting but also more broadly set this cinema apart. These critical moments of excess and the bending of realist possibility occur in myriad forms and, as I demonstrate throughout this book, are the indelible instances of performance in these films. But unlike in the previous chapters, I suggest that the cinematic car crash is specifically a performance that has worldmaking potential insofar as it is not only a spectacle that diverts the narrative, such as dance, but is also a rupture and an event that permanently and destructively transforms the cinematic space. As one of cinema's most self-reflexive tropes, the car crash may be the condition for the cinematic mode in the first place. Like the films themselves, the car crashes quite literally send us off on different paths and trajectories to see the world in alternative ways. In this sense, the world of the scrapheap is not simply a nihilistic one of death and destruction, but more accurately a deterritorializing one. Here Bruckner astutely remarks, "But this terrain in which the narratives' accident victims find themselves is too contingent and unstable to be categorized simply as space, no matter how open. It can be described as *nonspace*—placeless, deterritorialized, fantasmatic—but, more pointedly, as a productive kind of post-traumatic temporality" (2008, 367).

The locus of the crash is perhaps the most fitting example of what Petzold himself refers to as the space of the "mobile immobilities, the so-called transit zones, these non-places" that make up the modern world (Petzold quoted in Abel 2008a). As Bruckner illustrates in the above quote, there is a productive side to the crash that demands careful investigation. This is primarily the temporal space extended to a crash victim who through injury and trauma may have lost the capacity to process events and memories sequentially and narratively. A more comprehensive formulation, however, may be worked out by means of these films' performance of deterritorialization through the car crash.

Developed by Gilles Deleuze and Félix Guattari in *Anti-Oedipus* ([1972] 1983), the concept of deterritorialization is closely linked to capitalism and the advent of psychoanalysis, and can be read in a twofold manner. On the one hand, deteriorialization is the displacement of labor powers through industry and the psyche through Freud's Oedipal drama, what Marx would call the process of alienation; on the other hand, deterritorialization also embodies a mode of resisting these selfsame powers of alienation. Destabilizing mainstreams of thought, or Deleuze and Guattari's regulating "flows," deterritorialization enacts a critical process of constant undoing. They write: "That is what the completion of the process is: not a promised and pre-existing land, but a world created in the process of its tendency, its coming undone, its deterritorialization" ([1972]1983, 322). Processes of deterritorialization are the political movements and revolutions that block the regulating flows of hegemonic powers.

More broadly, the concept of deterritorialization has since been taken up by scholars to refer to a crucial and relentless process of resistance. I find this felicitous in the context of the cinematic car crash in terms of both its conceptual and literal significance. To deterritorialize means to uproot or to be uprooted from a place (a territory) of belonging or positioning, to exit a space of normativity, or to veer off from the regular spatial flow. In very real ways, the car crash exemplifies a form of deterritorialization, for it almost always implies a dangerous veering off the road—to that part which is blocked off, to a place where automobiles do not belong. As precisely the nature of the machine—real, symbolic, and imaginary— to which Deleuze and Guattari metaphorically refer, the (cinematic) automobile is a fitting instrument of deterritorialization. Both in its action and in its aftermath, the car crash breaks the barriers that quell flows of excessive movement—it wields lines of flight. Its forceful displacement of people, lives, technology, and landscape makes it an important phenomenologically and ontologically reflexive feature of so many Berlin School films. The car crash both evokes the notion of the automobile's role as the cinema machine and, at the same time, destroys that machine as a means of renewal. Destruction creates an opening for something new. In all of these films, the car crash does not bear narrative finitude; instead, it is a slippage into the nonnarrative and the nonnormative space of contingent phenomenological perception and experience. Deterritorialization as the selfdestructive work of film is a way of worldmaking, a mode of (dis)organization, that critically remains incomplete, as Altman (1992), Deleuze ([1983] 1986), and Cavell (1979) have all argued. Although deterritorialization as a destructive force appears to be precisely the opposite of the creative force of worldmaking, it is deterritorialization's incursion of resistance that allows us to see this differently. Not unlike Muñoz's employment of disidentificatory performance as a strategy of disavowal of a hegemonic culture that consequently becomes a site of emergence and the impetus for queer worldmaking, the deterritorializing car crash in many Berlin School films may serve a similar purpose of deforming and reforming worlds.

The cinematic car crash emblematizes the work of deterritorialization by quite literally providing what Muñoz has referred to in the context of performance as "a ground-level assault on a hegemonic world vision that substantiates the dominant public sphere" (1999, 196). It is the assault on the viewer's senses and perception that forces a constant refocusing and revisioning. I consider more broadly what this revisioning might entail and how it gestures to the performance politics of these films. Inasmuch as Petzold's crash scenes tend to arise as a symbolic injury to socioeconomic conditions and relationships (the car as a symbol of the bourgeoisie and capitalism, especially for Godard and certainly also for Petzold), heteronormativity also strikingly comes into play as a target for dissolution in some of the Berlin School films. In the following section, I shift my focus from Petzold's films first to Valeska Grisebach's film, *Sehnsucht*, and then to Christoph Hochhäusler's film *Falscher Bekenner*. These two features have some structural similarities but are most significantly linked by their materially contused mise-en-scènes. Both opening with an anonymous car wreck, they immediately confront the viewer with a bewildering site of both excess and loss.

The Primal Accident in Sehnsucht and Falscher Bekenner

Postmortem, postcoital, posttraumatic: the films *Sehnsucht* and *Falscher Bekenner* begin in the aftermath, in the condemningly empty yet still potential state of the "post." Although the two respective main protagonists are not directly involved in car accidents in these films, they are eyewitnesses and the first on the scene. Their encounters with these anonymous crashes have unexpected effects that play out over each film. In his text *The Primal Accident* (2007), Paul Virilio explores the accident as an initiating site of both trauma and suppressed fantasy that thrusts the witness into an altogether unfamiliar state. Stressing the futurity of the accident not only as the result of technological production and invention but moreover as an uncanny means of revealing what is to come, Virilio asserts: "Creation or collapse, the accident is an unconscious oeuvre, an *invention* in the sense of uncovering what was hidden, just waiting to happen" (9, emphasis in original). Virilio's approach evokes the productive possibility of the accident that needs to be examined and harnessed. He states further, "It is no longer a matter as it was in the past, of covering up an accident or failure, but indeed of making it productive" (84). The opening accidents in *Sehnsucht* and *Falscher Bekenner* resonate with a primal event and the emergence of something new. With his study on American accident-driven cinema, Bruckner remarks that "the accident has the capacity to reveal things undreamed-of and paths unknown" (2008, 7). The revelatory power of the accident as it smashes the surface of the present flings us into terra incognita. These untrodden paths of the new, the unfamiliar, and even the undreamed-of are the registers that incite this examination of the car crash and its wake.

Citing Freud's "primal scene," the libidinal resonance of Virilio's notion of the "primal accident,"[23] adds an interesting dimension and strikes a chord with the role of the car crash in *Sehnsucht* and (especially) *Falscher Bekenner* that reverberates with the shame and trauma of bearing witness to an accident. The spectacle of destruction of the car crash follows in this vein—destruction gives way to absence and loss. That sexuality appears to be curiously linked to the shaming encounter of the primal accident (qua scene) in these two films, fits this line of thought. While *Sehnsucht* is not exactly a sexually transgressive film (unlike *Falscher Bekenner*), it does explore sexuality beyond the norm and offers an affront to heteronormativity and conventional values of monogamy insofar as it is essentially a tale about an extramarital affair and one man's insatiable love and desire for two different women. *Sehnsucht* begins with Markus's (Andreas Müller) encounter with a wrecked car wrapped around a tree. As we subsequently learn, a man and a woman have attempted to take their lives by deliberately driving head-on into the tree. In the initial shots, however, the mise-en-scène and shot scale do not provide a clear image of the situation. The first shot is a close-up of Markus as he desperately attempts to help stabilize one victim of the crash. The jerkiness of the handheld camera used in this shot and the proximity to Markus's face moving in and out of the frame as he frantically performs first aid on the victim (whom the viewer does not see in this first shot) are both claustrophobic and disorienting. In this initial scene, it is almost as though Markus is metaphorically struggling with the film (or perhaps the viewer) itself—desperately trying to resuscitate it. "Do you hear me?" ("Hören Sie mich?"), he seems to say to nobody. Even before there is an image, through the black screen the viewer can hear the sound of an automobile stop and someone rush out. Only in the second shot (twenty seconds later) does the viewer see the immobilized body of the victim lying next to Markus. The second victim and the bolus of the wrecked car first appear several shots later. In his reading of this opening sequence, Abel observes that its aesthetics resemble a kind of documentary realism (2011, 209); while I agree, I propose further that there is something underlying in this initial scene that postulates its cinematic reflexivity. What is underscored is the crisis of the film and its world. As Beckman astutely suggests, "Crash films are cinematic quests, undertaken in the spaces whose outer limits are marked by terrestrial speed taking flight on the one hand, and by the mutilated body on the other; by the immobilized corpse, which throws film into crisis, and the speeding imagination taking a camera for a ride" (2010, 7).

It is evident that this crash scene immediately opens up a fragile diegetic world. The film story reflects this fragility insofar as the car crash directly represents the rupture and disturbance of a community and way of life. The long shot of Markus positioned next to the victim cuts to two subsequent landscape shots of swaths of idyllic village life—kids on bicycles and a sunrise over a meadow dotted with family homes. Accompanying these images, however, is the abrasive cry of a siren and dogs barking uncontrollably. This aural disturbance almost seems to serve as a wake-up call to the villagers (and volunteer rescue workers), who can be seen in small groups presumably slowly making their way to the site of the accident. *Sehnsucht* is not only a film found on a scrapheap but also a film about a world found on a scrapheap. When asked in an interview how the story for this film developed, Grisebach also elucidates this: "I searched for a story in the wake of a dramatic moment that would be the expression of longing: where something suddenly tears, the framework no longer holds. An event that can no longer be reversed, where something akin to fate occurs" (2006).[24] The car crash performs precisely this dramatic moment and event in the film, where at once everything begins but also seems to end. Not unlike Petzold's *Yella*, the film appears to be working on a dimension of "borrowed" time.

Unlike with the Petzold films, however, the viewer does not witness the car crash nor even catch a glimpse of the corpse of the woman who died in the accident, because she is quickly covered with a blanket. Grisebach prefers to work on a principle of implicit and even latent violence. From the car crash to the way Markus and his wife, Ella (Ilka Welz), so desperately and aggressively make love, and finally to Markus's attempted suicide near the close of the film, this so-called love story has an unexpected violent vein. The film's latent violence resonates with Catherine Wheatley's characterization of *Sehnsucht* as a type of new *Heimatfilm*. Wheatley posits that *Sehnsucht* employs elements of the *Heimatfilm* genre reflexively as a means of critiquing and reframing it (2011, 145). Indeed, unlike in the traditionally parochial *Heimatfilm* (von Moltke 2005), the violence and rupture of the establishing scene of the fateful car crash in this seemingly bucolic village of Zühlen (in Brandenburg) in *Sehnsucht* ushers in an alternative and destabilizing world in which traditional values and conventions have evidently already begun to disintegrate and a bout of repressed desires and transgressions rears its ugly head.

The car crash, as the epitome of technology, speed, and excess, is expressly in tension with the notion of *Heimat* and the machinations of the *Heimatfilm*, which is, in Johannes von Moltke's words, "against urbanization . . . against the increase of speed and mobility, or time-space compression." (13). It follows that the car crash has a deterritorializing effect that is not reconciled (as would be the case in the *Heimatfilm*) in the film and instead surges beyond it. *Sehnsucht* appears to embrace—to even be consonant with—the car crash in its subtly obsessive preoccupation with what Beckman calls "the experience of aftermath" and "living on after a disaster" (2010, 205). The film evokes the similarly tragically toned accident-driven performance and narrative of most crash films, such as Krzysztof Kieślowski *Trois Couleurs: Bleu* (1993) and Atom Egoyan's *The Sweet Hereafter* (1997). But rather than giving itself over to bleakness and melancholy, Grisebach's somewhat understated creation of a world in the aftermath of a car crash adopts a fairytale articulation that points to the surreal. This world locates itself in Petzold's "transit-zone," between life and death and dream and reality. The crash at the beginning of the film (perhaps there is an intertext to *Yella* here) is a primal scene that is at once violently and shockingly real to the witness but also traumatically baffling. Unable to reconcile what he has experienced, in an unexpected turn of events Markus has an affair with another woman, Rose. His subsequent feelings of guilt—or simply his inability to live without his wife, who discovers his affair and kicks him out—drives Markus to suicide. The reverberation of the car crash's unsettling destruction resounds throughout the film. Symbolically, the warning cry of the deafening siren at the beginning of the film never quite dissipates. This is a film of swelling excess, death, and failure. Yet even in its bruised and broken state, it stretches the limits and pushes us—if not forward—somewhere off in a new (possibly diagonal) direction.

Duly preoccupied with creating alternate worlds and realities, the final film I consider in this chapter is Christoph Hochhäusler's *Falscher Bekenner*. This film also begins at the site of the wreckage of an anonymous crash. Similar to Grisebach's *Sehnsucht*, the viewer does not actually witness the crash in *Falscher Bekenner*. But the young Armin (Constantin Jascheroff), who rather arbitrarily happens on the wreck of a car while aimlessly wandering along the highway one night, does not attempt to rescue the victim of the crash or even contact the police. The image of a bloody corpse with its disfigured head tucked forward against the steering wheel provides a shocking detail of gore. Armin looks on not in disgust and in fear but in unabashed wonder and curiosity. The crash as a spectacle of violence, excess, and destruction draws both character and viewer in. Indeed, accidents often attract an audience of voyeuristic onlookers. If the film had been made just a few years later, Armin might have been shown pulling out his smartphone to take pictures or film the scene. Instead, he steals a piece from the car wreck—a souvenir—and takes it home. As the film progresses Armin's rather callous reaction in the first scene is gradually replaced by the trauma of what he witnessed. He seeks out the identity of the car crash victim in the newspaper and even attends the deceased man's funeral, after which he fitfully weeps. Wracked with guilt or, as some critics have claimed, eager to rebel against the malaise of his family's middle-class coddling and meddling, Armin anonymously claims responsibility for the crash and other accidents in the area.

Following this violent sight/site of the establishing scene, Armin is presented as an errant teenager: unable to find work, unable to find a girlfriend, and generally arrested in an adolescent existence of play and irresponsibility. While we might assume that Armin's experience of the crash site has no direct bearing on his character, as the scene that opens the film and introduces us to Armin, we cannot ignore its chronological and structural significance for the entire film. It takes up Beckman's claim that filmmaking is "one form of this living on in the wake of accidents, disasters, uncertainty, and failure" (2010, 205). Even beyond the narrative events that are a direct result of the first scene (the funeral, the anonymous letters to the police), Armin's experience of this primal accident actually unravels as the impulse for his dreamlike transgressions and sexual fantasies. Hochhäusler explains that the car crash at the beginning of the film both literally and symbolically conjectures that "etwas aus der Bahn gerät" ("something gets off track") (filmmaker's audio commentary with the DVD). The car crash is the result of a derailment or a literal "getting off track" (off the highway—the autobahn) that also gestures toward the elliptical flow of the film and the perceived delinquency of young Armin.

By way of escaping the mundane, heteronormative, bourgeois everyday of his parents' home, where Armin appears to suffocate under the pressure to find a good job and settle down like his older brothers, Armin finds reprieve in nightly visits to a public restroom just off the highway near his home in the industrial small town of Mönchengladbach (close to Düsseldorf), actually known for its multiple highway intersections. Armin's nightly cruising of the toilets and regular sexual encounters with a gang of motorbikers are part of what appear to be the film's fantasyscapes. That is, it is never clear if these encounters actually occur or are part of Armin's dreams. Nevertheless, there is an indelible correlation between the accident and Armin's sexual awakening in the film. On his discovery of the wrecked car at the opening of the film, Armin's point of view lands on a mysterious phallic-looking object (apparently, the car's stabilizer arm for the steering bank), which he picks up and takes home as a kind of strangely perverse souvenir. When in the next scene he awakens in the morning safe and sound in his bed, it almost appears as though the car crash was merely a product of his dreams. Immediately after rising out of bed, however, he eyes the souvenir taken from the crash site and triumphantly reaches out to pick it up. In a startling close-up, we see Armin's disembodied hand reach out for the object resting on his desk. Something of a motif, or a "magisches Objekt" ("magical object"), as Hochhäusler calls it (in the audio commentary for the DVD), its alien-like shape and appearance seem to hold a mesmerizing power over Armin, who tenderly fondles it. That this object should somehow be the evidence that eventually incriminates Armin at the end of the film is at least symbolically apt. Caught in the folds of guilt or excitement, or both, Armin begins to write letters to the police anonymously claiming responsibility for the car crash and several other local accidents, including arson and a motorcycle accident. These crimes, or simply the fantasy of these crimes, metamorphose into extended transgressive behavior that include illicit homosexual encounters.

One of the few more prominently LGBTQI films of the Berlin School (with the exception of Jan Krüger's features), *Falscher Bekenner* duly explores the possibilities of nonnormative sexuality and desire as a direct assault of sexual transgression against heteronormativity. This film definitively engages a comparative reading of the car crash and queerness as both, what Muñoz would call "essentially about the rejection of a here and now" (2009, 1). Taking the destructive and mysterious car crash as a point of departure, as Hochhäusler posits in the audio commentary for the film, this is decidedly a tale about sexual identity that purposefully blurs the boundaries between reality and fantasy. Armin's fascination and even fetish for motor vehicles, also evinced in the vast number of model cars on display in his bedroom, finds its felicitous pairing with sex. In one scene, while receiving fellatio in the public bathroom Armin fantasizes about driving on the open highway atop a motorbike. In a later scene in his bedroom, he engages in intercourse with a motorbiker who rather fetishistically remains in full gear. Finally, a less explicit but also suggestive scene shows Armin adroitly performing mechanical work on a neighbor's car, and his father arrives to coolly collect him. The expressions on both of their faces seem to indicate that Armin was in the midst of doing something shameful. Just as Armin's interest in cars must be sidelined and he must find a proper bourgeois office job, so too must his queer desires be suppressed. In this vein, the film is at least thematically reminiscent of David Cronenberg's 1996 psychological thriller *Crash*, which similarly questions bourgeois morality and identity. Criticized for its strong entanglement of (nonnormative) sexuality and violence, and admittedly much more (porno) graphic than *Falscher Bekenner*, *Crash* explicitly links sexual transgression or at least nonnormative sexual drives and car crashes in cinema. But where *Crash* overtly pathologizes unconventional desire as the aberrant underside of an ailing society in its acts of forced pleasure, *Falscher Bekenner* creates a cinematic dream world of violence and destruction that actually avows desire and liberation.

A "rejection of the here and now," queerness, Muñoz states, is also "an insistence on potentiality or concrete possibility for another world" (2009, 1). The futurity of queerness finds some compelling parallels in the generative forces of deterritorialization. While the work of renewal serves as more of a gesture in *Falscher Bekenner*, as well as in the other films of the Berlin School cinema, this provocative claim resides. More affirming than negating, Hochhäusler's film embraces nonmainstream queer representation and aesthetics, and effectively interweaves these with the assault of the site of disruption of the car crash as not only a destructive affront to (hetero)normative sensibilities but also as a place of new beginnings. In *Feeling Backward* (2009) about the potential to be found in the queer history of feeling bad and backward, Heather Love poignantly begins with the following words: "A central paradox of any transformative criticism is that its dreams for the future are founded on a history of suffering, stigma, and violence" (1). This vividly encapsulates the transformative potential of these films founded and found on a scrapheap—worldmaking on the ruins of history. As a bookend, in her epilogue Love invokes Benjamin's memorably melancholic "Theses on the Philosophy of History" and its angel of history as the key figure of "loss and the politics of memory, trauma, and history" (148). Famously, Benjamin's metonymic angel faces toward the past, toward a history marked by a singular disastrous event. This negative account of history is the nimbus that unhinges perception and disorients. Although we perceive the past as a teleological chain of events, the angel sees only one catastrophe whose repercussions form a progression of scrap piles. According to Love, it is of less importance that Benjamin's angel of history is not a redemptive one, as even in its backward turning it cannot tarry in the past but is instead propelled forward into the future. What matters for Love, and for this chapter, is that this encounter and bearing witness to the wreckage of what now lies in the past is inherent to a kind of transformative performance of the future. This is also the germ of Muñoz's project of worldmaking through disidentificatory performance, whose approach, despite an undeniable ethos of utopianism, does specifically acknowledge the instrumental role of the negative, the feeling bad, and gay shame as critical components of queer worldmaking. If worldmaking is always a form of remaking the world then it always responds to something; that is, it is reaction to or against a dominant state.

The politics of the performance of Berlin School cinema is one of refusal—a refusal to remain within the boundaries, a refusal to go slow, a refusal to follow the line and obey the limit. The prevalence of the destructive car crash as the evocation of both extreme shock and sensation as well as a cultural metaphor of leveling make way for new (at least cinematic) worlds of change. In its transformative capacity, the Berlin School engages in a form of worldmaking that self-reflexively critiques the scrapheap as both a source of cinematic creativity and a violent act of capitalist commodity, territorial expansion, and death. The scrapheap proffers a worldness of sheer waste and excess often overlooked in Berlin School scholarship that generally focuses on the movement's minimalism, its slowness, and its vacuousness. Demonstrated in the myriad examples of the car crash in the Berlin School films, there appears to be a willful pursuit of destruction of the present that I argue becomes a means of opening up the film to something new and yet unknown—to a future. As a mode of deterritorialization the car crash violently takes us beyond the limits of movement and space to untrodden paths of possibility. It is the car crash as accident and failure which opens itself up to promise because it comes precisely, as Muñoz declares, as "a rejection of normative protocols of canonization and value" (2009, 153). Even death itself is not presented as a finitude in these films, but more as a form of excess through its dramatic, even theatrical, mode of the spectacle of the car crash. Speaking more generally, then, as I close this chapter, I suggest that there is a futurity of the Berlin School cinema that permeates a sense of possibility, even when this possibility is cloaked in ambiguity. If we abide by Lauren Berlant's call for the utopianism inherent in the aesthetic to provide "a better idea than the one that governs actual living" (2011, 139), then these films may be called utopian. But I resist taking them that far. In the vein of this chapter, the politics of performance of the Berlin School is to destroy and to subsequently move on from this new place of far-flung consequence with a renewed perception and vision of things.

Notes

1. It bears noting that the autobahn was indeed a major project taken up by the Nazis after its planning was not realized in the Weimar Republic period. This quote originates from Bitomsky's film and is quoted here from Pantenburg (2005, 23): "Wie schön es sich auf der Autobahn fährt! Die Blicke jagen den Bildern nach. Die Straße scheint fürs Sehen gedacht, ein Medium. Ein Medium, das Bilder und gleichzeitig auch tote Augenblicke produziert."
2. Kopp (2010) gives Kaspar Heidelbach's thriller *Polski Crash* (*Polish Crash*) (1993) and Oskar Roehler's *Silvester Countdown* (*In the New*) (1997) as examples of films that present stories of Germans traveling to Poland who become victims of crime.
3. The absence of subtitles is common in Berlin School films. There are numerous occasions when Polish, Turkish, French, or English is spoken and there are no subtitles to assist the viewer. The few exceptions include Thomas Arslan's *Der schöne Tag*, in which the conversation between Deniz (in German) and her mother (in Turkish) is subtitled, and his recent film *Gold*, in which brief conversations in English are translated with German subtitles.
4. The driver yells in Polish, "What are you looking at?" "What are you staring at?" "Get the fuck out of here!" "Fuck off!" (I am indebted to David Malinowski for his translation of the Polish into English.)
5. This scene calls to mind the various driving scenes in Jean-Luc Godard's classic *Breathless* (*À bout de* soufflé, 1960), which appear discontinuous and extended through their multiple employment of shots.
6. "Viel gereist wird im neueren deutschen Kino. Die Menschen sind auf der Suche, nach Orientierung, nach Sinn, nach Sicherheit und Geborgenheit. Auch Jan Krügers erster Langfilm ist so etwas wie ein Roadmovie."
7. "Windschutzscheibe und Leinwand: Zwei *Screens*, die unseren Blick auf die Landschaft rahmen, zwei Sichtmembrane, die zwischen unterschiedlichen Räumen vermitteln" (Pantenburg 2010, 94).
8. Indeed, in Benjamin Heisenberg's film *Sleeper* (*Schläfer*, 2005) the main character's favorite computer game is race car driving.
9. "Ein Film müsste eine Welt so anschaulich machen, dass man ihn nur erzählen kann, wenn man ihn ergänzt mit dem eigenen Leben, ihn mitnehmen muss ins Leben."
10. This quote originates from an interview with Thomas Arslan and Angela Schanelec conducted by Julian Hanich (2007). It is quoted from Baer (2013). The translation is from Baer. The original reads: "Dabei muss man dem Zuschauer einen Spielraum geben."
11. The curious intertext of this scene is also striking. Once we finally see the driver we recognize the French actor Aurélien Recoing from his celebrated role in Laurent Cantent's *L'emplois du temps Time Out* (*L'emplois du temps*, 2001), in which he finds distraction and repose perpetually driving around France and Switzerland after he loses his job.
12. It should be noted that the film in fact opens with a point-of-view shot of the passing landscape as Yella arrives in Wittenberge on the train. Of course, as the establishing shot in the film, this mobilized gaze should not be overlooked, but I argue that there is an important distinction between the train and the automobile in terms of their relationship to ownership, power, and flexibility. While mobilized, Yella's gaze is also restricted. She is not driving the train and cannot choose her path.

13. Fisher (2011b) suggests that this second gaze belongs exclusively to Yella; however, I would argue that once Ben exits his Range Rover, Wittenberge appears eerily desolate to both figures, as we do have point-of-view shots for both.

14. "Ich kann mir gar nicht vorstellen, anders als mit O-Ton zu arbeiten."

15. Consider, for instance, the off-screen dance scene examined briefly in the second chapter, where the young girl Clara (Clara Enge) asks her babysitter to dance for her to Schubert's "Erlkönig," which she presumably does. We only see Clara watching her and never see a reverse shot of the babysitter dancing, however.

16. Already in her introduction to *The Ends of Performance* (1998), edited with Jill Lane, Phelan does not recant her earlier argument but she expands her definition of performance as something that wields affective and even political consequences.

17. There are (more narratively minor) car accidents and collisions in number of other films as well, such as Maria Speth's *In den Tag hinein* (*The Days Between*, 2001), Henner Winckler's *Klassenfahrt* (*Class Trip*, 2002), Christoph Hochhäusler's *Milchwald* (*This Very Moment*, 2003), and Jan Krüger's *Auf der Suche* (*Searching for Simon*, 2011).

18. Setting the tone for this dispute, Phelan famously declared that "performance . . . becomes itself through disappearance" (1993, 146).

19. "dann dreht sich Kino um das Außergewöhnliche, um den Einbruch des Schicksals in den täglichen Trott."

20. As a ridiculous crash scene that brings two strangers together, this scene in *Jerichow* is somewhat reminiscent of a scene in Wim Wenders's road movie *Im Lauf der Zeit* (*Kings of the Road*, 1976), when the depressed Robert (Hanns Zischler) races his VW beetle into a lake and then climbs out unharmed. All the while, Bruno (Rüdiger Vogler) watches the spectacle in amusement.

21. Ali's suicide may also be connected to his recent cancer diagnosis, which he revealed to his wife, Laura, in the preceding scene.

22. Some critics have pointed out the possible symbolic connection between *Jerichow* and the biblical city of Jericho, which may find visual articulation in this final scene.

23. It bears mentioning that *The Primal Accident* (*L'accident originel*) can also been translated as *The Original Accident*, as is the case of the book I reference here, but the possible Freudian allusion is still relevant. Indeed, in his own translation of the text, Brian Massumi cannily translates it as *The Primal Accident*.

24. "Ich habe für die Geschichte nach einem dramatischen Moment gesucht, der Ausdruck der Sehnsucht wird: wo plötzlich etwas reißt, das Gerüst nicht mehr hält. Ein Ereignis, das nicht mehr rückgängig zu machen ist, wo so etwas wie Schicksal passiert."

5 Nina Hoss's Performance of the Fugitive Body; or, What to Do with Movement

The title of this final chapter does not offer a choice between two possibilities; rather, it implies relationality. The relationality of performance and movement is indeed one concern, if not the primary concern, of *Movement and Performance in Berlin School Cinema*. But how is performance rooted in movement and vice versa, without one simply being reduced to the other? This chapter takes up the more categorical question of the *what*: What is this performance? Does it have a figuration? A name? Here I seek to extend this book's focus on movement in the Berlin School to a direct analysis of how movement assumes more generic qualities in some of its later films, expressed by means of the performance of the actress Nina Hoss. Although Hoss's performance does not yield a conclusive paradigm within which the performance aspects of all Berlin School films may be diagnosed and classified, it nonetheless points this study in sanguine new directions. Continuing the voyage through these films, then, our traveling and mapping assumes a distinct form—and a body. But this turn to Hoss is by no means inspired by an arbitrary desperation for legibility or even genre. Instead, it speaks to a gap: a study on the performance of the Berlin School without a due nod to Hoss would be incomplete. It goes without saying that Hoss is the putative face (and body) of the Berlin School. Hoss has shaped the Berlin School as much as it has shaped her as an actress and a German film star. Her collaboration with the Berlin School's most preeminent filmmaker, Christian Petzold, with whom she has made six films and one theater play to date, is not only significant but also begs closer investigation.[1]

Without veering too far afield into the business of star studies,[2] we can observe patterns of performance both attached to Hoss's body and by way of which she inhabits roles in the Berlin School films. It is therefore crucial to think of performance beyond basic mimetic principles and the characteristics of specific roles and scripts. In terms of acting and performance in film, Richard Dyer has famously observed that "performance is what the performer does in addition to the actions/functions s/he performs in the plot and the lines s/he is given to say. Performance is how the action/function is done, how the lines are said" (1998, 97).

This excess, or surplus, is of course the classical locus of performance, in other words, its perlocutionary rendering. Things often happen in the Berlin School films in the absence of direct intentionality, what Victor Turner would call the liminoid of performance, or what Bert O. States refers to as "the ghost of self in performance" (1983, 361), which in the case of Hoss is hauntingly apt. Cinematically speaking, it is that which habitually emerges and takes shape visually but is not rigidly enclosed in the textual narrative of a film. I especially appreciate Anne Rutherford's recasting of James Naremore's definition of performance of the actor with a greater focus on the somatic and relational nature of bodies on-screen, as that which "go[es] beyond the dimension of characterization to generate a direct bodily connection between actor and spectator" (2015, 319).

But here I am concerned with the double-edged potential of performance as both tangible and legible. In this chapter, I propose that performance communicates something beyond itself. To put it slightly differently, Hoss's performance adopts a pattern, a design. This is not a typical characterization, but more of a figuration that strives for palpability without being a typical personification, such as a nymphet or a femme fatale. It is a fugacious performance marked *by* movement *in* the throes of movement. It is the performance of fugitivity. Oksana Bulgakowa's audiovisual work on the cultural coding of gesture and body language in film, particularly with regard to locomotion, offers a vocabulary of the body on-screen from which to draw (2008). Hoss's overall performance is decidedly economical in terms of its gestural repertoire, but it is neither flat nor dilatory. Perhaps Hoss's performance is best described as diffuse but animated, a quality shared by many Berlin School actors. Yet where conventional gesture might appear drained, movement bears its own tangible and to some extent legible substitution. "Concentrating on gesture," José Esteban Muñoz writes, "atomizes movement. The atomized and particular movements tell tales of historical becoming" (2009, 67). The interconnectivity of gesture and movement, directly expressive or not, manifestly orients this study of Hoss's performance of the fugitive body.

I take up the challenge of investigating Hoss's performance and steady our focus on several of the Berlin School's later films not thoroughly considered in earlier chapters. It is thus through the variegated and exuberant performances of Hoss that this final chapter traces and ambitiously carves out a more enfolded performance bent of the more recent years of the Berlin School. A period marked by an ineluctable shift in style, the Berlin School films since 2012 offer new and more formally accessible frames of analysis. The following pages pursue an investigation of Hoss's roles in three Berlin School films released after 2012: Petzold's *Barbara* (2012), Thomas Arslan's *Gold* (2013), and Petzold's *Phoenix* (2014). These features, historically set, track varying permutations of what I will demonstrate as Hoss's performance of the fugitive body—that is, her performance on the move.

Movement as Performance

My ongoing charge to (re)think the Berlin School beyond its earlier branding as phlegmatic, idle, brooding, and even vapid, that is, as just another candidate for the generic likes of "slow cinema" (de Luca 2016; Schoonover 2012; Flanagan 2008; Ciment 2003), bears new fruit with an investigation of the school's more recent features. While these films do (continue to) employ a cinematic idiom often synonymous with slow cinema, such as long takes, minimalistic editing, understated acting, and watered-down narratives, the panoptic term *slow* cannot be more misleading in these later films. Mostly it fails to account for the intense diegetic movement within the moving images of the Berlin School that I have sought to underscore throughout these chapters. The Berlin School's modus operandi is one not of deferred action but one of felt possibility and corporeal agitation—yes, even movement. Nowhere is this claim more resoundingly apropos as in an examination of the performance and kinesthetic strivings of the Berlin School's grande dame, Nina Hoss.

Hoss's overall style and performance visibly inhere in a mode of *being on the move*, condensed in a form of bodily insurgency—of perpetually running away from or searching for something. Sometimes it is a combination of both. Moreover, these acts of running and searching are always in a man's world, with all its added obstacles. The figures Hoss performs never fully escape nor do they realize their teleologically set goals. It follows that a tenor of disorientation manifests itself throughout Petzold's films. His characters are frequently set to a kind of less-than-grandiose wandering that overwhelmingly results in an extended sequence of wrong turns that nonetheless play out in interesting ways. Marco Abel keenly observed that in Christian Petzold's films "being out of place, out of sorts, oddly unhinged, askew, in a word: lost" is the idiom which conditions all of his narratives and characters (2013, 72). But such lack of direction certainly does not altogether belie the possibility of movement. It makes movement contingent and hopeful, even. Petzold's characters seem to frequently find moments of reprieve and even immunity in movement, which begins as a momentary means of escape and gradually becomes a performance—what I refer to as a performance of the fugitive body. Fugitivity is flight, movement of dissent. This figuration of movement as the performance of the fugitive body, of course, extends to sociopolitical frames of subordination, where, for instance, movement might be attached to feminist and race discourses. Notwithstanding the weightiness of movement and flight in related migrant and diaspora studies, where these often adopt qualities of vulnerability and precarity, movement can also affirm freedom and identity for those bodies culturally, politically, and socially delimited to stasis. The mobilization of these bodies can yield compelling implications of liberty and renewed subjectivity.

Consider a rather inconsequential sequence in *Barbara*. Along a narrow unpaved path, flanked by an expansive row of towering deciduous trees violently sighing in the wind, a cyclist comes a-racing. This initial extreme long shot is accompanied by an audio track of original sound amplified: wind, seagulls, sea. The architecture of the shot is decidedly painterly. The image has no doubt attributed to the art historian–inspired reading of the film as aesthetically Romantic. Although the churning of the sea à la Caspar David Friedrich remains beyond the viewer's field of vision in this image, its presence is certainly felt aurally. But the cyclist is evidently part of this image and not interested in contemplating it. Indeed, the cyclist's own sealike, dark-blue tones of dress and windblown hair set her as visually part of this landscape. The kinetic esprit with which the cyclist moves is both in sync with the inundating freneticism of nature and apparently uninhibited by it. This mobile dot on the landscape thus swiftly expands as it draws nearer. A long-shot pan follows the cyclist as she expertly and dexterously takes a bend and traverses the path further. She takes another bend, struggling only slightly now against the rush of the wind. A second shot shows the cyclist arriving just in time to catch a train at the local train station. The single-car locomotive gradually chugs up just as she herself does. Shot three: cyclist turned passenger boards the train and sits. Without a minute lost, the train begins its journey again and the passenger bounces along against the backdrop of a passing rural landscape. Several shots later, the passenger turned pedestrian appears to make her way along a quietly idyllic riverside path to an isolated inn. At long last, the cause for the woman's marathon-like endeavor arrives at a denouement. At the inn, the woman must collect a note and money from her West German lover via a young waitress. But this sequence that hardly ends here (it shows the return trip in great detail too) is not simply a teleological means to an end. These four and a half minutes of pure motion demonstrate the mode of fugitive performance as nothing more and nothing less than an ontology of movement. Described here is one of the myriad sequences of the movement of Hoss's eponymous figure from *Barbara*, whose kinetic navigations through a small provincial East German town are tirelessly and often beautifully rendered. While the nominal motivation for Barbara's movement is eventual escape from this town in the coastal state of Mecklenburg-Vorpommern in the former German Democratic Republic, as, for instance, her collection of the money is destined to be the payment for her illegal emigration, it is easy to forget this narrative and to simply be consumed by the spectacle of motion. For although Barbara is geographically trapped, she regularly seizes the freedom manifested in her body on the move through space.

Though there is a copious repertoire of Berlin School films that would provide fitting studies on Hoss and her performance of movement, the following engages a slender scope in its attempt, on the one hand, to catch up with some of the Berlin School's more recent features and, on the other, to sharpen our thinking about what performance can do and its place in these films. The first films I consider here more closely are Christian Petzold's *Barbara* and Thomas Arslan's *Gold*. These have represented, for many, the first signs of a shift in the Berlin School's style, as both can be described as period pieces that bend toward more mainstream aesthetics and genre-oriented narratives. Historically set, *Barbara* takes place in 1980 in the German Democratic Republic and *Gold* tells a story of the Klondike Gold Rush in Western Canada in 1898. Such historical settings may appear to buckle, even trouble, performance, as the contemporaneous quality of liveness risks being suspended. But as Rebecca Schneider has assiduously examined and revealed, history and historical reenactment do not foreclose the possibility of performance. History is not a problem for performance. Through performance, or "the syncopated time of reenactment," "the *then* and *now* punctuate each other" (2011, 2, emphasis in original). It follows that, if anything, these unique historical contexts offer compelling formal frameworks for such an analysis of performances of resistance and dissent. Indeed, Joseph Roach has argued that the most dynamic and informative medium of history and historical processes is the body of the living.[3] Like Roach, I suggest that the emphasis on performance in these films is one of embodiment and consequently the embodiment of specific times, places, and stories. In a final Petzold film to be considered in this chapter, *Phoenix*, Hoss's performance of the fugitive body transmogrifies more explicitly into a performance of the traumatized body. An implicit but omnipresent quality of the performance of the fugitive body, the traumatized body is correspondingly the devastated and unsettled body propelled into motion with the intent of reorienting itself. *Phoenix* follows in the historical fashioning of *Barbara* and *Gold*. Set amid the rubble of postwar Berlin, in this later Petzold film Hoss's figure is a fugitive body traumatized by war, genocide, and displacement.

This historical vector also guides me to the framing text of this chapter and study of the performance of the fugitive body. Exploring the performance acts of resistance of African Americans during the long postbellum period, Daphne A. Brooks's monograph, *Bodies in Dissent: Spectacular Performances of Race and Freedom, 1850–1910* (2006), presents a rich conceptual model of the fugitive body as a means to analyze performance as eruption and resistance through movement. Indeed, Black studies scholars such as Brooks, Saidiya Hartman, Fred Moten, and Alexander G. Weheliye have underscored the urgency of thinking about the body in flight or in pain as a site of performance and even resistance.[4] For those who may protest the engagement with black studies concepts beyond their disciplinary scope, Weheliye offers a pointed argument in favor of a rethinking of black studies as not merely an approach to be applied exclusively to black narratives and black history but with a scope that is exceedingly more comprehensive, indeed, as the study of the human condition tout court. Positioned in abolitionist studies but offering an extensive reach, Brooks's study focuses on the performance of individuals in the cultural margins, especially African American women. Again, a turn to this text may seem out of place here, as race and the history of slavery are not categories of representation or exploration in *Barbara*, *Gold*, or *Phoenix*. But this turn to Brooks's project underscores a conceptual kinship uninhibited by a divergence in scholarly objects of study. Brooks's brilliant layering of movement, historical performance, and resistance is indispensable to a pursuit of Hoss's figures in these later films. A direct overlap may be noted with regard to the topos of gender, which is crucial both to Brooks's study and to these films. The title figures in *Barbara*, *Gold*, and *Phoenix* are women who struggle against the grain of social and patriarchal conventions in their respective historical settings. As I will demonstrate, Brooks's attention to performance *on the move*, or as she puts it, "on the run" (1), as an eruption "out of putative 'stillness'" (6) is vividly resonant with the type of movement found in these films. With her bold proclamation that movement embraced is movement restored, and that movement means history, identity, and freedom, Brooks offers a concept of the fugitive body that helps to set up a rigorous and thematically contextualized approach to movement—and more specifically the act of fleeing—as performance in these films.

The premise of flight bears a long and transformative genealogy in film studies discourse, where flight means escape as well as subversion. Without labeling these films political or feminist, I suggest that they spur Deleuzian "lines of flight" in a uniquely literal way, such that they overtly perform what Steven Shaviro has called "potentials for resistance and subversion . . . latent within [even] mainstream, narrative film" (1993, 11). That is to say, they present themselves even in the most unexpected of places. Shaviro wrote this line as a criticism of Laura Mulvey's still influential essay "Visual Pleasure and Narrative Cinema" ([1975] 1990) by way of proposing, counter to Mulvey's famous argument, a less totalizing account of narrative cinema as irresolvably antifeminist. In *A Thousand Plateaus*, Gilles Deleuze and Félix Guattari develop the term "line of flight" (*ligne de fuite*) in a slightly different direction. Concretely put, a line of flight directly constitutes an alternative parallel route or path preserved as a means of escape in a dire situation or an impasse. At the same time, they describe lines of flight as not about escaping the world as such, but rather, in their words, about "causing runoffs, as when you drill a hole in a pipe" ([1980] 1987, 7). Flight thus takes on a Foucauldian charge, by way of which freedom is relative to power and not necessarily opposed to it. While Deleuze and Guattari were in certain ways more radical than their contemporary Michel Foucault about the energies at our disposal and the possibilities of escape and freedom that could be wrought, in the case of the films I consider here the lines of flight available to Hoss's protagonists are not substratal breakthroughs but instead subtle achievements of wiggle room, or perhaps these may be better worded as *movement spaces*. Hoss forges these apertures by means of her performance of the fugitive body.

In its application of the plentitude of movement and its implication of freedom and identity through movement, the cinematic performance of the fugitive body intervenes and rewrites the narrative of, for example, female immobility. It offers a compelling figure through which to analyze the gender performance of Hoss's protagonists in *Barbara*, *Gold*, and *Phoenix*. In one of the few feminist readings of the Berlin School films, "Women's Lab: The Female Protagonist in the Berlin School," Rajendra Roy examines the important role of women in many of the Berlin School films and emphasizes a shared aim to "regain mobility" out of "a profound sense of being stuck, both collectively and personally" (2013, 48). Further, once such mobility has been regained it is a matter of staying in motion, for that is, she asserts, "the only way for a rebel to survive" (49). This does not underscore movement for movement's sake, but rather movement for the sake of survival. Hoss's protagonists are not flaneuses; their movement is always goal driven, even if that goal is never actually reached. At the same time, however, Hoss's figures are concerned not simply with getting from A to B but also with the pleasures and perils of being a body in motion and the at least temporary freedom this kinetic state can offer. An emphasis on pleasure, peril, and freedom highlights the significance of movement as the performance of self and the agency of Hoss's figures. Hoss often occupies and actualizes transient positions, which I read against the grain as more than merely precarious; these instabilities are equally performative and even generative. Brooks's work in this direction, in her affirmation of movement and transience against the backdrop of slavery, insightfully renders displacement and roaming part of a willful performance. These are the qualities that also link Hoss's performances.

Linking this all back to the body on-screen, its unique gestural language achieved through sundry corporeal movements, finally brings me to the pioneering work of Bulgakowa and her extensive study on the historical employment of gesture in Soviet film, from standing and bending to walking and kissing, the feature-length video essay *The Factory of Gestures: Body Language in Film* (2008). As a means of devising a taxonomy of bodily movements performed by Hoss in *Barbara*, *Gold*, and *Phoenix* that cohere with performance narratives of fugitivity, I will compose a kind of repertoire of gestures of my own, though on a much smaller scale. Without giving in to the impulse to over read the body, it will draw from Bulgakowa's example as a methodological frame with a directed focus on posture, walking, and riding (a bike and a horse). What precisely is the promissory figuration of the fugitive in these films? How does she move? What are the lines and thresholds of this process? A body language is called in not so much to prescribe meaning as to concretize performance, give it a design.

Barbara: The Escape Artist in Training

Hoss's performance of the fugitive body, a breaking out of idleness and an escape from its imposing powers, finds formulation and motivation in the narrative of Petzold's film *Barbara*. The title figure, Barbara Wolf, is a doctor, formerly at the renowned Charité in East Berlin but now banished to a provincial pediatric clinic in a small coastal town in the state of Mecklenburg-Vorpommern. The reason: she applied for an exit visa. It requires no explanation that the German Democratic Republic (GDR) was a state keenly invested in controlling the movement of its citizens. Many are well aware of the legacy of the East German Ministry for State Security (*Stasi*), one of the most notorious and repressive intelligence agencies in history. Hence Barbara's request to leave the GDR (and emigrate to the West) is met with a harsh penalty. Her freedom of movement and mobility become decidedly more restricted, to a point where even a few hours of absence are met with disciplinary measures. Yet Petzold's depiction of the mechanisms of power in the GDR is one of regulation rather than possession. The violence visited on her body is brutal, as Jaimey Fisher also emphasizes (2013, 142), but it is not utterly debilitating. No doubt Barbara's banishment to this small town has the aim to isolate, police, and ultimately immobilize her. Petzold seems to draw a clear line back to Foucault ([1975] 1977, 27), whereby the power of the state is at once exercised on Barbara's body and invests her with the pressure to struggle against it. But modes of surveillance are not what is at stake in this film. The viewer is not overwhelmed with an inundating sense of panoptic observation and the feeling of anxiety this typically incurs. If anything, the way in which Barbara gives herself so freely and without qualms to the work of resistance and regularly seeks out the possibilities for movement and leverage within power's reign is stunning. What critics and scholars frequently neglect to mention is that this is a phenomenologically exhilarating film.

Barbara is never still. She is quite literally a fugitive and an escape artist in training, as the film does build up to an escape narrative. "Motion, migration, and flight," which Brooks calls "operative tropes" (2006, 67), are applicable to the historical context of the GDR. More than half a million citizens fled the GDR during its forty-one years of existence; at least a third of these were through unofficial (and illegal) means of escape—escape from repression and sometimes even persecution. Framed by the broader historical narrative of escape from the GDR, Barbara's fugitive status is produced by the very conditions that confine her. She never actually escapes the GDR, though the opportunity to do so does eventually arise. Instead, what I will focus on here is the slice of freedom that Barbara seizes on a regular basis by means of movement. Barbara's mobile body lends this film—ostensibly, a story of entrapment and surveillance—a feeling of freedom, spatial latitude, and possibility. Hailed as a new kind of film about the

GDR, *Barbara* does not generate the repressive feeling of imprisonment that one might expect. It forecloses the hackneyed images of historically preemptive sites of power: the Berlin Wall, border crossings, prisons. There is a modality of surveillance that at times appears inundating, as Barbara is frequently shown furtively looking over her shoulder, but it is ultimately rendered intrusive and not frightfully threatening. Alternatively, what often wrests the viewer's attention is the beauty of the film's images: densely atmospheric long shots and landscape shots of forests, unkempt country roads flanked with wild English-style gardens, and the breathtaking chromatic scale of the blue, gray, and black of the Baltic. Petzold has disclosed the desire to introduce an unexpectedly rich color palette to his mise-en-scène in *Barbara* as a contrast to so many films about the GDR that are sentenced to a fate of dreary achromatism (Petzold quoted in Nord 2012).[5] While Barbara's motility and this aesthetic and affective celebration of space in the film should not be confused with freedom in any real sense, they do offer the cinematic fantasy space of freedom through movement despite its limitations.

Like so many of Petzold's films, *Barbara* begins with an incipient arrival. The establishing shot shows Barbara standing on a crowded bus on her way to her first day of work at the clinic. Like so many Berlin School films, in *Barbara* various modes of transportation not only appear but also serve to define and categorize their owners or commuters. In Petzold's films, typically only men drive cars; this is also the case in *Barbara*. As she is first forced to be at the whim of the erratic bus schedule and then coerced to accept a ride from her new supervisor, Dr. André Reiser (Ronald Zehrfeld), Barbara's introduction is reminiscent of that of Hoss's protagonists in Petzold's earlier films, especially *Toter Mann* (*Something to Remind Me*, 2001), *Wolfsburg* (2003), and *Yella* (2007), in which riding shotgun habitually has a violently fateful outcome. *Barbara* unfolds differently. From the moment Barbara resourcefully repairs the bicycle tire in a dramatically charged scene sharply set with operatic accompaniment, namely, the thrillingly heady overture to Carl Maria von Weber's *Der Freischütz*, she seizes as much independence and freedom of movement as she possibly can. The phenomenological ease and knowledge of place with which she navigates the country roads of this small town by foot or on her bicycle are striking, as they seem to visually suggest that she has lived there her whole life. Considered more carefully, this might appear remarkable with regard to the fact that Barbara has only just arrived in this town; it was crucial to Petzold, however, that Barbara (indeed, Hoss herself) possess a "bodily relationship" to the spaces in and through which she moves (Pinfold 2014, 283). For this reason, Hoss reportedly spent time prior to filming exploring the areas and inhabiting the spaces where the film would be set.

Emancipation through mobility in *Barbara* manifests itself not as a "great escape," as the film's narrative misleadingly sets up, but rather through the daily moments of movement. As much for the viewer as for the protagonist, these moments of movement serve as minor escapes from the construct of stasis and confinement so inherent in prominent (cinematic) imaging of the GDR, especially in the post-2000 examples *Das Leben der Anderen* (*The Lives of Others*, 2006), *Good Bye, Lenin!* (2003), and *Der Tunnel* (*The Tunnel*, 2001). As Petzold explains, once Barbara makes up her mind to leave the GDR "her senses are numbed" to everything around her; she is not interested in making connections or seeing beauty (Leweke 2013, 33). At one point in the film, Barbara exclaims that she could be a candidate for brain surgery, as not unlike a patient in their care who suffers from a traumatic brain injury she appears to have lost all of her affective capacity. Indeed, Barbara appears unable to get beyond exteriority. This numbness could also offer a metacommentary on Hoss's overall acting style, which is frequently characterized as antimelodramatic and minimalist. According to Verena von Eicken, Hoss's training at the Berlin Ernst Busch Academy, renowned as a school of dramatic art strongly informed by a tradition of Brechtian epic acting, fostered her unemotional and distanced style (2014, 114). In Barbara's case, as often happens in the Berlin School films, emotion and expression are filtered through a diffuse gestural language. But this is not one of charged underperformative alienation or irony (à la Brecht or Fassbinder) so much as it is an ever-exteriorized manifestation of sheer physicality, which communicates by means of phenomenological and affective orientations of the body through movement.

Consider Barbara's stiff straight line and tense back throughout the film. Could this be Soviet-influenced, militarized stiffness? Or, perhaps a display of unadorned uneasiness? I read Barbara's comportment slightly differently. Although her eyes frequently dart about nervously, her body always maintains its uncompromising straight line, even in movement. What is certain is that Barbara refuses to be physically broken down by the state. Even her almost ritualistically crossed arms in the film demonstrate a flinty assertion of dramatic refusal to partake of this normative social production of stuckness, both narratively and performatively. In fact, she is a paragon of corporeal self-confidence and even gracefulness. She walks, never runs. Her gait is ballet-inspired. Her legs cross agilely with each step and her toes pointed slightly outward. She is always in a skirt, never pants; her long, limber legs reveal themselves in frequent long shots. Even when she is on a bicycle, Barbara's legs bend and flex with unhindered grace, and her long back sustains an almost perfect forty-five-degree-angled arch. Barbara's body on the move is one of poise and pluck. Her spirit of fugitivity inheres in a design of absolute lissomeness.

It is not Barbara, however, but rather one of her patients, the pregnant teenager Stella (Jasna Fritzi Bauer), who is the real escape artist in this film. Stella escapes from the notoriously formidable juvenile detention center, Torgau,[6] and then finally from the GDR. Yet the film establishes some salient parallels between the two women—a relationship dynamic that Petzold refers to as a possible rebirth for Barbara (Ratner 2012, 20). A doppelganger motif yields a compelling line of thought, but it does not account for the reciprocity of their relationship, which posits a corporeal kinship marked by movement and invested in forging hodological space. The scene of Stella's escape from Torgau directly cuts to an image of Barbara once again on her bicycle as she rides home from the train station one morning after a clandestine sleepover in East Berlin with her West German paramour, Jörg (Mark Waschke). This second scene ends in Barbara's abrupt interception by the *Stasi* and another incursive search of her apartment and body. On precisely the night that Barbara has planned for her own escape from the GDR, the runaway Stella collapses at her door. After treating Stella's wound, inflicted by the barbed-wire fence at the perimeter of Torgau, Barbara takes Stella to the seaside, whence Barbara is due to flee the GDR. From Barbara's house the two quietly escape into the night on her bicycle. Medium close-up shots of first Barbara and then Stella show the two on bicycle as they travel in silence through the steely-blue hues of a moonlit night. The two have serene, almost mirthful, expressions on their faces. In this fleeting set of shots, these two women are ensconced in a shared peacefulness of silent trust and the freedom afforded through their movement. The fugitive bodies of these two heroines are linked, as Stella lovingly grasps Barbara's waist. It is unclear at this point if Barbara intends to escape with Stella or if she already decided to send Stella to the West in her stead. While the latter proves to be the case, in the end it does not seem to matter.

Coming Undone: Shedding the Image through Movement in *Gold*

Thomas Arslan's *Gold* unfolds as a western-inspired tale about a rather unconventional woman who breaks free from her ill-paid job as a housemaid and joins a group of fellow German émigrés on a treacherous adventure to search for gold in the Klondike region. With the exception of a brief prologue that historically establishes the film's setting and narrative, *Gold* begins with all the same symbolic incipience as *Barbara*—with an arrival. Here Hoss's protagonist, Emily Meyer, arrives on a steam engine train in Ashcroft, British Columbia. The viewer does not see Emily on the train; instead, a brief tracking shot follows the train sidelong as it chugs along in barren mountain terrain. In this establishing scene, Arslan adds an unaccustomed—in this case original—musical score of minimalist electronic beats by Dylan Carson's band Earth. Extradiegetic music at once dulcetly and forebodingly ushers in this tale of adventure. Emily disembarks from the train looking rigidly dignified in a Victorian-style riding habit, including a tailored jacket fit with a corset, a long skirt, a top hat, and even a necktie. She is the picture of conservative femininity. An opening masquerade of historically, socially, and even geographically imposed womanliness, this telltale costume gradually and symbolically comes undone over the course of the film. The image of Emily as she emerges from the train thus (at least extradiegetically) aligns with Mary Ann Doane's account of feminine masquerade, "the masquerade, in flaunting femininity, holds it at a distance" (1990, 13). Hoss does not perform this role in excess of her own body; with her removed style of acting, she also does not appear to overly identify with this image. Instead, she clearly sets the distance between herself and her image, and as such indicates the flexibility of the latter as nothing more or less than artificial. Arlan's characteristic eschewal of subjective point-of-view shots is emphatically reprised in *Gold* in these earlier scenes as a means of forging such distancing and to emphasize Hoss's figure as one (at least initially) at a remove.

Similarly drawing on the historical period of western expansionism and settler life, *Gold* thematically and affectively demonstrates parallels with Kelly Reichardt's western *Meek's Cutoff* (2010), which is loosely based on a true story about three pioneer families' unsuccessful attempt to navigate the Oregon Trail in 1845. In an ecstatic and forsakenly barren landscape where the regulatory structures of institutional (read male) power are absent, the main female protagonist (played by Michelle Williams) in this slightly earlier film seizes agency and tips the scales of the otherwise staunchly patriarchal gender dynamic of the group. *Gold* is similarly about the erasure of social dispositions, functionings, and relations. In both films' acts of undoing dominant narratives, genre itself—that is, the western—also ebbs. (That *genre* shares etymological roots with the word *gender*, and the two words still bear the same meaning in French, is worth noting.) Therefore, even as the Berlin School seems to have taken a turn toward more conventional and genre-oriented films in recent years, this turn may simultaneously involve a detectable unraveling of the generic logic that undergirds upheld cultural and social rituals.[7]

In terms of its relationship to power, *Gold* is quite distinct from *Barbara*, in which structures of power and tensions remain intact, albeit tractable. Yet *Gold* likewise relies on the exercise of individual power through tireless movement. To read Emily as a fugitive body may seem like a bit of a stretch. Unlike, for example, her fellow traveler and eventual paramour, Carl Böhmer (Marko Mandic), she is not running away from likely assassins. Her trek into the wilderness nevertheless does position her as a fugitive from the stifling social conventions of class and gender that initially, quite literally, cling tightly to her body. In this sense, Emily may be characterized as a fugitive from the repressive scripting of late nineteenth-century Victorian society, which decreed women's silence and immobility. As Jennifer Duncan observes in the preface to her study about women who braved the Klondike trail, *Frontier Spirit: The Brave Women of the Klondike*, "These were women who strove to escape the confines of Victorian propriety and the prison of the domestic sphere. The frontier gave them the greatest opportunity of this emancipation" (2003, vii). But it is not explicitly the lawlessness and isolation of frontier life that affords Emily the opportunity for emancipation. Rather, it is through the kinetic strivings of her ever-unraveling nomadic mode with all the expansive potential of embodiment, presentness, and mutability that such a differentiated subjectivity through movement permits.

Through the lens of performance, movement literally becomes a formative means of subjectivization. An eruption from stillness and immobility, Emily's performance of liberation, emancipation, and self-actualization does not occur abruptly but rather it unfolds gradually over the course of the film. Katja Nicodemus astutely avers, "Only through movement and through the tasks along the way does Emily invent herself as a protagonist, in action before our eyes" (2013, 76). In the case of Emily, the performance of the fugitive body is a performance of *undoing*, that is, an undoing of her image of femininity. Arslan formulates this gradual undoing in an interview: "Jacket torn, hat dirty, hair disheveled, these are people on the verge of existence, whose only concern it is to take the next step" (2013).[8] Returning, then, to the earlier description of Emily's outfit on her arrival in Ashcroft at the beginning of the film, let us once again take stock of her image and the articles of her traditional lady's riding habit: a tailored jacket, a corset, a blouse, a long thick skirt, a top hat, and a necktie. Considered standard attire of the period for women to go riding, the riding habit was in reality extremely constrictive and hardly conducive to the constant movement involved in a months-long trek through the mountainous terrain of the interior of British Columbia. Shortly after stepping off the train, Emily discreetly removes her necktie. This minor gesture subtly initiates Emily's performance of undoing. Several scenes later she opens the buttons of her rigid jacket, finally removing it altogether along with the hat on route. Her hair, which had been placed up in a tight bun atop her head, gradually loosens. In a telling scene, the viewer glimpses Emily washing her corset in a river, thence to be shed entirely. The shedding of the corset cannot be overstated here. As a result, Emily's body releases tension and becomes more agile. She achieves a new mastery over her body and a new freedom of movement. Christiane Peitz's description of Emily's transformation into a western heroine is especially apt: "She descends from the train, clean and tidy with a hat and a necktie and an ironed blouse. She looks around searchingly, Emily Meyer, a German emigrant in British Columbia, it is the period of the Klondike gold rush. A hundred film minutes later, this stranger has transformed into a heroine of a western, a woman who has asserted herself in a man's world, who has learned how to ride horses and knows the mountains and the forests, the greed for gold, hardship, love, death" (2013).[9] But Peitz seems to take this reading off course when she further suggests that Emily "loses herself" along the way. What Emily loses is the masquerade, her image of femininity, through this transformation. Emily's undressing, as it were, assumes an altogether unique charge that is not coterminous with sexualization; this is not a striptease. Bulgakowa holds that the relaxing of the female body with the casting off of the corset in the early part of the twentieth century actually coincided with modern art's emphasis on women's curves and the new sinuous line of the body (2008). Emily's unlaced body, however, is not simply put in the service of the male gaze by other means. It in fact remains invisible beneath her rather shapeless attire: a thick, long, flowing skirt and a high-collared blouse.

While Emily, like Barbara, maintains Hoss's undeniable straight line and her perfect posture, her bearing and movement gradually fall into step with that of the men. When she is riding on horseback, her torso begins to roll instead of stiffly wobble with each jaunt of the horse. The hand that at first desperately clenches the saddle in a monkey grip for support eventually comes to occupy itself with the task of leading another horse alongside. This transformation of corporeal flexibility and the achievement of a new kind of bearing comes alive in the weave of the film and is in my reading uncompromisingly affirmative and emancipatory. For in contrast to her male counterparts, all of whom die, go mad, or are forced to abandon the journey, Emily is not broken down or punished film noir or Hitchcockian style for seeking the freedom and agency that is not initially in her possession and may be male-coded. [10] Even at moments when the weight of the arduous expedition devolves into an inuring existence of mere survival, Emily is undefeatable. Her tractability thus becomes her preservation.

Emily's performance of undoing is cautiously executed. Although she sheds a number of the vestiges of nineteenth-century femininity, her performance is not one of transvestitism or even drag. Further, her body does not become a site of excess. Emily quietly performs a loosening of rigid femininity, not as a means of fitting in or passing in this men's world but in order to emerge from the stillness cast on her body so that she may navigate the world on her own terms—to seize mobility and ultimately to survive. The residual effect of this performance is an irresolvable stripping down of identity interpellation and the artificial and reductive binary of feminine weakness and immobility versus masculine power and mobility. In the final scene of the film, Emily is now completely alone on her journey, for she is the only surviving traveler. She emerges from the inn in Telegraph Creek ready to set out again to the ever more remote destination of Dawson City, much as she does at the beginning of the film, when she descends from the train in Ashcroft. In this later instance of setting out, Emily is visibly transformed. This transformation is not revealed to the viewer through dialogue or even expressive close-ups; instead, her movements and attire deliver the palpable clues. Donning her dead lover's wool jacket, her hair loose, Emily confidently and expertly saddles up her horses and swiftly trots out of town, stopping only briefly at a small graveyard to stoically salute Carl's grave before she rides into the wilderness and becomes a speck against the ominous expanse of mountain landscape. The extreme long shot that ushers the film to a close visually casts a sense

Figure 5.1. Closing with a gallop across the wilderness stage in *Gold*, 2012. © Schramm Film Koerner & Weber

of isolation and perhaps even mystery to Emily's character. Yet it also formally establishes the context for movement in the final scene and image, in which for the first time in the film Emily gallops in an exhilaratingly mad dash across the screen (see figure 5.1). A final release comes with the increase in speed, what Bulgakowa interprets as the ultimate bodily liberation. That the adventure continues beyond the formal borders of the film is abundantly evident.

Performance within Performance: The Flight of (the) *Phoenix*[11]

Nina Hoss's performance, her augmented body *on the move*, adopts a palpably different form with an exploration of her most recent Berlin School film and collaboration with Christian Petzold, *Phoenix*. Hardly an undue finale for this study on the cinematic performance of the fugitive body, Hoss's performance in *Phoenix* is nonetheless much more complexly layered than those in *Barbara* and *Gold*. It is Germany 1945; the Jewish returnee Nelly Lenz (Hoss) has just escaped from the concentration camp (secondary sources seem to indicate Auschwitz) and an almost inevitable death. In some ways, Hoss's performance of the fugitive body here operates at the level of postperformance—a performance imbricated in the processing of the corollaries of escape and the trauma dispensed on her body through hate, war, and violence. In the final chapter of Brooks's book on fugitivity (2006), she turns to the performance of divas. I read the diva performance as the phenomenon of performance within performance. To speak of performance within performance is not to speak of a metaperformance or simply what James Naremore refers to as professional acting (in a film) versus a Goffmanian presentation of self in society (1988, 70). Instead, a performance within a performance designates a performance scenario, for instance, with an embedded and dynamic audience, a cinematic mise en abyme. Via diva performances, Brooks traces configurations of spectacle and audience. Specifically, she traces the color line politics (in the spirit of W. E. B. Du Bois) and the contact zone of the black (often female) performer and the predominantly white audience. Like Brooks, I am compelled by the performative moment that emerges by means of this fraught encounter, where identity, history, and culpability reawaken and are brought to presence in powerful form. The diva performance provides the contours for the performance configuration also present in Hoss's performance of Nelly, a figure beset by trauma, violence, and disfigurement, who must gradually pull herself up.

Hoss's overall performance in *Phoenix* stands out for its culturally and ethnically charged portrayal of a Jewish concentration camp survivor. It might be added that Hoss is not Jewish. But the film's play with identity and its layers of performance emphatically and creatively throw notions of authenticity into question. An entire post–Des Presian discourse on the importance of bearing witness despite the complex ethos of representation may be considered in this instance.[12] Adam Lowenstein emphasizes the importance of the representation of such traumatic events as the Holocaust, as critical to "the shaping of our contemporary world" (2005, 5), even at the risk of forsaking the authenticity of the survivor experience. According to Lowenstein, an utter lack of representation would be almost as detrimental as irresponsible representations. Still, the precarious and complex nexus of authenticity, history, and representation cannot be ignored. Hinting at an unspoken self-reflexivity, *Phoenix* instead fosters performance both in lieu of direct (re)presentation and as circumvention of the potentially messy dialectic of aesthetics and experience. Identity and subjectivity are aptly presented in a kind of flux. In its postwar rendering, the film trembles with the aftershocks of violence, destruction, and hate that constantly threaten any kind of subjective stability. But in a film in which ambiguity prevails, Hoss's fugitive performance wrenches life from death and identity from invisibility not from a blazing flame as the phoenix but from a national slate wiped desperately clean.

Yet another arrival, if one may call it that, opens this Petzold film. Nelly has been miraculously rescued from a concentration camp, where she had been shot in the head and left for dead. *Phoenix* begins with a crossing of the border from Switzerland into Germany. Nelly's rescuer, Lene (Nina Kunzendorf), is a Jewish friend and a lawyer for the Jewish Agency[13] who survived the war by fleeing to Switzerland. The two women arrive in Germany and are stopped at a makeshift border checkpoint controlled by American GIs. A soldier demands to see their passports, which Lene provides, but the soldier aggressively insists on seeing what is hidden beneath Nelly's entirely bandaged and bloody face. Defensively, Lene retorts, "She's not Eva Braun" (Hitler's long-term female companion). Yes, but who is she? This is the question that indicatively thrusts the film forward. Satisfied neither with that response nor with the explanation that she's "from the camps," the soldier vehemently repeats, "I want to see her face!" With sobs of anguish and fear, Nelly is forced to unwrap her bandages and show him the devastated flesh that was once a human face. But the promise of truth and revelation in this establishing scene never comes to fruition for the viewer. Nelly's face remains an absent center, a hollow abyss. There is no reverse shot. The viewer does not see what the soldier does or does not see. The foreclosure of the shot–reverse-shot formation feels like a partial blindfold, an extra layer of mediation. In a medium close-up the viewer can only observe the response of the soldier to this image: a mixed mien of shock, disgust, sadness, and shame crosses his face as he now recognizes what he failed to recognize earlier—absence in all its bloody horror. Recoiling, he looks away and quietly apologizes. The opacity of Nelly's (nonexistent) face is the film's blind spot. It is the central void around which the film's story and performance evolve.

The viewer does not witness the act of violence visited on Nelly's body that has resulted in her damaged flesh and bodily trauma. Nelly's escape and rescue from Auschwitz are not shown in the film; Petzold began to film that scene but discarded it after the first day of shooting. Nonetheless, the state of flight is not simply ancillary to the film so much as it is refigured. Compared to Hoss's other roles, her performance of the fugitive body in *Phoenix* is more ontologically entangled in the state of her traumatized body. Flight persists, but it is marked by the crisis of (dis)orientation. Driven by a force to rise out of a paralysis inflicted by another, here the fugitive body strives to reposition itself in the world. In its displacement and disorientation, it is thrust into a reorientation and a turning toward new directions. Sara Ahmed observes throughout her study *Queer Phenomenology* (2006) that it is through turning that reorientation becomes possible. In the case of *Phoenix*, this revolution develops into a circuitous flight of turning back as a way forward.

Once in Berlin, Nelly undergoes reconstructive surgery on her face. A pre-surgery consultation with the doctor gives rise to an oddly comical discussion about appearance and identity. The doctor, who is evidently a film fan, drolly muses that he could make Nelly look like Zarah Leander or Kristina Söderbaum, both film stars of the Nazi era. He then follows up with the comment: "They're not really in style anymore, though." ("Aber sie sind wohl aus der mode.") Nelly firmly counters that she would like to look like her old self, but the surgeon advises against this, since an exact reconstruction will not be possible, and he adds that it is advantageous to have a new identity. Notwithstanding *Phoenix*'s horror elements—the inscrutable woman without a face—which echo to some extent Georges Franju's macabre *Les yeux sans visage* (*Eyes without a Face*, 1960),[14] which shares a postwar setting of disfigurement and identity whitewashing—*Phoenix* also proffers a degree of performative playfulness. In a rather ironic twist of extrafilmic performance, Nelly is not made to look like the old film stars of the

Nazi era; instead, she is made to look like a new German film star—Nina Hoss. By means of this physical transformation from a faceless concentration camp survivor to a beautiful film star, Petzold opens up the possibility of representation and belief. If the viewer felt compelled to suspend belief with regard to Hoss's performance of a Jewish Holocaust survivor, she can now accept Hoss in this role in all of her putative "old-style movie-star glamour and Aryan ideals of feminine beauty," as *New York Times* film critic A. O. Scott (2009) described her, because Hoss ultimately performs herself in *Phoenix*. Thus, the textural complexity of this performance is already established in the first few scenes of the film.

Once the cast falls and Nelly symbolically encounters her transformed self in the shards of a mirror among the ruins of her old house, a Lacanian crisis of the body as an unrecognizable object ensues. Overcome with shock and even abjection, Nelly flees this strange specular self-image. This crisis sets Nelly to a different kind of fleeing from that of Barbara and Emily: she flees from her (non) self. But fleeing, like Ahmed's principle of "turning," is in like manner an act of orienting oneself along new lines of flight. Citing Paul Jefferson, Brooks states that "the act of fleeing is an existential act of self-creation" (2007, 69). Nelly's existential flight is not only a flight from the uncanny but also explicitly an attempt at self-(re)creation. For nearly the first quarter of the film Nelly is invisible: her head remains tightly wrapped in a skull cast and bandages. Even her body moves with an awkward, almost robotic stiffness, as though unsure of how to use her body, of where to place her feet or even rest her gaze. Nelly carries her body with heaving unease. In an interview, Hoss explains that at the beginning she tried to give Nelly a childish, erratic, and weak quality to match her corpse-like appearance of pallid skin, bruised face, and ashen hair. It is only with time that Nelly forms her body again and begins to recognize who she is. "She needs self-awareness, she has to trust herself in order to hold up her body."[15]

Nelly's pursuit of self-recognition unfolds as a desperate search for her errant husband, Johnny (Ronald Zehrfeld). The only problem is that he presumes her dead, as he was the one who directly or indirectly orchestrated her capture by the Nazis and her deportation to Auschwitz. Roaming the streets of the rubble-filled, kaput city of Berlin, Nelly stumbles on him one night in a makeshift cabaret for American soldiers appropriately called Phoenix. In this and subsequent scenes at said club, Petzold appears to apply all the mise-en-scène conventions of New German Cinema in the spirit of Fassbinder (garish color and lighting, theatrical spectacle, unnatural blocking). In Rainer Werner Fassbinder's postwar classic *Die Ehe der Maria Braun* (*The Marriage of Maria Braun*, 1979), the eponymous figure (played by Hanna Schygulla) eventually gives up searching for her husband and procures work at a bar for American soldiers. Indeed, Elena del Río's suggestive reading of the figure of Maria as a body beset by the national and historical trauma of Nazi Germany whose movement is coded by a "self-conscious choreography" removed from "natural-looking flow" (2012, 78–79) astutely speaks to Nelly's own kinetic awkwardness in these earlier scenes. Unlike Maria, though, Nelly is not a representative figure who can be read hermeneutically. Her performance is more subjective and direct; without being overwrought with pathos, it leans toward pure presentation. Consider Nelly's first encounter with Johnny. Her desire for a familiar object by means of which she may align and reorient herself is at first shattered. Her attempt to turn toward the past is met with repudiation. She is unrecognizable to Johnny as Nelly. Ahmed observes that *turning* in phenomenology also lends itself to strategies of subject formation of address. While Judith Butler, following Louis Althusser, famously argued that the "turning around" that transpires when one is hailed by a person of authority is a forced form of subject constitution that needs to be deconstructed, for Ahmed the physical turning that occurs in this "turning around" can also be affirmative insofar as it "might take subjects in different directions," where "different worlds might even come into view" (2006, 15).[16] By contrast, in reverse-Althusserian manner, the absence of (the reciprocated) address becomes a form of renewed debilitation and even trauma for Nelly, because it leaves her nowhere to turn. In this scene, Nelly appears in a close-up as she calls out Johnny's name, and in a reverse shot he looks up but there is no eye contact, and no subsequent eyeline match from the perspective of Johnny. Instead, he darts his eyes around the room in a confused manner. Not only does it appear as though he has not seen a familiar face, he does not seem to see anyone with whom he could match this voice. It is as though this woman standing before him does not exist at all. Once again, Petzold's foreclosure of classical continuity editing serves as a method of displacement and renewed disorientation, both for Nelly and for the viewer.

On a textual level, the film invites a curiously enfolded Hitchcockian narrative, in which Johnny eventually spies something familiar in Nelly's wan appearance and beckons her into a scheming thespian plot to procure his deceased wife's (her own) estate. A number of scholars, including Petzold himself, have been quick to point out the film's clear homage to Alfred Hitchcock's *Vertigo* (1958) (Nayman 2014). Johnny's aim in this scheme is to transform this shadow of a woman into the image of the scintillating woman he once loved. Unlike Scottie in Hitchcock's film, Johnny, broken down by war and loss, is not interested in love or sexual desire; he simply wants the wealth that would allow him the chance to start over. As he indicates, he plans to leave Germany once he has secured the money. Convinced that through her husband's eyes she too will be able to pick up the broken pieces of her body and reorient herself, Nelly goes along with his scheme. But as Johnny stubbornly tries to shape Nelly into "his Nelly" it becomes evident that his memory of his wife is more fantasy than anything else. From the writing of a shopping list, to the descending of stairs, the length of her dress and the color of her hair, Johnny coerces Nelly into a fetishistic performance of his fantasy. This is not merely a male, Oedipal fantasy, as Laura Mulvey definitively delineated in the case of *Vertigo* (1990, 37–38), but a national historical fantasy based on the inability to face German guilt. In protest Nelly weakly explains that no one will believe that she would return from the camps looking like her old self, dressed to go celebrate in a red dress and stylish shoes from Paris. This is where she errs: belief here is relative and therefore suspended. More important is what people want to see. Indeed, Nelly's second (feigned) arrival in Berlin, which she and Johnny meticulously planned, is not to prove her physical existence to their former circle of friends, because they too are perceptibly involved in the plot to wangle Nelly's money. Adding insult to injury, the ensuing superfluous performance of arrival and reconciliation stands out more as a symbolic alleviation of guilt than as any course of action within their broader plan.

But something goes awry in this performance. The woman who emerges from the train in this second arrival (what Petzold has called "the *real* beginning of the film" [Nayman 2014]) is one we have not yet met, or perhaps there is an interfilmic note at work here. Nelly does not simply act in this scene—she acts out. She is what Brooks calls in the final chapter of her book *Bodies in Dissent* a "diva" (if I may borrow the term traditionally bestowed on trailblazing women of color) with a "diasporic consciousness," a woman of "quietly fierce mettle" (2007, 281). Unlike her cinematic stepsister in *Vertigo*, Madeline/Judy, Nelly will not be silenced by death (or attempted reconciliation, for that matter) and instead ends the film in this final sequence on her own terms—that is, through *her own* performance. After a decisively contrived train station welcome, followed by lunch, drinking, and hammy toasts celebrating her return, Nelly beckons the party into a music hall with the promise of a duo performance performed by her and Johnny for old time's sake. As we have learned throughout the film, Nelly was a singer before the war and previously performed with her pianist husband. A confused but willing participant, Johnny takes his spot at the piano and at Nelly's request begins to play "Speak Low." A musical motif in the film, common to Petzold features, this standard jazz tune can be heard on a number of occasions, both diegetically on a Kurt Weill record and extradiegetically in an instrumental version as an overture to the film. Nelly's performance begins slowly, hesitantly, quietly. In near-whispering tones, she mouths the first few lines of the song. But a willful transformation gradually transpires. Nelly is made present.

In this theatrical mise-en-scène, Nelly appears imposing. She towers over a diminutive-looking Johnny in her vertical position next to the piano. Adding to this larger-than-life perspective of Nelly, the camera matches Johnny's perspective from below, forced into an upward cant in order to gaze at her. At one moment, in what might be described as cinema's most rarefied look of loathing, Nelly casts her gaze down at Johnny and then begins to *really* sing. The beauty and talent of her voice is hauntingly electric and disarming. Immediately recognizing her true identity through the power and beauty of her voice, Johnny rests his eyes on the number tattooed on her left arm, the indissoluble physical trace of her internment at Auschwitz, and he ceases to play the piano. With a look of utter consternation, now slumped down at the piano, he freezes entirely. Having brought the scene to an abrupt abeyance (in a reverse shot the small audience now also looks on almost comically stupefied), Nelly picks up her coat and walks toward the door. In typical Petzoldian fashion, this final shot shows Nelly's red silhouette as it turns away, awash with light and visually obfuscated as though viewed through tear-filled eyes. But this is not the point of view of any diegetic perspective; Nelly's exit is for the viewer only.

Hoss's diva performance at the close of *Phoenix* is quite possibly her most powerful cinema performance of all time. The theatrical performance embedded in this film, with its stage and additional spectators, illuminates the performer (here Nelly/Hoss) as pure presence. Shane Vogel asserts that "while the musical diva may be difficult to reach offstage, onstage she offers everything in her performances; she elaborates a social, corporeal, and affective excess that marks pure presence" (2009, 168). Nelly certainly sings herself into a vibrant presence in this scene, whose performance's overwhelming sensuous spirit contrasts with her character's otherwise childlike demureness throughout the film—indeed, her hitherto utter lack of presence. The dramatic fusing of performance and performativity here yields Nelly's long sought after moment of self-actualization and emancipation and proffers an absorptive spectacle of liveness. Finding her voice and rendering herself visible again, Nelly ironically does not give the audience what it seeks but in fact the opposite. There are parallels to be drawn between Nelly's performance as a concentration camp survivor to a non-Jewish German audience in the immediate postwar period and an African American singer to a white American audience in the Reconstruction era. Brooks's concept of the "contact zone," inherent to much black postbellum performance, was where "many white audiences witnessed and experienced black cultural workers on stage for the first time" (2007, 297). Through certain performances, such an experience had the effect of precisely the reconciliation that Nelly's spectators seek, in which they may find a moment of recognition followed directly by exoneration and even "disavowal for their complicity" with the narrative of slavery (or with the Holocaust, for that matter)—a swift process of open and shut (298). Instead, Nelly opens the narrative of complicity and guilt, and denies its closure. Presenting the audience with "the real Nelly," this performance within a performance (within a performance) spectacularly intervenes in Johnny's and his fellow spectators' own performance of historical amnesia and elision. In the end, she is without pity for her stone-faced audience and continues to sing over the deadening silence of the piano, stretching out her notes, manifesting her presence, relentlessly pursuing her freedom.

That Nelly's stunning subjectivizing performance becomes most palpable with her minor flight mid song underscores its element of fugitivity. In its radical "turning away" and refusal to participate, the performance of flight proffers an arrestingly continuous quality that demands the intensity of the present tense. It resists infinitely. A body given to flight, a body perpetually in motion: such is the performance of the fugitive body. Reading Hoss's performances in *Barbara*, *Gold*, and *Phoenix* along reoccurring patterns of flight, this chapter has sought both to hail her important work in the Berlin School into a viable discourse and to understand her instrumental place in this cinema by dint of movement and performance. While based on the premise of escape, the performance of the fugitive body is not so much about getting away as it is about mobilizing the body out of stillness. Brooks describes this as something like an act of "instill[ing] movement in 'free' yet socially, politically, and culturally circumscribed bodies" (8). The performance of the fugitive body is invested in the transitory moments when movement and mobility become subversive acts of breaking free from the stasis induced by political and social imperatives. I argue that Hoss performs the figures of Barbara, Emily, and Nelly like abolitionist performers before her, at "the tensions between captivity and escape, oppression and insurgency, stasis and mobility" (189). In its emphasis on the body in action and transformation, movement presents a bodily performance of resistance against confinement, immobility, and dependence. Even as movement seems to make a spectacle of the body, potentially placing it in a position of hypervisibility and even vulnerability, animated by movement and agility, the spectacle of Hoss's gendered body charts the viewer through an undoing of dominant epistemologies of femininity (especially of earlier historical periods) so often enfolded in negating categories of stillness and inertia.

Thinking about the broader context of Hoss's performance of the fugitive body, in closing I propose that such a material performance-movement/movement-performance pattern permeates and even shapes these later Berlin School films, and certainly the way in which they are viewed. Enacted through the iconic body of Hoss, whose movements and gesturing have become indelibly traceable and assertively habitual to this cinema, such an account of performance through movement becomes not only conceivable but perhaps even requisite when speaking of the Berlin School. With this final chapter I present a categorical figure for thinking about movement and performance in the Berlin School films. The performance of the fugitive body should add to but not eclipse the previously investigated instances of performance, given breath and breadth in this book. In so doing, it affirms and affords yet another rich example of Berlin School performance crossed over with all the physical movement and dynamism that is such a significant dimension of these films and their feel of contingency, and liveness. The Berlin School's immense potential as a film movement that offers new points of entry for thinking about cinema as a performance-based medium that explores and expands the ecstatic experience of the live.

Notes

1. These collaborations include *Toter Mann* (*Something to Remind Me*, 2001), *Wolfsburg* (2003), *Yella* (2007), *Jerichow* (2008), *Barbara* (2012), *Phoenix* (2014), and a production of Arthur Schnitzler's dramatic work *Der einsame Weg* (*The Lonely Path*), which premiered in 2009 at the Deutsches Theater in Berlin.
2. For a rich star studies reading of Nina Hoss, see von Eicken (2014).
3. Roach has famously investigated bodily performance as precisely a kind of surrogation of memory and historical processes meant to interrogate but also reinvent. He writes: "Voices of the dead may speak freely now only through the voices of the living" (1996, xiii).
4. See, for instance, Moten (2003); Harney and Moten (2013); Hartman (1997), and Weheliye (2014). The two earlier texts are also extensively cited in Brooks's study.
5. One might compare *Barbara* to the slightly earlier film about the GDR, the award-winning *Das Leben der Anderen* (*The Lives of Others*, 2006), which according to Fisher was celebrated for its accentuated minimalist, dark, and dreary aesthetics. These apparently accurately rendered the memories of socialist Germany (2013, 140).
6. From 1950 to 1990, Torgau-Fort Zinna served as an East German penal institution for juvenile offenders. It was considered the harshest detention center of the GDR, where youths were under strict control and forced to perform hard labor. There are few English-language sources about Torgau. For a comprehensive study in German see Krausz (2010).
7. This is also observable in Valeska Grisebach's 2017 film *Western*, which clearly subverts genre expectations in its depiction of a team of male German contractors in rural Bulgaria.
8. "Das Sakko gerissen, der Hut fleckig, das Haar zerzaust, es sind Menschen in Auflösung, denen es nur noch darum geht, den nächsten Schritt zu Machen."
9. "Sie steigt aus dem Zug, sauber zurechtgeputzt, mit Hut und Tuch und gebügelter Bluse. Sie schaut sich suchend um, Emily Meyer, eine deutsche Auswanderin in British Columbia, es ist die Zeit des Klondike-Goldrauschs. Hundert Filmminuten später hat sich die Fremde in eine Westernheldin verwandelt, eine Frau, die sich allein in einer Männerwelt behauptet, die reiten gelernt hat und die Berge und Wälder kennt, die Gier nach dem Gold, die Mühsal, die Liebe, den Tod."
10. One might easily recall the figure of Melanie Daniels (Tippi Hedren) in Alfred Hitchcock's *The Birds*. She is wealthy and independent and has desires. Melanie is the one to pursue Mitch, not the other way around. As Susan Lurie famously claimed, Melanie is threatening to the male because of her strength and perceived wholeness; therefore, she must be castrated or punished. See Modleski (2016, 2).
11. Parts of this section were previously published in *Film-Philosophy*. See Landry, "A Body without a Face: The Disorientation of Trauma in *Phoenix* (2014) and New Holocaust Cinema" (2017).
12. In his famous article "Holocaust *Laughter*?" (1988), Terrence Des Pres discusses the limitations of the received ethical parameters of Holocaust representation that dictates that Holocaust must be represented truthfully and without artistic intervention. This claim offers

a backlash against Theodor W. Adorno's prominent postwar injunction that representing the Holocaust through art and especially poetry was barbaric ([1967] 1983, 34).

13. The Jewish Agency (now the Jewish Agency for Israel) was an organization established in the late 1920s as part of the Zionist movement to encourage and assist Jews to immigrate to what was then Palestine. The organization was especially instrumental in seeking and identifying Jews displaced and/or murdered during the Nazi period.

14. While Franju's film is the one most often cited as a cinematic model for *Phoenix*, I would also add Delmer Daves's film noir classic *Dark Passage* (1947) and especially the Japanese postwar drama *The Face of Another* (1966), directed by Hiroshi Teshigahara. In the lesser-known latter film, a man experiences a work-related accident and the flesh on his face is singed. He is forced to cover his entire face in bandages. Tired of the way he is treated, he decides to undergo an experiment in which a doctor will use the face mold of another, much younger man to create a mask that allows him to start a new life, but things go awry when he uses this new identity to seduce his wife. There is also the Austrian horror film, Veronika Franz and Severin Fiala's *Ich seh, ich seh* (*Goodnight Mommy*, 2014). In the latter film, the mother returns home after full facial plastic surgery. Her face is likewise cast in bandages. She seems different, and her sons begin to believe that she is not their mother, but an intruder. Horror ensues.

15. The entire quote, which originates from an interview, titled "Der Riss," with Hoss, Petzold, Ronald Zehrfeld, and Nina Kunzendorf printed in the accompanying DVD booklet for *Phoenix*, reads: "Ich habe versucht, der Nelly am Anfang etwas kindliches, auch etwas Fahriges, Haltloses zu geben, so wie ihre Haare, da ist alles so grau und eigentlich nicht da.... Und mit der Zeit formt sich der Körper wieder, sie fängt wieder an zu wissen, wer sie ist. Sie muss wieder ein Selbstbewusstsein haben, sie muss auf sich vertrauen können, um ihren Körper aufrecht zu halten." ("I tried to give Nelly a childish quality, also agitated, and weak, just like her hair, which is all gray and not really there.... And with time her body takes shape again, she begins to recognize who she is. She has to have self-assurance again, she has to be able to trust herself so that she can hold her body.")

16. I read *Phoenix* with reference to Sara Ahmed's theory of disorientation in an earlier article. See Landry (2017).

Conclusion
Performance on the Move

The Berlin School moves. It performs through movement. Its performance is one of kinetic force. This much is evident. We began with a departure from stasis and slowness, as the given (rather narrow) precepts of much contemporary global cinema. A departure from the same becomes an aperture to the dynamic and the mobile. The Berlin School films possess a vitalism hitherto elided by critics and scholars. This book energetically brings these scenes of dynamism into relief, into presence. But this is not the half of it. What is at the heart of *Movement and Performance in Berlin School Cinema* is the performance possibilities to be found in movement. This is for the most part a movement stripped of its hermeneutic and semiotic weightiness. Its heady promise instead churns in an unexpected abundance of effervescence and sentience. The scene of movement is a scene of performance in these films. It offers a spectacle of the body that at times with grandeur and at other times with painstaking subtlety consumes space and marks boundaries. That said, movement on-screen is not always performance; such is not the full argument I hope to have made here. And when observed in isolation, movement in the Berlin School may not readily strike the viewer as performance, that is, as anything out of the ordinary, anything beyond the utilitarianism of movement as such. Considered in its rhythmic recurrence across these films, and distilled in this book, movement develops patterns, designs, and qualities that bid our attention and take us for a ride. Performance thus bears out in movement. If movement is performance's catalyst, then performance in turn gives it form and a figuration.

Performance itself may assume myriad forms. The definition I assign to performance is not strict but it is applied consistently. What is performance? Performance is the spectacle of the body in motion that effusively draws its spectators in to partake of its motion. Throughout this book, I have looked for moments where diegetic movement yields thresholds of relationality. Over these thresholds of simmering movement, the viewer is invited to engage in vivid experiences of spatiotemporal liveness and presence, what I have referred to throughout as being-there and being-with. Beholding motion sets the film world alive and pulls the viewer into the tussle of moving, living bodies. The sense of being present to the film world, of being there, is critical to my pursuit of performance here.

Being present likewise underpins the sense of being proximate to the scene of these bodies. Proximity, and even interaction and reciprocity, triggered through this experience of presence and its affective power, in turn releases an experience of being with the bodies in this world where corporeal address and response become possible. Tracking performance in the Berlin School films is the task of tracking these moments of effusion, which pulse with energy.

A resistance to the static and a challenge to the slow in an era where these seem to be the overwhelming antidote to and even reaction against our accelerated lives is a move against the grain that boldly sets up this study. Indeed, the turn to the aesthetics and politics of slowness appears to permeate every last corner of the humanities of late. Lutz Koepnick's monograph *On Slowness: Toward an Aesthetic of the Contemporary* (2014) is an example of the heightened concern with this contemporary widespread phenomenon of idleness. Included among his numerous and varied objects of study, the films of the Berlin School are central to this contemporary shift in the structures of temporality. Yet this book's penchant for movement is not completely at odds with this nominal zeitgeist of languidness. A focus on movement in film does not necessarily propose a speeding up of time, but it does trouble the assumed tangle of time and movement. Slowing things down does not automatically mean foreclosing movement. When Koepnick describes slowness via Giorgio Agamben as a kind of contemporaneousness in which engagement and even copresence become possible (6), he inadvertently slips into a designation of performance. Contemporaneousness hinges on experiences of presence and proximity. Slow cinema's almost ritualistic propensity for long takes and wide framing is taken up in many Berlin School films, but instead of casting the cinematic image into a realist-inspired photographic verisimilitude, this style of cinematography opens up the material world of film. The mise-en-scène and its quality and tradition of theatrical staging, as that which is "put on stage," becomes fixed in the camera's gaze. Needless to say, mise-en-scène contains the germ of spectacle and movement inherent in performance. Alexandre Astruc famously formulates mise-en-scène as "a certain way of extending states of mind into movements of the body" (1985, 267). "It is," he adds, "a song, a rhythm, a dance" (ibid.). The spatialized and temporalized creative energy of the mise-en-scène, of what is put on stage or into the scene, is what Anne Rutherford incisively describes as "the moment of experience, how the spectator is drawn into the scene at the moment of its unfolding" (2003, 5). The film frame becomes a kind of proscenium for contemporaneous movement and intensity to which the viewer is drawn. Mise-en-scène becomes a mode of experience. Treating the film frame as a stage upon which action unfolds and movement is navigated is a neat and important metaphor for the performance of the Berlin School, but this is only part of a larger argument I am making with this book.

Performance's own speculative status as something that refuses to hold to any one definition additionally offers a new threshold of possibility for film. It calls for a levity of theory and structure, while weighted concepts and modes of permissibility fall through its semantic floor of straw. To seek a place for film in performance studies thus also invites a deepening of our understanding of performance, which I argue is made possible by thinking about its affinity to the body, and by extension to liveness, movement, affect, and sensation. Bringing together two highly suggestive and semantically drifting terms such as *film* and *performance* via kinesthetic force finds ontological grounding in chapter 1's investigation of film's mediatic encounter with photography and surveillance. If film is already a "mongrel medium," as Karen Beckman (2010, 3) and others claim, then this quality is brought to presence through film's juxtaposition with other media. Although this technique may seem utterly exhausted, it delivers a robust place for further examination that ultimately leads to unheralded revelations. This act of remediation evident throughout many of the Berlin School films demonstrates film's deep ties to the spatiotemporal effects of copresence and even liveness, both through difference and affinity. Still media (for instance, the photograph) clashes with mobile media (film, surveillance video footage), however, not in simple binary terms. By drawing a set of complex mediatic interrelations, these films bubble energetically where intersections as well as frays of movement, film, and performance vigorously play out. Ontological difference and similarity operatively give prominence to the undeniable quality of the *moving* image.

As chapters 2 and 3 also reveal, film's relationship to corporeal movement can always be uncovered, even in what might appear to be the unlikeliest of places. This study explores the plethora of diegetic movement. It brings into relief the importance and relevance of movement within the frame: the runner, the walker, the dancer, the cyclist, the driver. While certainly not all identical, the figure of the body in movement is central to many Berlin School films, and their overall architecture of the mise-en-scène and the composition of space. A shift in focus from movement of the frame (cinematography, editing) to movement within the frame, offers a rethinking of Gilles Deleuze's famous narrative of cinema history from the movement-image to the time-image. He proposed the formal transformation from the movement-image to the time-image as one chiefly established through an alteration in editing practices, wherein the erstwhile linear continuity editing that steadfastly matches narrative action becomes replaced by long takes meant to serve viewer observation ([1985] 1989, xi). Movement in the image does not simply cease to exist with a lack of cuts and a dearth of tracking shots, however. Indeed, some of cinema's most kinesthetic moments emerge from the early "cinema of attractions," considered at length in chapter 2, at a time when the mobile camera was still unthinkable. Yet the effects of movement and spectacle still shock and agitate. The long take set at a distance actually makes diegetic movement all the more visible in these films. It provides, in Steven Shaviro's words (drawing on André Bazin), "an originary, phenomenological plentitude of perception" (1993, 17). Again, we observe how movement occurs across the film frame as though across a stage. The stage as metaphor and the physical act of staging are foundational aspects of this study's interrogation of a performance of film that frequently comes in tandem with the effects of live experience and presence. In the case of dance, I propose a thinking about theatricality in line with Erika Fischer-Lichte ([2004] 2008), in contrast to Platonic traditions, as a shedding of artifice and a breaking down of the fourth wall. Dance prompts a bodily authenticity that draws the viewer in. At first glance, the nature of these theatrical moments of dance appear as anomalies in the films but they ultimately permeate the film world, even bleed into the frame. As I see it, dance's theatricality therefore opens up the ontological potential of film even further.

Announcing new readings of both the Berlin School films and film more generally, the preceding pages strive to demonstrate how the films may alter the way we think about and experience the moving image through a multifaceted (and an utterly less ideologically burdened) *point of sense* rather than through the scopic regime of the *point of view*. The point of sense directs the viewer's experience of the film scene through sensory perception and facilitated by the mobile body that beckons the viewer's attention. It privileges our tendency toward objects in movement. Gravitational force draws our bodies in. Knowledge becomes bodily. By way of this proposed epistemology of live experience, I have hoped to demonstrate how film may call itself a performance-based medium incidentally propelled toward liveness, theatricality, and interactivity. This epistemology bears out in close analyses of the Berlin School films here in particular, but it has been my intention to present these as paradigmatic examples. While it would be foolhardy to suggest that performance and live experience are the only measures of cinema, current and past, they nonetheless eke out new directions where the ostensible impasses of digitalization and fragmentation of the post-cinematic age of rapid streaming and recording may otherwise appear to foreclose such paths.

The new turn to/in affect coincides with the post-cinematic mood. A turn toward affect in chapter 3 is not only a turn toward contemporary film scholarship, in which affect is increasingly gaining traction, but also a necessary grounding for examining the body and its enormous potential at a moment when it becomes tricky to speak of the cinematic body. For some, affect as an approach has become the sinuous alternative to phenomenological film theory, which reached its height in the mid to late 1990s and whose influence has been slowly receding. Affect provides a noncognitive somatic language that relies neither on structured (shall we also say, moralized) emotional capacity—what Lauren Berlant (2011) refers to as "genre"—nor even on the body as anchor. Affect's autonomy is its currency, not to mention its contagion. But in my reading of affect with performance, affects do not emerge ex nihilo, nor do bodies simply *catch* affects, as proposed by many affect theorists; instead, bodies produce them. Film phenomenology continues to teach us that the body on-screen holds a power over the viewer, regardless of the quality or size of the screen or the quality (theatrical or ordinary) of the movement. Bodily performance is highly affective. My interest in reading affect through phenomenology is twofold. First, it follows a similar reconfiguration of theatricality as a mode of presence, proximity, and authenticity. Affect is a communicative measure between bodies and things, which at the same time orients bodies toward and away from those same things. Through these processes, affect generates atmospheres of experience that are first and foremost embodied. Ultimately, though, and this brings me to the second point, affect through phenomenology is a critical rivet that links performance to a robust genealogy of embodiment and relationality in film and film studies. Thus, I do not propose that performance replaces affect in a theoretical trajectory from materiality to phenomenology and affect; rather, performance becomes a viable next step, a stepping out, a fleshy extension. The paradigm of film performance is one that holds to the boundlessly energetic materiality of the body.

This book also attends to modes of movement that are quite ordinary. The pedestrian is the main figure in the scenes of performance of the everyday. Motion is seamless but rendered with such realism that the viewer drifts along too. Corporeality floats in these many sensory encounters in which walking alone invites a following, a falling into step. The body is also registered in ordinary movement, and it directs attention through filmic space where it bumps into free-floating affects and the stochastic objects and people of the everyday on the street. In these films, the ordinary is not just the dull, the static, or the habitual per se, but, as Kathleen Stewart claims, also that which "can turn on you" (2007, 106). Particularly when movement speeds up, the ordinary can take off in other directions.

Propinquity to the materiality of bodies and things (cars, for instance) in the throes of movement is of course not without its jolts—both exciting and dangerous. Automobility features prominently in many of the Berlin School films. Without shifting away from the body, the automobile becomes the cinematic body in full throttle, as it were. It is a kind of body (and definitely a sight) prosthesis and the cinematic camera ersatz all wrapped into one. I liken driving to film viewing, a rote comparison, but one effortlessly applicable here. The windshield becomes the rectangular frame of our mobile field of vision, what Volker Pantenburg terms "the automobilization of the gaze" (2010). This is the gaze in motion but with exhilaratingly greater speed and steadiness. Even when lolling lazily on our couch (or behind the wheel, for that matter), we can take in the world agog as it affectively rushes toward us. What a thrill! What wonder!

Performance's relational demand slides into an interactive state at such moments. The viewer becomes driver. This is the opening premise and promise of chapter 4. But the automobile, and its propensity for speed in particular, formidably places the pleasure of participatory looking from a mediated distance under duress. When movement escalates, we are thrown off course. Flung from a bridge or a precipice, hurled onto the shoulder in minor flight, the recurring car crash not only recalibrates our experience but also assails our senses. Pleasure is not necessarily annulled in these moments but rather transformed into a vertiginous feeling. We become present at the site of destruction. The crest of the crash and its aftermath do not simply punish or doom for chances too hastily taken when movement stakes are high. The high stakes of movement are part of the promise of the unfolding present, maybe even a glimpse into the future. The purport of performance of the scrap pile, an ostensibly static state, is its worldmaking force. Figured as an event in which present zoning and spatial boundaries of existence are thrown asunder, the car crash is a violent opening, a threshold of new possibility on which the film world of the Berlin School turns.

What my investigations of the confluence of movement and performance in chapters 4 and 5 seek to teach us about the Berlin School and its potentially more transcendental motives is drawn more broadly with the consideration of the ramifications of the event of the car crash and finally with the figure of the fugitive body of the actress Nina Hoss, as a performance of atomized movement in the service of historical recasting. These turns explore to some extent the afterlife of movement. Not meant to be diagnostic, they nonetheless point us to new worlds, new modes of worldmaking, for as Diana Taylor boldly avers, "Performance is world-making. We need to understand it" (2016, 208). If tracking performance shapes the first part of the present book, then understanding performance and its sanguine effect/affect in these film worlds is more explicitly the aim of the latter part. In all these chapters, I take on the challenge of thinking film through performance categories, such as liveness, theatricality, presence, affect, interactivity, transformation, and historical processes of embodiment. Through this engagement, both the films and these topics are reanimated and reframed in provocative ways. The tone of this book is curiously mobilizing and even life-giving. Even when death and destruction appear to attenuate all possibility, the performance path I follow is unmistakably affirmative, edging on the utopian.

Concluding with a more emblematic example of performance in film, that is, with the performance of a singular body and how it is shaped through movement, chapter 5's focus on Nina Hoss offers a distillation of the direct concatenation of movement and performance. The fugitive body is not the body of the criminal on the run from justice, or at least, not the way we might think. It is the unadorned body in motion whose kinetic gestures tell tales of freedom. These are tales somatically felt through the body. If, according to Rutherford, the performing body on-screen adopts the traits of the cinematic body, as it develops an intrinsic relationship with the space of the frame and the materiality of the diegetic world (2015, 320), then the cinematic body is still indelibly formed by and of the performing body. Swelling to fit the frame, this said body is imbued with a power that penetrates the viewer's senses with rhythmic notes of liveness, presence, relationality, and interaction and whose role and place in the Berlin School has hopefully, in sum, been given its due scrutiny.

What does it mean, then, to turn to performance? A performance turn in film, if you will, is certainly in part a redirecting of the body in cinema and its unbounding potential. It is also about catching the drift of contemporary technologies all the while maintaining our hold on the material and the live. It is about staying proximate and acute to scenes of vitality and resonance and the bodies that populate them. It is about looking for and successfully finding a renewal of ontological energy on the site of ostensible obsolescence through capaciously interdisciplinary measures and pathways. By way of this winding adventure, I hope I have conveyed the exigency to foster a more productive and full dialogue between film and performance studies, as two disciplines whose alliances may move beyond design but are nevertheless intuitive and generative. The aims of this book are multiple but interconnected. From film studies and performance studies to German studies and beyond, I draw on the brilliant insight of many scholars and theorists throughout this book and propose an interdisciplinary approach that no doubt may seem unconventional. This is entirely intentional.

Drawing broadly and concluding thus, it has been my hope that an approach of performance will ultimately contribute to a more nuanced reading of the rich possibilities of the Berlin School as well as a recalibration of aspects of film theory that draw new lines of thought about the body, movement, spectacle, sensation, and spectatorship. *Movement and Performance in Berlin School Cinema* pointedly carries this through in a period where film studies and film theory practices appear to have been further flung into a state of instability and fragmentation with the nominal "death of cinema" and the advent and proliferation of new kinds of media. As a matter of course, it asks the ever-pervasive metaphysical questions about the nature of film without reducing itself to a threadbare method of metaphysics. That this book tracks a potentially new paradigm of performance in film and film studies, I am convinced; that it offers insight into thinking about contemporary film more broadly, I leave to the reader to decide. As the Berlin School expands in new directions, or, for some, simply dissipates, there is still much scholarly work to be done as we try to understand these perplexing films and this important movement.

Filmography

3 Dreams of Black. Dir. Chris Milk. Milk Studies, 2011.
40 qm Meter Deutschland / 40 Square Meters of Germany. Dir. Tevfik Başer. Perf. Özay Fecht and Yaman Okay. Tevfik Başer Filmproduktion, 1986.
71 Fragmente einer Chronologie des Zufalls / 71 Fragments of a Chronology of Chance. Dir. Michael Haneke. Perf. Gabriel Cosmin Urdes, Lukas Miko, and Otto Grünmandl, Zweites Deutsches Fernsehen (ZDF), 1994.
2001: A Space Odyssey. Dir. Stanley Kubrick. Perf. Keir Dullea and Gary Lockwood. Metro-Goldwyn-Mayer, 1968.
Alice in den Städten / Alice in the Cities. Dir. Wim Wenders. Perf. Rüdiger Vogler and Yella Rottländer. Produktion 1 im Filmverlag der Autoren, 1974.
Alle Anderen / Everyone Else. Dir. Maren Ade. Perf. Birgit Minichmayr and Lars Eidinger. Komplizen Film GmbH, 2009.
Amarcord. Dir. Federico Fellini. Perf. Bruno Zanin, Magali Noël, and Pupella Maggio. Warner Bros, 1973.
Aprilkinder /April Children. Dir. Yüksel Yavuz. Perf. Erdal Yıldız, Bulent Sharif, and Senem Tepe. Zero Fiction Film GmbH, 1998.
Auf der Suche / Looking for Simon. Dir. Jan Krüger. Perf. Corinna Harfouch and Nico Rogner. Schramm Film Koerner & Weber, 2011.
Band à part / Band of Outsiders. Jean-Luc Godard. Perf. Anna Karina, Sami Frey, and Claude Brasseur. Columbia Pictures, 1964.
Barbara. Dir. Christian Petzold. Perf. Nina Hoss, Ronald Zehrfeld, and Rainer Bock. Schramm Film Koerner & Weber, 2012.
Benny's Video. Dir. Michael Haneke. Perf. Arno Frisch, Angela Winkler, and Ulrich Mühe. Wega Filmproduktionsgesellschaft mbH, 1992.
Bilder der Welt und Inschrift des Krieges / Images of the World and Inscription of War. Dir. Harun Farocki. Harun Farocki Filmproduktion, 1988.
Bildnis einer Trinkerin / Ticket of No Return. Dir. Ulrike Ottinger. Perf. Tabea Blumenschein. Zweites Deutsches Fernsehen (ZDF), 1979.
Blow-Up. Dir. Michelangelo Antonioni. Perf. David Hemmings and Vanessa Redgrave. Bridge Films and MGM, 1966.
Blue Steel. Dir. Kathryn Bigelow. Perf. Jamie Lee Curtis, Ron Silver, and Clancy Brown. Metro-Goldwyn-Mayer, 1990.
Böse Zellen / Free Radicals. Dir. Barbara Albert. Perf. Kathrin Resetarits, Ursula Strauss, Georg Friedrich. Coop 99 Filmproduktion, 2003.
Breathless / À bout de souffle. Dir. Jean-Luc Godard. Perf. Jean-Paul Belmondo, Jean Seberg, and Daniel Boulanger. Les Films Impéria, 1960.
Caché / Hidden. Dir. Michael Haneke. Perf. Juliette Binoche and Daniel Auteuil. France 3 Cinéma, 2005.
Carnival of Souls. Dir. Herk Harvey. Perf. Candace Hilligoss. Herts-Lion International Corp, 1962.

Caro Diario / Dear Diary. Dir. Nanni Moretti. Perf. Nanni Moretti, Giovanna Bozzolo, and Sebastiano Nardone. Dendy Films, 1993.
The Conversation. Dir. Francis Ford Coppola. Perf. Gene Hackman, John Cazele. Paramount Pictures, 1974.
Crash. Dir. David Cronenberg. Perf. James Spader, Holly Hunter, and Elias Koteas. Alliance Communications, 1996.
Das Fahrrad / The Bicycle. Dir. Evelyn Schmidt. Perf. Heidemarie Schneider, Roman Kaminiski, and Anke Friedrich. DEFA, 1982.
Das Leben der Anderen / The Lives of Others. Dir. Florian Henckel von Donnersmarck. Perf. Martina Gedeck, Ulrich Mühe, and Sebastian Koch. Wiedemann & Berg Filmproduktion, 2005.
Dealer. Dir. Thomas Arslan. Perf. Tamer Yigit, Idil Üner, and Birol Ünel. Trans-Film GmbH, 1999.
Der Himmel über Berlin / Wings of Desire. Dir. Wim Wenders. Perf. Bruno Ganz, Solveig Dommartin, Otto Sander. Argos Films, 1987.
Der Räuber / The Robber. Dir. Benjamin Heisenberg. Perf. Andreas Lust and Franciska Weisz. Nikolaus Geyrhalter Filmproduktion GmbH, Peter Heilrath Filmproduktion e.K., 2010.
Der schöne Tag / A Fine Day. Dir. Thomas Arslan. Perf. Serpil Turhan and Bilge Bingül. Pickpocket Filmproduktion, 2001.
Der siebente Kontinent / The Seventh Continent. Dir. Michael Haneke. Perf. Birgit Doll, Dieter Berner, and Leni Tanzer. Wega Filmproduktionsgesellschaft mbH, 1989.
Der Tunnel / The Tunnel. Dir. Roland Suso Richter. Perf. Heino Ferch, Nicolette Krebitz, Alexandra Maria Lara, and Sebastian Koch. TeamWorxX Television & Film GmbH, 2001.
Deutschland 09. 13 Kurze Filme zur Lage der Nation: Séance / Germany 09: 13 Short Films about the State of the Nation. Dir Christoph Hochhäusler. Herbstfilm Produktion GmbH, 2009.
Die innere Sicherheit / The State I Am In. Dir. Christian Petzold. Perf. Julia Hummer, Barbara Auer, Richy Müller, and Bilge Bingül. Schramm Film Koerner & Weber, 2000.
Easy Rider. Dir. Dennis Hopper. Perf. Peter Fonda, Dennis Hopper, and Jack Nicholson. Columbia Pictures, 1969.
Eine Minute Dunkel / A Minute of Darkness. Dir. Christoph Hochhäusler. Perf. Stefan Kurt and Eberhard Kirchberg. Heimatfilm GmbH + Co KG, 2011.
Enemy of the State. Dir. Tony Scott. Perf. Will Smith, Gene Hackman, and Jon Voight. Touchstone Pictures, 1998.
Etwas Besseres als den Tod / Beats Being Dead. Dir. Christian Petzold. Perf. Jacob Matschenz and Luna Mijović. Schramm Film Koerner & Weber, 2011.
Factory of Gestures: Body Language in Film, The. Dir. Oksana Bulgakowa. PPMedia & Stanford Humanities Lab, 2008.
Fallen / Falling. Dir. Barbara Albert. Perf. Nina Proll, Birgit Minichmayr, and Kathrin Resetarits. Coop99 Filmproduktion, 2006.
Falsche Bewegung / Wrong Move. Dir. Wim Wenders. Perf. Rüdiger Vogler, Hans-Christian Blech, and Hanna Schygulla. Westdeutscher Rundfunk (WDR), 1975.
Falscher Bekenner / I Am Guilty. Dir. Benjamin Heisenberg. Perf. Constiani von Jascheroff, Manfred Zapatka, and Victoria Trauttmansdorff. Heimatfilm GmbH, 2005.

Funny Games. Dir. Michael Haneke. Perf. Susanne Lothar, Ulrich Mühe, and Arno Frisch. Wega Filmproduktionsgesellschaft mbH, 1997.
Geschwister-Kardeşler / Siblings. Dir. Thomas Arslan. Perf. Savas Yuderi, Tamer Yigit, and Serpil Turhan, 1997.
Gespenster / Ghosts. Dir. Christian Petzold. Perf. Julia Hummer, Sabine Timoteo, Marianne Basler. Schramm Film Koerner & Weber, 2005.
Gold. Dir. Thomas Arslan. Perf. Nina Hoss, Uwe Bohm, Marco Mandić. Schramm Film Koerner & Weber, 2012.
Good Bye, Lenin! Dir. Wolfgang Becker. Perf. Daniel Brühl and Katrin Sass.
Hundstage / Dog Days. Dir. Ulrich Seidl. Perf. Maria Hofstätter, Alfred Mrva, Erich Finsches. Allegro Filmproduktions GmbH, 2001.
Ich seh ich seh / Goodnight Mommy. Dir. Veronika Franz and Severin Fiala. Perf. Susanne Wuest, Elias Schwarz, and Lukas Schwarz. Ulrich Seidl Film Produktion GmbH, 2014.
Il sorpasso / The Easy Life. Dir. Dino Risi. Perf. Vittorio Gassman, Jean-Louis Trintignant. Fair Film, 1962.
Im Juli / In July. Dir. Fatih Akın. Perf. Moritz Bleibtreu, Christiane Paul. Wüste Filmproduktion, 2000.
Im Lauf der Zeit / Kings of the Road. Dir. Wim Wenders. Perf. Rüdiger Vogler and Hanns Zischler. Westdeutscher Rundfunk (WDR), 1976.
Import/Export. Dir. Ulrich Seidl. Perf. Ekateryna Rak, Paul Hoffmann, and Michael Thomas. Ulrich Seidl Filmproduktion, 2007.
In den Tag hinein / The Days Between. Dir. Maria Speth. Perf. Sabine Timoteo and Hiroki Mano. November Film GmbH, 2001.
Jerichow. Dir. Christian Petzold. Perf. Nina Hoss, Hilmi Sözer, and Benno Fürmann. Schramm Film Koerner & Weber, 2008.
Klassenfahrt / Class Trip. Dir. Henner Winckler. Perf. Steven Sperling and Sophie Kempe. Schramm Film Koerner & Weber, 2002.
Kroko. Dir. Sylke Enders. Perf. Franziska Jünger, Alexander Lange, and Hinnerk Schönemann. Luna-Film GmbH, 2003.
Ladri di biciclette / Bicycle Thieves. Dir. Vittorio De Sica. Perf. Enzo Staiola and Lamberto Maggiorani. Produzioni De Sica, 1948.
La Jetée. Dir. Chris Marker. Perf. Hélène Chatelain, Davos Hanich. Argos Film, 1962.
La Notte / The Night. Dir. Michelangelo Antonioni. Perf. Marcello Mastronianni, Jeanne Moreau, and Monica Vitti. United Artists, 1961.
La peau douce / The Soft Skin. Dir. François Truffaut. Perf. Jean Desailly, Françoise Dorléac, Nelly Benedetti. Athos Film, 1964.
Le gamin au vélo / The Boy with a Bike. Dir. Jean-Pierre Dardenne and Luc Dardenne. Perf. Thomas Doret and Cécile de France. Diaphana Films, 2001.
Le mépris / Contempt. Dir. Jean-Luc Godard. Perf. Brigitte Bardot, Jack Palance, and Michel Piccoli. Embassy Pictures, 1963.
L'emplois du temps / Time Out. Dir. Laurent Cantet. Perf. Aurelien Recoing, Karin Viard, and Serge Livrozet. Haut et Court, 2001.
Leningrad Cowboys Go America. Dir. Aki Kaurismäki. Perf. Matti Pellonpää, Kari Väänänen, and Leningrad Cowboys. Orion Classics, 1989.
Lisbon Story. Dir. Wim Wenders. Perf. Rüdiger Vogler and Patrick Bauchau. Axiom Films, 1994.

Lola rennt / Run Lola Run. Dir. Tom Tykwer. Perf. Franka Potente and Moritz Bleibtreu. X-Film Creative Pool GmbH, 1998.
Lost Highway. Dir. David Lynch. Perf. Bill Pullman, Patricia Arquette, and Balthazar Getty. Assymetrical Productions, 1987.
Mach die Musik leiser / Turn Down the Music. Dir. Thomas Arslan. Perf. Andreas Böhmer, Marco Garmund, and Andy Lehmann. Cine-Image München, Schramm Film Koerner & Weber, ZDF, 1994.
Madonnen / Madonnas. Dir. Maria Speth. Perf. Sandra Hüller, Luisa Sappelt, and Coleman Orlando Swinton. Pandora Filmproduktion GmbH, 2007.
Marnie. Dir. Alfred Hitchcock. Perf. Tippi Hedren and Sean Connery. Universal Studios, 1964.
Marseille. Dir. Angela Schanelec. Perf. Maren Eggert. Schramm Film Koerner & Weber, 2004.
Meek's Cutoff. Dir. Kelly Reichardt. Perf. Michelle Williams, Bruce Greenwood, and Paul Dano. Evenstar Films, 2010.
Mein langsames Leben / Passing Summer. Dir. Angela Schanelec. Perf. Ursina Lardi, Andreas Patton, Anne Tismer, Schramm Film Koerner & Weber, 2001.
Mein Stern / Be My Star. Dir. Valeska Grisebach. Perf. Nicole Gläser, Monique Gläser, and Christopher Schöps. Filmakademie Wien, 2001.
Metropolis. Dir. Fritz Lang. Perf. Alfred Abel, Brigitte Helm, Gustav Fröhlich. Ufa, 1927.
Milchwald / This Very Moment. Dir. Christoph Hochhäusler. Perf. Sophie Charlotte Conrad, Leonard Bruckmann, Judith Mattis, Hörst-Günter Marx. fieberfilm, ZDF, Colonia Media Filmproduktion GmbH, 2003.
Montag kommen die Fenster / Windows on Monday. Dir. Ulrich Köhler. Perf. Isabelle Menke and Hans-Jochen Wagner. Ö-Filmproduktion Löprich & Schlösser GmbH, 2006.
Mulholland Drive. Dir. David Lynch. Perf. Naomi Watts, Laura Harring, and Justin Theroux. Assymetrical Productions, 2001.
My Own Private Idaho. Dir. Gus Van Sant. Perf. River Phoenix and Keanu Reeves. Fine Line Features, 1991.
Orly. Dir. Angela Schanelec. Perf. Natacha Régnier, Bruno Todeschini, Mireille Perrier, and Maren Eggert. Nachmittagfilm, Ringel Filmproduktion, 2010.
Paradies: Glaube / Paradise: Faith. Dir. Ulrich Seidl. Perf. Maria Hofstätter, Nabil Saleh, and Natalia Baranova. Ulrich Seidl Film Produktion GmbH, 2012.
Paradies: Hoffnung / Paradise: Hope. Dir. Ulrich Seidl. Perf. Melanie Lenz, Vivian Daniel, and Joseph Lorenz. Ulrich Seidl Film Produktion GmbH, 2013.
Paradies: Liebe / Paradise: Love. Dir Ulrich Seidl. Perf. Margarethe Tiesel, Peter Kazungu, and Inge Maux. Ulrich Seidl Film Produktion GmbH, 2012.
Permanent Vacation. Dir. Jim Jarmusch. Perf. Chris Parker. Cinesthesia, 1980.
Phoenix. Dir. Christian Petzold. Perf. Nina Hoss, Ronald Zehrfeld, and Nina Kunzendorf. Schramm Film Koerner & Weber, 2014.
The Piano. Dir. Jane Campion. Perf. Holly Hunter, Harvey Keitell, and Sam Neill. Miramax Films, 1993.
Pickpocket. Dir. Robert Bresson. Perf. Martin LaSalle and Marika Green. Agnès Delahaie Productions, 1959.
Pierrot le fou / Pierrot the Madman. Dir. Jean-Luc Godard. Perf. Jean-Paul Belmondo and Anna Karina. Société Nouvelle de Cinématographie (SNC), 1965.

Plätze in Städten / Places in Cities. Dir. Angela Schanelec. Perf. Sophie Aigner. Schramm Film Koerner & Weber, 1998.
Polski Crash / Polish Crash. Dir. Kaspar Heidelbach. Perf. Miroslaw Baka, Klaus J. Behrendt, and Jürgen Vogel. Westdeutscher Rundfunk (WDR), 1994.
Postman Always Rings Twice, The. Dir. Tay Garnett. Perf. Lana Turner, John Garfield, and Cecil Kellaway. Metro-Goldwyn-Mayer, 1946.
Reichsautobahn. Dir. Harmut Bitomsky. Big Sky Film, 1984–86.
Rückenwind / Light Gradient. Dir. Jan Krüger. Perf. Sebastian Schlecht and Eric Golub. Edition Salzberger & Co. Medien GmbH, 2009.
Sans toit ni loi / Vagabond. Dir. Agnès Varda. Perf. Sandrine Bonnaire, Macha Méril, and Yolande Moreau. MK2 Diffusion, 1985.
Scener ur ett äktenskap / Scenes from a Marriage. Dir. Ingmar Bergman. Perf. Liv Ullmann and Erland Josephson. Cinema 5 Distribution, 1973.
Schläfer / Sleeper. Dir. Benjamin Heisenberg. Perf. Bastian Trost, Mehdi Nebbou, and Loretta Pflaum. Coop99 Filmproduktion GmbH, 2005.
Schlafkrankheit / Sleeping Illness. Dir. Ulrich Köhler. Perf. Pierre Bokma, Jean-Christophe Folly. Komplizen Film GmbH, Ö-Film GmbH, Why Not Productions, 2011.
Sehnsucht / Longing. Dir. Valeka Grisebach. Perf. Andreas Müller, Ilka Welz, and Anett Dornbusch. Peter Rommel Productions, 2006. TeamWorxX Television & Film GmbH, 2001.
Silvester Countdown / In the New. Dir. Oskar Roehler. Perf. Rolf Peter Kahl, Marie Zielcke, and Robert Viktor Minich. ErdbeermundFilm, 1997.
SOURCE, THE. Dir. David Aitkin. Perf. Aaron Koblin, Alice Waters, Tilda Swinton. Video Installation, 2014.
Sweet Hereafter, The. Dir. Atom Egoyan. Perf. Ian Holm, Maury Chaykin, and Peter Donaldson. Ego Film Arts, 1997.
Teorema. Dir. Pier Paolo Pasolini. Perf. Terence Stamp, Laura Betti, and Silvana Mangano. Euro International Film, 1968.
Thelma & Louise. Dir. Ridley Scott. Perf. Susan Sarandon, Geena Davis, and Harvey Keitel. Metro-Goldwyn-Mayer, 1991.
Thomas Arslan über GESCHWISTER. Dir. Thomas Arslan. Perf. Thomas Arslan. Filmgalerie 451, 2011. (Included in the DVD copy of *Geschwister*).
Titanic. Dir. James Cameron. Perf. Kate Winslet, Leonardo Dicaprio. Paramount Pictures, 1997.
Toter Mann / Something to Remind Me. Dir. Christian Petzold. Perf. Nina Hoss, André M. Hennicke, and Sven Pippig. TeamWorxX Television & Film GmbH, 2001.
Treeless Mountain. Dir. So Yong Kim. Perf. Hee Yeon Kim, Song Hee Kim, Soo Ah Lee. Oscilloscope Pictures, 2008.
Trois Couleurs: Bleu. Dir. Krzysztof Kieślowski. Perf. Juliette Binoche, Benoît Régent, and Emmanuelle Riva. Miramax, 1993.
Uccellacci e uccellini / The Hawks and the Sparrows. Dir. Pier Paolo Pasolini. Perf. Totò, Ninetto Davoli, Femi Benussi. Arco Film, 1966.
Unter dir die Stadt / The City Below. Dir. Christoph Hochhäusler. Perf. Robert Hunger-Bühler, Nicolette Krebitz, and Mark Waschke. Heimatfilm GmbH + Co KG, 2010.
Unterwegs / On the Road. Dir. Jan Krüger. Perf. Anabelle Lachette, Florian Panzner, and Martin Kiefer. Schramm Film Koerner & Weber, 2004.
Vertigo. Dir. Alfred Hitchcock. Perf. James Stewart, Kim Novak. Paramount Pictures, 1958.

Viaggio in Italia / Journey to Italy. Dir. Roberto Rossellini. Perf. Ingrid Bergman and George Sanders. Titanus Distribuzione, 1954.

Wadjda. Dir. Haifaa al-Mansour. Perf. Waad Mohammed, Reem Abdullah, and Abdulrahman al-Guhanni. Razor Filmproduktion, 2012.

Weekend. Dir. Jean-Luc Godard. Perf. Mireille Darc and Jean Yanne. Athos Films, 1967.

Wendy and Lucy. Dir. Kelly Reichardt. Perf. Michelle Williams. Field Guide Films, 2008.

Western. Dir. Valeska Grisebach. Perf. Meinhard Neumann, Reinhardt Wetrek, and Syuleyman Alilov Letifov. Komplizen Film GmbH, 2017.

Wolfsburg. Dir. Christian Petzold. Perf. Benno Fürmann and Nina Hoss. TeamWorxX Television & Film GmbH, 2003.

Yasemin. Dir. Hark Bohm. Perf. Ayşe Romney, Uwe Bohm, and Şener Şen. Zweites Deutsches Fernsehen (ZDF), 1988.

Yella. Dir. Christian Petzold. Perf. Nina Hoss, Devid Striesow and Burghart Klaußner. Schramm Film Koerner &Weber, 2007.

References

Abel, Marco. 2007. "Tender Speaking: An Interview with Christoph Hochhäusler." *Senses of Cinema* 42, no. 4 (February). http://www.sensesofcinema.com/2007/42/christoph-hochhausler/. Accessed 5 Mar 2011.
———. 2008a. "The Cinema of Identification Gets on My Nerves: An Interview with Christian Petzold." *Cineaste* 33, no. 3 (Summer). https://www.cineaste.com/summer2008/the-cinema-of-identification-gets-on-my-nerves/?rq=The%20cinema%20of%20identification%20gets%20on%20my%20nerves. Accessed 5 Mar 2011.
———. 2008b. "Intensifying Life: The Cinema of the 'Berlin School.'" *Cineaste* 33, no. 4 (Fall). https://www.cineaste.com/fall2008/intensifying-life-the-cinema-of-the-berlin-school/?rq=Intensifying%20life. Accessed 1 Mar 2011.
———. 2010. "Imaging Germany: The (Political) Cinema of Christian Petzold." In *The Collapse of the Conventional*, edited by Jaimey Fisher and Brad Prager, 258–84. Detroit: Wayne State University Press.
———. 2011. "'A Sharpening of Our Regard': Realism, Affect and the Redistribution of the Sensible in Valeska Grisebach's *Longing* (2006)." In *New Directions in German Cinema*, edited by Paul Cooke and Chris Homewood, 200–218. London: I. B. Tauris.
———. 2013. *The Counter-Cinema of the Berlin School*. Rochester, NY: Camden House.
Abel, Marco, and Jaimey Fisher, eds. 2018. *The Berlin School and Its Global Contexts: A Transnational Art Cinema*. Detroit: Wayne State University Press.
Adorno, Theodor W. (1967) 1983. "Cultural Criticism and Society." In *Prisms*, translated and edited by Samuel Weber and Shierry Weber, 17–34. Cambridge, MA: MIT Press.
———. (1970) 1997. *Aesthetic Theory*. Edited by Gretel Adorno and Wolf Tiedemann. Translated by Robert Hullot-Kentor. London: Athlone.
Adorno, Theodor W., and Max Horkheimer. (1987) 2002. *Dialectic of Enlightenment*. Translated by Edmund Jephcott. Stanford, CA: Stanford University Press.
Ahmed, Sara. 2006. *Queer Phenomenology: Orientations, Objects, Others*. Durham, NC: Duke University Press.
———. 2010. *The Promise of Happiness*. Durham, NC: Duke University Press.
———. 2015. *Cultural Politics of Emotion*. 2nd ed. London: Routledge.
Altman, Rick. 1992. "General Introduction: Cinema as Event." In *Sound Theory, Sound Practice*. Edited by Rick Altman, 1–14. London: Routledge.
Arslan, Thomas. 2013. "Die Pferde sind weich gefallen." Interview by Christine Peitz. *Der Tagesspiegel Online*, 9 Feb 2013. http://www.tagesspiegel.de/kultur/thomas-arslan-im-interview-die-pferde-sind-weich-gefallen/7758046.html. Accessed 27 Mar 2013.
Astruc, Alexandre. 1985. "What Is Mise-en-Scène?" Translated by Liz Heron. In *Cahiers du Cinema: The 1950s*, edited by Jim Hillier, 266–68. Cambridge, MA: Harvard University Press.
Augé, Marc. (1992) 2000. *Non-Places: An Introduction to an Anthropology of Supermodernity*. Translated by John Howe. London: Verso.

Auslander, Philip. 2008. *Liveness: Performance in a Mediatized Culture*. 2nd ed. London: Routledge.
Austin, J. L. 1975. *How to Do Things with Words*. 2nd ed. Cambridge: Harvard University Press.
Baer, Hester. 2013: "Affectless Economies: The Berlin School and Neoliberalism." *Discourse* 35, no. 1 (Winter): 72–100.
Balázs, Béla. (1924) 2010. *Early Film Theory: Visible Man and The Spirit of Film*. Edited by Erica Carter. Translated by Rodney Livingstone. New York: Berghahn.
Balfour, Ian. 2010. "Nancy on Film: Regarding Kiarostami, Re-Thinking Representation (with a Coda on Claire Denis)." *Journal of Visual Culture* 9, no. 1 (April): 29–43.
Barker, Jennifer. 2009. *The Tactile Eye: Touch and the Cinematic Experience*. Berkeley: University of California Press.
Barnes, John. 1996. *The Beginnings of the Cinema in England 1894-1901*. Vol. 2. Exeter: University of Exeter Press.
Barnett, David. 2005. *Rainer Werner Fassbinder and the German Theatre*. Cambridge: Cambridge University Press.
Barthes, Roland. 1977. *Image-Music-Text*. Translated by Stephen Heath. London: Fontana.
———. (1980) 2000. *Camera Lucida: Reflections on Photography*. Translated by Richard Howard. London: Vintage Classics.
Baute, Michael, Ekkehard Knörer, Volker Pantenburg, Stefan Pethke, and Simon Rothhier. [2006] 2010. "The Berlin School—A Collage." *Senses of Cinema*. 55 (July). http://sensesofcinema.com/2010/feature-articles/the-berlin-school-%e2%80%93-a-collage-2/. Accessed 8 Feb 2012.
Bazin, André. (1967) 2005. *What Is Cinema?* Vol. 1. Translated by Hugh Gray. Berkeley: University of California Press.
Beckman (Redrobe), Karen. 2010. *Crash: Cinema and the Politics of Speed*. Durham, NC: Duke University Press.
Beckman (Redrobe), Karen, and Jean Ma, eds. 2008. *Still Moving: Between Cinema and Photography*. Durham, NC: Duke University Press.
Benjamin, Walter. (1936) 1968. "The Work of Art in the Age of Mechanical Reproduction." In *Illuminations: Essays and Reflections*, edited by Hannah Arendt, translated by Harry Zohn, 217–52. New York: Schocken.
———. (1940) 1968. "Theses on the Philosophy of History." In *Illuminations: Essays and Reflections*, edited by Hannah Arendt, translated by Harry Zohn, 253–64. New York: Schocken.
———. (1940) 1999. *The Arcades Project*. Translated by Howard Eiland and Kevin McLaughlin. Cambridge, MA: Belknap.
Berlant, Lauren. 2011. *Cruel Optimism*. Durham, NC: Duke University Press.
Berlant, Lauren, and Lee Edelman. 2014. *Sex, or the Unbearable*. Durham, NC: Duke University Press.
Biendarra, Anke S. 2011. "Ghostly Business: Place, Space, and Gender in Christian Petzold's *Yella*." *Seminar* 47 (4): 465–78.
Bolter, Jay David, and Richard Grusin. 2000. *Remediation: Understanding New Media*. Boston: MIT Press.
Bonitzer, Pascal. 1980. "Le hors-champ subtil." *Cahiers du Cinéma* 311 (May): 4–7.
Bordwell, David. 1985. *Narration in the Fiction Film*. Madison: University of Wisconsin Press.

Bradatsch, Reinhard. 2006. "Generation des Scheiterns." allesfilm.com. http://www.allesfilm.com/show_filmkritik.php?id=23141 (website no longer accessible). Accessed 27 May 2012.

Brandstetter, Gabriele. 1995. *Tanz-Lektüren. Körperbilder und Raumfiguren der Avantgarde*. Frankfurt am Main: Fischer.

Brannigan, Erin. 2011. *Dancefilm: Choreography and the Moving Image*. Oxford: Oxford University Press.

Breger, Claudia. 2012. *An Aesthetics of Narrative Performance: Transnational Theater, Literature, and Film in Contemporary Germany*. Columbus: Ohio State University Press.

Brinkema, Eugenie. 2011. "The Critique of Silence." In "The Sense of Sound," edited by Rey Chow and James A. Steintrager. Special issue, *differences: A Journal of Feminist Cultural Studies* 22 (2–3): 211–34.

———. 2014. *The Forms of the Affects*. Durham, NC: Duke University Press.

Brooks, Daphne A. 2006. *Bodies in Dissent: Spectacular Performances of Race and Freedom, 1850–1910*. Durham, NC: Duke University Press.

Bruckner, René Thoreau. 2008. "Lost Time: Blunt Head Trauma and Accident-Driven Cinema." *Discourse* 30 (3): 373–400.

Burns, Rob. 2007. "Towards a Cinema of Cultural Hybridity: Turkish-German Filmmakers and the Representation of Alterity." *Debatte: Journal of Contemporary Central and Eastern Europe* 15 (1): 3–24.

Buß, Christian, and Birgit Glombitza. 2004. "In den Tag hinein: Die Kühlschränke der Hauptstadt." filmportal.de. http://www.filmportal.de/node/40569/material/618672. Accessed 20 Apr 2012.

Carlson, Marvin. 2004. *Performance: A Critical Introduction*. 2nd ed. London: Routledge.

Cavell, Stanley. 1979. *The World Viewed*. Cambridge, MA: Harvard University Press.

———. 1981. *Pursuits of Happiness: The Hollywood Comedy of Remarriage*. Cambridge, MA: Harvard University Press.

Ciment, Michel. 2003. "The State of Cinema." Address speech at the 46th San Francisco Film Festival. http://unspokencinema.blogspot.com/2006/10/state-of-cinema-m-ciment.html. Accessed 28 July 2018.

Cohan, Steven, and Ina Rae Hark, eds. 1997. "Introduction." In *The Road Movie Book*, 1–16. London: Routledge.

Cook, Roger F. 2013. "Ambient Sound." In *Berlin School Glossary: An ABC of the New Wave in German Cinema*, edited by Roger F. Cook, Lutz Keopnick, Kristin Kopp, and Brad Prager, 27–34. Bristol: Intellect.

Corrigan, Timothy. 1991. *A Cinema without Walls: Movies and Culture after Vietnam*. New Brunswick, NJ: Rutgers University Press.

Crafton, Donald. 1995. "Pie and Chase: Gag, Spectacle and Narrative in Slapstick Comedy." In *Classical Hollywood Comedy*, edited by Kristine Brunovska Karnick and Henry Jenkins, 106–19. New York: Routledge.

Crary, Jonathan. 1990. *Techniques of the Observer: Vision and Modernity in the Nineteenth Century*. Minneapolis: Minnesota University Press.

De Certeau, Michel. (1980) 1984. *The Practice of Everyday Life*. Translated by Steven F. Rendall. Berkeley: University of California Press.

Dehn, Moritz. 1999. "Die Türken vom Dienst." *Freitag Online*, 26 Mar 1999 https://www.freitag.de/autoren/der-freitag/die-turken-vom-dienst. Accessed 22 Mar 2016.

Deleuze, Gilles. (1983) 1986. *Cinema 1: The Movement-Image*. Translated by Hugh Tomlinson and Barbara Habberjam. Minneapolis: University of Minnesota Press.

———. (1985) 1989. *Cinema 2: The Time-Image*. Translated by Hugh Tomlinson and Robert Galeta. Minneapolis: University of Minnesota Press.

———. 1997. "Spinoza and the Three Ethics." Translated by Daniel W. Smith and Michael A. Greco. In *The New Spinoza*, edited by Warren Montag and Ted Stolze, 21–36. Minneapolis: University of Minnesota Press.

Deleuze, Gilles, and Félix Guattari. (1972) 1983. *Anti-Oedipus: Capitalism and Schizophrenia*. Translated by Robert Hurley. With a preface by Michel Foucault. Minneapolis: University of Minnesota Press.

———. (1980) 1987. *A Thousand Plateaus: Capitalism and Schizophrenia*. Translated by Brian Massumi. Minneapolis: University of Minnesota Press.

del Río, Elena. 2012. *Deleuze and the Cinemas of Performance: Powers of Affection*. Edinburgh: Edinburgh University Press.

de Luca, Tiago. 2016. "Slow Time, Visible Cinema: Duration, Experience, and Spectatorship." *Cinema Journal* 56, no. 1 (Fall): 23–42.

de Luca, Tiago, and Nuno Barradas Jorge, eds. 2016. *Slow Cinema*. Edinburgh: Edinburgh University Press.

Derrida, Jacques. (1988) 1997. *Limited Inc*. Translated by Samuel Weber. Evanston, IL: Northwestern University Press.

———. (1993) 1994. *Specters of Marx: The State of the Debt, the Work of Mourning & the New International*. Translated by Peggy Kamuf. New York: Routledge.

Des Pres, Terrence. 1988. "Holocaust Laughter?" In *Writing and the Holocaust*, edited by Berel Lang, 216–33. New York: Holmes & Meier.

Doane, Mary Ann. 1990. "Film and Masquerade: Theorizing the Female Spectator." In *Issues in Feminist Film Criticism*, edited by Patricia Erens, 41–57. Bloomington: Indiana University Press.

———. 2002. *The Emergence of Cinematic Time: Modernity, Contingency, the Archive*. Cambridge, MA: Harvard University Press.

Duncan, Jennifer. 2003. *Frontier Spirit: The Brave Women of the Klondike*. New York: Doubleday.

Dyer, Richard. 1998. *Stars*. London: British Film Institute.

Elsaesser, Thomas. 2005. "Cinephilia or the Uses of Disenchantment." In *Cinephilia: Movies, Love and Memory*, edited by Marijike de Valck and Malte Hagener, 27–44. Amsterdam: Amsterdam University Press.

Elsaesser, Thomas, and Malte Hagener. 2015. *Film Theory: An Introduction through the Senses*. 2nd ed. New York: Routledge.

Eschkötter, Daniel. 2011. "Phantombilder der abstrakten Existenz. Die Szene der Überwachung bei Christian Petzold." In *Public Enemies. Film zwischen Identitätsbildung und Kontrolle*, edited by Winfried Pauleit, Christine Rüffert, Karl -Heinz Schmid, and Alfred Tews, 88–100 Berlin: Bertz + Fischer.

Everett, Wendy. 2009. "Lost in Transition? The European Road Movie, or a Genre 'Adrift in the Cosmos.'" *Literature/Film Quarterly* 37, no. 3 (January): 165–75.

Feuer, Jane. 1983. "The Concept of Live Television: Ontology of Ideology." In *Regarding Television: Critical Approaches—An Anthology*, edited by E. Ann Kaplan, 12–21. Frederick, MD: University Publications of America.

———. 1993. *The Hollywood Musical*. 2nd ed. Bloomington: Indiana University Press.

Fisher, Jaimey. 2010. "Kreuzberg as Relational Place: Respatializing the 'Ghetto' in Bettina Blümner's Prinzessinnen (Pool of Princesses, 2007)." In *Spatial Turns: Space, Place, and Mobility in German Literary and Visual Culture*, edited by Jaimey Fisher and Barbara Mennel, 421–26. Amsterdam: Editions Rodopi B. V.

———. 2011a. "German Autoren Dialogue with Hollywood? Refunctioning the Horror Genre in Christian Petzold's *Yella* (2007)." In *New Directions in German Studies*, edited by Paul Cooke and Chris Homewood, 182–99. London: I. B. Tauris.

———. 2011b. "Globalization as Uneven Geographical Development: The 'Creative' Destruction of Place and Fantasy in Christian Petzold's Ghost Trilogy." *Seminar* 47, no. 4 (September): 447–64.

———. 2013. *Christian Petzold*. Urbana: University of Illinois Press.

Fisher, Jaimey, and Brad Prager, eds. 2010. *The Collapse of the Conventional*. Detroit: Wayne State University Press.

Fischer-Lichte, Erika. (2004) 2008. *The Transformative Power of Performance: A New Aesthetics*. Translated by Saskya Iris Jain. London: Routledge.

Flanagan, Matthew. 2008. "Towards an Aesthetic of Slow in Contemporary Cinema," *16:9* 6, no. 29 (November). English edition. www.16-9.dk/2008-11/side11_inenglish.htm. Accessed 12 Nov 2015.

Foucault, Michel. (1975) 1977. *Discipline and Punish: The Birth of the Prison*. Translated by Alan Sheridan. New York: Vintage Books.

Franzel, Sean. 2013. "Dorfdiskos." In *Berlin School Glossary: An ABC of the New Wave in German Cinema*, edited by Roger F. Cook, Lutz Keopnick, Kristin Kopp, and Brad Prager, 93–100. Bristol: Intellect.

Gallager, Jessica. 2006: "The Limitation of Urban Space in Thomas Arslan's Berlin Trilogy." *Seminar* 42, no. 3 (September): 337–52.

Garczynski, Matt. 2011 "Symposium Discusses Berlin School, Individuality." *Dartmouth* 15 May 2011. http://thedartmouth.com/2011/05/16/arts/symposium-discusses-berlin-school-individuality. Accessed 13 Nov 2013.

Geuens, Jean-Paul. 2001. "Dogma 95: A Manifesto for Our Times." *Quarterly Review of Film and Video* 18 (2): 191–202.

Gleber, Anke. 1997. "Women on the Screens and Streets of Modernity: In Search of the Female Flâneur." In *The Image in Dispute: Art and Cinema in the Age of Photography*, edited by Dudley Andrew, 55–86. Austin: University of Texas Press.

Goffman, Erving. 1959. *The Presentation of Self in Everyday Life*. New York: Anchor Books.

Göktürk, Deniz. 2000. "Turkish Women on the Streets: Closure and Exposure in Transnational Cinema." In *Spaces in European Cinema*, edited by Myrto Konstantarakos, 64–75. London: Exeter.

———. 2001. "Turkish Delight—German Fright: Migrant Identities in Transnational Cinema." In *Mediated Identities*, edited by Deniz Derman, Karen Ross, and Nevena Dakovic, 131–49. Istanbul: Bilgi University Press.

Gordon, Avery F. 2008. *Ghostly Matters: Haunting and the Sociological Imagination*. Minneapolis: Minnesota University Press.

Goodman, Nelson. 1978. *The Ways of Worldmaking*. Indianapolis, IN: Hackett.

Gregg, Melissa, and Gregory J. Seigworth. 2010. "An Inventory of Shimmers." In *The Affect Theory Reader*, edited by Melissa Gregg and Gregory J. Seigworth, 1–25. Durham, NC: Duke University Press.

Grisebach, Valeska. 2001. "*Mein Stern*: Interview." fsk Kino: Das Kino am Oranienplatz. http://www.peripherfilm.de/meinstern/interview. Accessed 13 Mar 2012.

———. 2006. "Sehnsucht: Helden des eigenen Lebens—Interview." piffl-medien. http://www.piffl-medien.de/sehnsucht/html/interview.html. Accessed 13 Mar 2013.

Grundtner, Markus. 2006. "Sehnsucht—mit Regisseurin Valeska Grisebach." *MovieGod.de*, 19 Oct 2006. http://www.moviegod.de/kino/interview/822/sehnsucht-interview-mit-regisseurin-valeska-grisebach/seite-1. Accessed 12 Nov 2012.

Gumbrecht, Hans Ulrich. 2004. *The Production of Presence: What Meaning Cannot Convey*. Stanford, CA: Stanford University Press.

Gunning, Tom. 2006. "The Cinema of Attraction(s): Early Film, Its Spectator and the Avant-Garde." In *The Cinema of Attractions Reloaded*, edited by Wanda Strauven, 381–88. Amsterdam: Amsterdam University Press.

Hagener, Malte, Vinzenz Hediger, and Alena Strohmaier, eds. 2016. *The State of Post-Cinema: Tracing the Moving Image in the Age of Digital Dissemination*. London: Palgrave Macmillan.

Halberstam, Judith (Jack). 2011. *The Queer Art of Failure*. Durham, NC: Duke University Press.

Halle, Randall. 2014. *The Europeanization of Cinema: Interzones and Imagination Communities*. Urbana: University of Illinois Press.

Hanich, Julian. 2007. "Ein Recht auf Liebe gibt es nicht." *Der Tagesspiegel*, 13 Feb 2007. http://www.tagesspiegel.de/kultur/ein-recht-auf-liebe-gibt-es-nicht/810526.html. Accessed 5 Dec 2011.

Hansen, Miriam Bratu. 1995. "Early Cinema, Late Cinema: Transformations of the Public Sphere." In *Viewing Positions: Ways of Seeing Film*, edited by Linda Williams, 134–52. New Brunswick, NJ: Rutgers University Press.

Harney, Stefano, and Fred Moten. 2013. *The Undercommons: Fugitive Planning and Black Study*. New York: Autonomedia.

Hartman, Saidiya V. 1997. *Scenes of Subjection: Terror, Slavery, and Self-Making in Nineteenth-Century America*. Oxford: Oxford University Press.

Haupt, Friederike. 2011. "Drei Regisseure retten das deutsche Fernsehen." *Frankfurter Allgemeine Zeitung*, 28 Aug 2011. http://www.faz.net/aktuell/feuilleton/medien/2.1756/fernseh-dreiteiler-dreileben-drei-regisseure-retten-das-deutsche-fernsehen-11124911.html. Accessed 13 Nov 2012.

Hessel, Franz. 1929. *Ein Flaneur in Berlin*. Berlin: Arsenal.

Highmore, Ben. 2010. "Bitter after Taste: Affect, Food, and Social Aesthetics. In *The Affect Theory Reader*, edited by Melissa Gregg and Gregory J. Seigworth, 118–37. Durham, NC: Duke University Press.

Hinrichsen, Jens. "Im Zwischenreich." Film-Zentrale. http://www.filmzentrale.com/essays/gespenstertrilogiejh.htm. Accessed 2 Dec 2011.

Holden, Stephen. 2008. "When Selling a Soul, Consider the Price." *New York Times*, 16 May 2008. http://movies.nytimes.com/2008/05/16/movies/16yell.html.

Holl, Ute. 2012. "Cinema on the Web and Newer Psychology." In *Screen Dynamics: Mapping the Borders of Cinema*, edited by Getrud Koch, Volker Pantenburg, and Simon Rothöhler, 150–68. Vienna: Synema.

Hurley, Erin, and Sara Warner. 2012. "Special Section: 'Affect/Performance/Politics.'" *Journal of Dramatic Theory and Criticism* 26, no. 2 (Spring): 99–107.

Jaffe, Ira. 2014. *Slow Movies: Countering the Cinema of Action*. New York: Wallflower.

Jameson, Fredric. 1991. *Postmodernism, or, the Cultural Logic of Late Capitalism*. Durham, NC: Duke University Press.
Kammerer, Dietmar. 2004. "Video Surveillance in Hollywood Movies." In *Surveillance and Society CCTV special issue* 2 2/3, edited by Clive Norris, Mike McCahill, and David Wood, 464–73.
Kaye, Nick, and Gabriella Giannachi. 2011. "Acts of Presence: Performance, Mediation, Virtual Reality." *TDR: The Drama Review* 55, no. 4 (Winter): 88–95.
King, Alisdair. 2014. "Still Lives in Transit: Movement and Inertia in Angela Schanelec's *Orly* (2010)." *Studies in European Cinema* 11 (2): 139–50.
King, Geoff. 2000. *Spectacular Narratives: Hollywood in the Age of the Blockbuster*. London: I. B. Tauris.
Knörer, Ekkerhard. 2007. "Luminous Days: Notes on the New German Cinema." *Vertigo* 3, no. 5 (Spring). https://www.closeupfilmcentre.com/vertigo_magazine/volume-3-issue-5-spring-2007/luminous-days-notes-on-the-new-german-cinema/.
———. 2011. "Bewegung durch Berlin." DVDesk, *Die Tageszeitung*, 5 May 2011. http://www.taz.de/1/archiv/digitaz/artikel/?ressort=ku&dig=2011%2F05%2F05%2Fa0150&cHash=7901b908f3. Accessed 3 Aug 2013.
———. 2012. "Moveable Images on Portable Devices." In *Screen Dynamics: Mapping the Borders of Cinema*, edited by Gertrud Koch, Volker Panteburg, and Simon Rothöhler, 169–78. Vienna: Synema.
Koepnick, Lutz. 2013. "Cars." In *Berlin School Glossary: An ABC of the New Wave in German Cinema*, edited by Roger F. Cook, Lutz Koepnick, Kristin Kopp, and Brad Prager, 75–82. Bristol: Intellect.
———. 2014. *On Slowness: Toward an Aesthetic of the Contemporary*. New York: Columbia University Press.
Kopp, Kristin. 2010. "Christoph Hochhäusler's *This Very Moment*: The Berlin School and the Politics of Spatial Aesthetics in the German-Polish Borderlands." In *The Collapse of the Conventional: The German Film and Its Politics at the Turn of the New Century*, edited by Brad Prager and Jaimey Fisher, 285–308. Detroit: Wayne State University Press.
Kracauer, Siegfried. 1997. *Theory of Film: The Redemption of Physical Reality*. Princeton, NJ: Princeton University Press.
Krauss, Rosalind. 2000. *A Voyage on the North See: The Post-Medium Condition*. London: Thames & Hudson.
Krausz, Daniel. 2010. *Jugendwerkhöfe in der DDR: Der geschlossene Jugendwerkhof Torgau*. Hamburg: Diplomica.
Landry, Olivia. 2014. "Dance and the Theatricality of Berlin School Cinema." *The Germanic Review: Literature, Culture, Theory* 89 (1): 1–19.
———. 2017. "A Body without a Face: The Disorientation of Trauma in *Phoenix* (2014) and New Holocaust Cinema." *Film-Philosophy* 21 (2): 188–205. http://www.euppublishing.com/doi/abs/10.3366/film.2017.0043.
Lefait, Sébastien. 2013. *Surveillance on Screen: Monitoring Contemporary Films and Television Programs*. Plymouth, UK: The Scarecrow Press.
Leinkauf, Maxi, and Jan Pfaff. 2011. "Hardcore-Emanze." *Der Freitag*, 16 Sep 2011. http://www.freitag.de/alltag/1137-alles-ist-im-grunde-eine-beziehungskrise.
Lepecki, André. 2004. "Introduction: Presence and Body in Dance and Performance Theory." In *Of the Presence of the Body*, edited by André Lepecki, 1–12. Middleton, CT: Wesleyan University Press.

———. 2006. *Exhausting Dance: Performance and the Politics of Movement*. London: Routledge.
Lequeret, Elisabeth. 2004. "Allemagne: la génération de l'espace." *Cahiers du Cinéma*, no. 587 (February): 47–48, 50–51.
Levin, Thomas Y. 2002. "Rhetoric of the Temporal Index: Surveillant Narration and the Cinema of Real Time." In *Rhetorics of Surveillance from Benthan to Big Brother*, edited by Thomas Y. Levin, Ursula Frohne, and Peter Weibel, 578–93. Cambridge, MA: MIT Press.
Leweke, Anke. 2013. "French Cancan in the DDR: An Exchange with Christian Petzold." In *The Berlin School: Films from the Berliner Schule*, edited by Rajendra Roy and Anke Leweke, 32–43. New York: Museum of Modern Art.
Lie, Sulgi. 2016. "From Shame to Drive: The Waning of Affect; or, The Rising of the Drive Image in Contemporary Hollywood Cinema." *Social Text* 34, no. 2 (127) (1 June): 45–70.
Lim, Dennis. 2006. "Greetings from the Land of Feel-Bad Cinema." *New York Times*, 26 Nov 2006. https://www.nytimes.com/2006/11/26/movies/26lim.html. Accessed 3 Aug 2018.
———. 2012. "Summoning Halcyon Days of Failed Ideals." *New York Times*, 7 Dec 2012. https://www.nytimes.com/2012/12/09/movies/christian-petzold-directs-barbara-starring-nina-hoss.html. Accessed 3 Aug 2018.
Lim, Song Hwee. 2014. *Tsai Min-liang and a Cinema of Slowness*. Honolulu: University of Hawaii Press.
Love, Heather. 2009. *Feeling Backward: Loss and Politics of Queer History*. Cambridge, MA: Harvard University Press.
Lowenstein, Adam. 2005. *Shocking Representation: Historical Trauma, National Cinema, and the Modern Horror Film*. New York: Columbia University Press.
———. 2015. *Dreaming of Cinema: Spectatorship, Surrealism, and the Age of Digital Media*. New York: Columbia University Press.
Lünstedt, Claudius, and Ansgar Vogt. 2002. "Klassenfahrt: Ein Film von Henner Winckler." Peripherfilm, 4 Jan 2002. http://www.peripherfilm.de/klassenfahrt/interview.htm. Accessed 2 Aug 2018.
Marks, Laura U. 2000. *The Skin of the Film: Intercultural Cinema, Embodiment, and the Senses*. Durham, NC: Duke University Press.
———. 2016. "Workshopping for Ideas: Jacques Rivette's *Out 1: Noli Me Tangere*." *The Cine-Files* 10 (Spring): 1–8.
Massumi, Brian. 1995. "The Autonomy of Affect." *Cultural Critique* 31 (Autumn): 83–109.
———. 2002. *Parables for the Virtual: Movement, Affect, Sensation*. Durham, NC: Duke University Press.
Mazierska, Ewa, and Laura Rascaroli. 2006. *Crossing New Europe: Postmodern Travel and the European Road*. New York: Wallflower Press.
Mennel, Barbara. 2008. *Cities and Cinema*. London: Routledge.
Merleau-Ponty, Maurice. (1945) 2007. *Phenomenology of Perception*. Translated by Colin Smith. London: Routledge.
———. (1964) 1968. *The Visible and the Invisible*. Edited by Claude Lefort. Translated by Alphonso Lingis. Evanston, IL: Northwestern University Press.
Metz, Christian. (1971) 1974. *Film Language: A Semiotics of the Cinema*. Translated by Michael Taylor. Chicago: University of Chicago Press.
———. 1985. "Photography and Fetish." *October* 34 (Autumn): 81–90.

Miller, Matthew D. 2012. "Facts of Migration, Demands on Identity: Christian Petzold's *Yella* and *Jerichow* in Comparison." *The German Quarterly* 85, no. 1 (Winter): 55–76.
Modleski, Tania. 2016. *The Women Who Knew Too Much: Hitchcock and Feminist Theory*. 3rd ed. New York: Routledge.
Möller, Kristen. 2008. "Wald, Haus, Straße. Christian Petzolds *Die innere Sicherheit* (2000) & Jan Böttchers *Geld oder Leben*." In *Nachbilder der RAF*, edited by Inga Stephan and Alexandra Tacke, 181–96. Vienna: Böhlau.
Möller, Olaf. 2007. "Vanishing Point." *Sight and Sound* 17 (10): 40–42.
Moten, Fred. 2003. *In the Break: The Aesthetics of the Black Radical Tradition*. Minneapolis: Minnesota University Press.
Mulvey, Laura. (1975) 1990. "Visual Pleasure and Narrative Cinema." In *Issues in Feminist Film Criticism*, edited by Patricia Erens, 28–40. Bloomington: Indiana University Press.
———. 2006. *Death 24x a Second: Stillness and the Moving Image*. London: Reaktion.
Muñoz, José Esteban. 1999. *Disidentifications: Queers of Color and the Performance of Politics*. Minneapolis: University of Minnesota Press.
———. 2009. *Cruising Utopia: The Then and There of Queer Futurity*. New York: New York University Press.
Naficy, Hamid. 2001. *An Accented Cinema: Exilic and Diasporic Filmmaking*. Princeton, NJ: Princeton University Press.
Nancy, Jean-Luc. 2001. *L'evidence du film*. Brussels: Yves Gevaert Éditeur.
Naremore, James. 1988. *Acting in the Cinema*. Berkeley: University of California Press.
Nayman, Adam. 2014. "The Face of Another: Christian Petzold's *Phoenix*." *Cinema Scope* 61. http://cinema-scope.com/features/face-another-christian-petzolds-phoenix/. Accessed 12 Jun 2015.
Nessel, Sabine. 2008. *Kino und Ereignis. Das Kinematografische zwischen Text und Körper*. Berlin: Vorwerk 8.
———. 2009a. "Ferien vom Erzählen: Leerstellen, Ellipsen und das Wissen vom Erzählen im neuen Autorenfilm der Berliner Schule," In *Erzählen im Film: Unzuverlässigkeit—Audiovisualität—Musik*, edited by Susanne Kaul, Jean-Pierre Palmier, and Timo Skrandies, 105–19. Bielefeld: Transcript.
———. 2009b. "Ghost Dances: Tanzszenen im aktuellen europäischen Kino." *Ästhetik & Kommunikation* 40 (146): 61–68.
———. 2011. "Gespenster des Spätkapitalismus bei Christian Petzold." In *Geld und Kino*, edited by Margrit Fröhlich and Rembert Hüser, 203–16, Schüren: Marburg.
Ngai, Sianne. 2005. *Ugly Feelings*. Cambridge, MA: Harvard University Press.
Nicodemus, Katja. 2013. "On the Move: Thomas Arslan's Kinetic Cinema." In *The Berlin School: Films from the Berliner Schule*, edited by Rajendra Roy and Anke Leweke, 74–81. New York: Museum of Modern Art.
Nord, Cristina. 2005. "Mit geschlossenen Augen hören." *Die Tageszeitung*, 15 Feb 2005. http://www.taz.de/!643303/. Accessed 2 Apr 2013.
———. 2009. "Freiheit tut weh." *Die Tageszeitung*, 16 Jun 2009. http://www.taz.de/!36193/. Accessed 23 Jun 2013.
———. 2012. "Ich wollte, dass die DDR Farben Hat" (An Interview with Christian Petzold). *Die Tageszeitung* (11 Feb). http://www.taz.de/!5100957/. Accessed 5 Sep 2013.
Nyong'o, Tavia. 2009. "Performance." *Social Text* 27, no. 3 (100) (Fall): 171–75.

Organization for Economic Co-operation and Development (OECD). 2016. https://www.oecd.org/els/family/LMF2_6_Time_spent_travelling_to_and_from_work.pdf. Accessed 2 Aug 2018.

O'Sullivan, Simon. 2001. "The Aesthetics of Affect: Thinking Art Beyond Representation." *Angelaki* 6, no. 3 (December): 125–35.

Pantenburg, Volker. 2005. "Ansichtssache. Natur Landschaft Film." *Augenblick* ("Blicke auf Landschaften") 37, edited by Nils Path, 15–24. Marburg: Schüren.

———. 2010. "Raum Erfahren. Zur Automobilisierung der Blicke und Landschaften im Kino." In *Raum in den Künsten. Konstruktionen—Bewegung—Politik*, edited by Armen Avanessian and Franck Hoffmann, 101–14. Paderborn: Wilhelm Fink.

Peitz, Christiane. 2013. "'Gold': Eine Frau geht ihren Weg." *Der Tagesspiegel*, 14 Aug 2013. https://www.tagesspiegel.de/kultur/thomas-arslans-western-gold-gold-eine-frau-geht-ihren-weg/8639504.html. Accessed 20 Aug 2013.

Peters, Kathrin. 2005. "Orte im Off. Zum Fotographischen in Angela Schanelecs 'Marseille.'" *Nach dem Film* 1 (1 December). http://www.nachdemfilm.de/issues/text/orte-im. Accessed 1 Aug 2018.

Petzold, Christian. 2004. "*Gespenster*: Director's Note." http://www.gespenster-der-film.de/html/directorsnote_en.html. Accessed 28 Jul 2018.

Peucker, Brigitte. 2007. *The Material Image: Art and the Real in Film*. Stanford, CA: Stanford University Press.

Phelan, Peggy. 1993. *Unmarked: The Politics of Performance*. London: Routledge.

Phelan, Peggy, and Jill Lane, eds. 1998. *The Ends of Performance*. New York: New York University Press.

Pichler, Barbara, and Andrea Pollach, eds. 2006. "Moving Landscapes. Einführende Anmerkungen zu Landschaft und Film." In *Moving Landscapes. Landschaft und Film*, 15–24. Vienna: SYNEMA Gesellschaft für Film und Medien.

Pinfold, Debbie. 2006. "The End of the Fairy-Tale? Christian Petzold's *Barbara* and the Difficulties of Interpretation." *German Life and Letters* 67, no. 2 (April): 279–300.

Ratner, Megan. 2012. "Building on the Ruins: Interview with Christian Petzold." *Film Quarterly* 66, no. 2 (Winter): 16–24.

Rebhandl, Bert. 2006. "Realismus des Wünschens." *Spiegel Online*, 7 Sept 2006. http://www.spiegel.de/kultur/kino/sehnsucht-realismus-des-wuenschens-a-435454.html. Accessed 25 Oct 2014.

Reinecke, Stefan. 2003. "Das Kino als Versuchsanordnung. Ein Werkstattgespräch mit dem Regisseur Christian Petzold." *epd Film*, 2 Oct 2010. http://www.filmportal.de/node/263489/material/1020977. Accessed 3 Feb 2015.

Rentschler, Eric. 2000. "From New German Cinema to Post-Wall Cinema of Consensus." In *Cinema and Nation*, edited by Mette Hjort and Scott MacKenzie, 260–77. London: Routledge.

———. 2013. "The Surveillance Camera's Quarry in Hochhäusler's *Eine Minute Dunkel*." *German Studies Review* 36, no. 3 (October): 635–42.

Roach, Joseph. 1996. *Cities of the Dead: Circum-Atlantic Performance*. New York: Columbia University Press.

Rosen, Philip. 2001. *Change Mummified: Cinema, Historicity, Theory*. Minneapolis: University of Minnesota Press.

Rother, Ray. 2013. "No Solutions, Only Questions: An Encounter with Nina Hoss." In *The Berlin School: Films from the Berliner Schule*, 60–65. New York: Museum of Modern Art.

Roy, Rajendra. 2013. "Women's Lab: The Female Protagonist in the Berlin School." In *The Berlin School: Films from the Berliner Schule*, edited by Rajendra Roy and Anke Leweke, 46–57. New York: Museum of Modern Art.
Rutherford, Anne. 2003. "Cinema and Embodied Affect." *Senses of Cinema* 25 (March). http://sensesofcinema.com/2003/feature-articles/embodied_affect/. Accessed 23 Nov 2016.
———. 2015. "Walking the Edge: Performance, the Cinematic Body and the Cultural Mediator in Ivan Sen's Mystery Road." *Studies in Australasian Cinema* 9 (3): 312–26.
———. 2016. "Introduction: Keeping the Concept of Cinematic Affect 'In Play.'" *The Cine-Files* special issue "Dossier on Cinematic Affect" 10 (Spring): 1–5.
Sartre, Jean-Paul. (1943) 1977. *Being and Nothingness: A Phenomenological Essay on Ontology*. Translated by Hazel E. Barnes. New York: First Washington Square.
Schanelec, Angela. 2001. "Interview." By Antonia Ganz. *Revolver* 5, 8 Mar 2001. http://www.revolver-film.com/hefte/heft-05-schanelec/.
———. 2012. "Interview." By Christoph Hoschhäusler and Nicolas Wackerbarth. *Revolver* 26, 36–37. Frankfurt aM: Verlag der Autoren.
Schanelec, Angela, and Reinhold Vorschneider. 2005. "Interview." By Christoph Hochhäusler and Nicolas Wackerbarth. *Revolver Live!*, 6 Apr 2005. http://www.revolver-film.com/hefte/heft-13-schanelec-vorschneider/.
Schechner, Richard. 1995. *The Future of Ritual*. 2nd ed. London: Routledge.
———. 2006. *Performance Studies: An Introduction*. 2nd ed. London: Routledge.
Schick, Thomas. 2010. "'A Nouvelle Vague Allemande?' Thomas Arslan's Films in the Context of the Berlin School." *Acta Univ. Sapientiae: Film and Media Studies* 3: 143–55.
———. 2011. "Stillstand in Bewegung. Raum, Zeit und die Freiheit des Zuschauers in Thomas Arslans *Der schöne Tag* und Angela Schanelecs *Mein langsames Leben*." In *Kino in Bewegung: Perspektiven des deutschen Gegenwartskino*, edited by Thomas Schick and Tobias Ebbrecht, 79–103. Dresden: Springer.
Schneider, Rebecca. 2011. *Performing Remains*. London: Routledge.
Schoonover, Karl. 2012. "Wastrels of Time: Slow Cinema's Laboring Body, the Political Spectator, and the Queer." *Framework: The Journal of Cinema and Media* 53 (1): 65–78.
Scott, A. O. 2009. "Diary of Soviet Violence in a Conquered Capital." *New York Times*, 16 Jul 2009. http://www.nytimes.com/2009/07/17/movies/17woman.html?_r=0. Accessed Jun 2012.
Sedgwick, Eve Kosofsky. 2003. *Touching Feeling: Affect, Pedagogy, Performativity*. Durham, NC: Duke University Press.
Seel, Martin. 1995. "Fotografien sind wie Namen." *Deutsche Zeitschrift für Philosophie* 43 (3): 465–78.
Seidel, Gabriela. 2001. "*Der schöne Tag*: Thomas Arslan im Interview." *Peripherfilm*, 14 Jan 2001. http://www.peripherfilm.de/derschoenetag/dst2.htm#interview. Accessed 12 Nov 2011.
Shaviro, Steven. 1993. *The Cinematic Body: Theory out of Bounds*. Minneapolis: University of Minnesota Press.
———. 2010. *Post Cinematic Affect*. London: Zero Books.
———. 2015. *No Speed Limit: Three Essays on Accelerationism*. Minneapolis: University of Minnesota Press.
———. 2016. "Affect Vs. Emotion." *The Cine-Files* 10: 1–3.
Simmel, Georg. (1903) 1998. "The Metropolis and Mental Life." Translated by Kurt H. Wolff. In *Simmel on Culture*, edited by David Frisby and Mike Featherston, 174–86. London: Sage Publications.

Slevogt, Esther. 2009. "Der Kampf des Lebens mit seinem Preis." *Nachtkritik.de*, 14 Mar 2009. https://www.nachtkritik.de/index.php?option=com_content&view=article&id=2529:der-einsame-weg-christian-petzold-kaempft-mit-den-echtzeiten-von-theater-und-film-&catid=35:deutsches-theater-berlin&Itemid=100476. Accessed 29 Jul 2018.

Sloterdijk, Peter. 2006. "Mobilization of the Planet from the Spirit of Self-Intensification." Translated by Heidi Ziegler. *TDR* 50 (4): 36–43.

Sobchack, Vivian. 1992. *The Address of the Eye: A Phenomenology of Film Experience*. Princeton, NJ: Princeton University Press.

———. 2004. *Carnal Thoughts: Embodiment and Moving Image Culture*. Berkeley: University of California Press.

Sontag, Susan. 2001. *On Photography*. New York: Picador.

Spinoza, Benedict de. (1677) 1966. *Ethics*. Edited by William Hale White. Translated by James Guttmann. New York: Hafner.

States, Bert O. 1983. "The Actor's Presence: Three Phenomenal Modes." *Theatre Journal* 35 (3): 359–75.

———. 1996. "Performance as Metaphor." *Theatre Journal* 48, no. 1 (March): 1–26.

Stehle, Maria. 2012. *Ghetto Voices in Contemporary Germany: Textscapes, Filmscapes, and Soundscapes*. Rochester, NY: Camden House.

Stewart, Garrett. 1999. *Between Film and Screen: Modernism's Photosynthesis*. Chicago: Chicago University Press.

———. 2015. *Closed Circuits: Screening Narrative Surveillance*. Chicago: University of Chicago Press.

Stewart, Kathleen. 2007. *Ordinary Affects*. Durham, NC: Duke University.

Strathausen, Carsten. 2013. "Interiority." In *Berlin School Glossary: An ABC of the New Wave in German Cinema*, edited by Roger F. Cook, Lutz Koepnick, Kristin Kopp, and Brad Prager, 165–72. Bristol: Intellect.

Ströbele, Carolin. 2011. "Der letzte Tango in Frankfurt." *Die Zeit*, 30 Mar 2011. http://www.zeit.de/kultur/film/2011-03/film-unter-dir-stadt. Accessed Mar 3 2014.

Suchsland, Rüdiger. 2005. "Langsames Leben, Schöne Tage." Annährung an die 'Berliner Schule.'" *FILMDIENST* 58 (13): 6–9.

———. 2007. "Liebe in Zeiten der Heuschrecken." *Telepolis*, 15 Sep 2007. http://www.heise.de/tp/artikel/26/26195/1.html. Accessed May 11 2016.

Taylor, Diana. 2003. *The Archive and the Repertoire: Performing Cultural Memory in the Americas*. Durham, NC: Duke University Press.

———. 2016. *Performance*. Durham, NC: Duke University Press.

Thrift, Nigel. 2004. "Movement-space: The Changing Domain of Thinking Resulting from the Development of New Kinds of Spatial Awareness." *Economy and Society* 33 (4): 582–604.

Torlasco, Domietta. 2008. *The Time of Crime: Phenomenology, Psychoanalysis, Italian Film*. Stanford, CA: Stanford University Press.

Trigg, Dylan. 2014. *The Thing: A Phenomenology of Horror*. Winchester, UK: Zero Books.

Vinogradova, Maria. 2010. "The Berliner Schule as a Recent New Wave in German Cinema." *Acta Universitatis Sapientiae, Film and Media Studies* 3: 157–68.

Virilio, Paul. 2007. *The Original Accident*. Translated by Julie Rose. Cambridge: Polity.

Vogel, Shane. 2009. *The Scene of the Harlem Cabaret: Race, Sexuality, Performance*. Chicago: University of Chicago Press.

von Eicken, Verena. 2014. "German Actresses of the 2000s: A Study of Female Representation, Acting and Stardom." PhD diss., University of York.
von Moltke, Johannes. 2005. *Heimatfilm: No Place Like Home*. Berkeley: University of California Press,
Wagner, Brigitta B. 2010. "Vorschneider in Focus." *Film Quarterly* 63, no. 4 (Summer): 62–64.
Watkins, Megan. 2010. "Desiring Recognition, Accumulating Affect." In *The Affect Theory Reader*, edited by Melissa Gregg and Gregory J. Seigworth, 269–85. Durham, NC: Duke University Press.
Webber, Andrew J. 2011. "Topographical Turns: Recasting Berlin in Christian Petzold's *Gespenster*." In *Debating German Cultural Identity Since 1989*, edited by Anne Fuchs, Kathleen James-Chakraborty, Linda Shortt, 67–81. Rochester, NY: Camden House.
Weheliye, Alexander G. 2005. *Phonographies: Grooves in Sonic Afro-Modernity*. Durham, NC: Duke University Press.
———. 2014. *Habeas Viscus: Racializing Assemblages, Biopolitics and Black Feminist Theories of the Human*. Durham, NC: Duke University Press.
Wheatley, Catherine. 2011. "Not Politics but People: The 'Feminine Aesthetic' of Valeska Grisebach and Jessica Hausner." In *New Austrian Film*, edited by Robert von Dassanowsky and Oliver C. Speck, 136–50. Oxford: Berghahn.
Williams, Linda. 1999. *Hard Core: Power, Pleasure, and the "Frenzy of the Visible."* Berkeley: University of California Press.
Wolf, Sabine. 2009. "Die urbane Landschaft in den Filmen der Berliner Schule." *Cinema: unabhängige Schweizer Filmzeitschrift* 54: 39–50.
Wood, Jason. 2007. "Many Rivers to Cross." *Sight & Sound* 17, no. 10 (October): 42.
Worschech, Rudolf. 2004. "Unterwegs: Ein Roadmovie von Jan Krüger." *epd Film Online* 8, 2 Aug 2004. Republished on *Filmportal.de*: http://www.filmportal.de/node/20525/material/658545. Accessed Apr 2 2012.
Worthmann, Merthen. 2001. "Mit Vorsicht genießen: Angela Schanelecs Film Mein langsames Leben ist eine Meditation über die Neugier und ein abenteuerliches Spiel mit Auslassungen." *Die Zeit*, 27 Sep 2001. http://www.zeit.de/2001/40/200140_langs._leben.xml. Accessed 5 Jan 2012.
Zeller, Thomas. 2010. *Driving Germany: The Landscape of the German Autobahn 1930–1970*. Oxford: Berghahn.
Zimmer, Catherine. 2015. *Surveillance Cinema*. New York: New York University Press.
Zinsmaier, Markus. 2009. "Filmen fürs Leben. Eine Begegnung mit dem Filmemacher Christoph Hochhäusler, der als einer von 13 Regisseuren an Tom Tykwers Omnibusfilm 'Deutschland 09' mitgearbeitet hat." *Die Zeit*, 16 Feb 2009. http://www.zeit.de/online/2009/08/berlinale-christoph-hochhaeusler-film-deutschland-09.
Žižek, Slavoj. 1991. *Looking Awry: An Introduction to Jacques Lacan through Popular Culture*. Boston: MIT Press.

Index

Abel, Marco, 4, 15n3, 40, 57, 88, 117, 143, 144, 146, 149; *The Counter-Cinema of the Berlin School*, 4, 16n7, 17, 65–66, 110, 119, 139, 159
accelerationism, 14, 131. *See also* Shaviro, Steven
Address of the Eye, The (Sobchack), 80, 127
Ade, Maren, 2, 56, 76n2, 57, 70, 72, 75, 108
Adorno, Theodor W., 54, 87, 180n12
affect: affective atmospheres/affectspheres, 85, 86–87, 98, 100, 106, 113, 115, 117, 121; affective turn, 85; affectivity, 5; affect studies, 79, 184; affect theory, 8, 12, 84; *Affect Theory Reader, The* (Gregg and Seigworth), 84; autonomy of, 85, 104; definition and derivation of, 12 83-88; Gilles Deleuze's definition of, 85; embodied affect, 81; as experience, 12, 93, 95, 123; language of, 84, 89, 95, 184; as mood, 83; as participatory, 120, 126; production of, 115, 184; as relational, 126, 127; as transmissive, 89; waning of, 86. *See also* Stimmung
Ahmed, Sara, 6, 85, 104, 115, 119, 173–75, 180n16
Albert, Barbara, 68
Alice in den Städten (*Alice in the Cities*, 1974), 112
Alle Anderen (*Everyone Else*, 2009), 11, 51n13, 56–57, 70–75, 108
Altman, Rick, 138, 147
Amarcord (1973), 61
"ambulatory vision," 93, 111
Anti-Oedipus: Capitalism and Schizophrenia (Deleuze and Guattari), 146–47
Archive and the Repertoire, The (Taylor), 25
Arslan, Thomas, 2, 77n10, 80, 87–90, 93–99, 107n8, 107n13, 167–69; on cinema and movement, 88–89; on participatory spectatorship, 122

Astruc, Alexandre, 182
Auf der Suche (*Looking for Simon*, 2011), 32, 108, 156n17
Augé, Marc, 112
aura, 87, 128. *See also* Benjamin, Walter
Aus der Ferne (*From Afar*, 2006), 108
Auslander, Philip, 10, 18, 39, 49, 54, 132. *See also* liveness
Austin, J. L., 6
automobile, 13, 120-25, 130, 139, 140, 141, 147, 149, 186; automobile travel, 14, 109, 127–28; automobility, 15, 108, 109, 110, 118, 124, 185; automobilized gaze, 13, 118, 120–27, 136, 143, 185; "automobilization of the gaze," 7, 13, 109, 111, 118–20, 185. *See also* Pantenburg, Volker

Baer, Hester, 4, 89, 96, 121, 155n10
Balázs, Béla, 12, 58, 82–84, 87
Band à part (*Band of Outsiders*, 1964), 61
Barbara (2012), 51n12, 157n1, 158, 160–68, 170, 171, 178, 179n1, 179n5
Barker, Jennifer, 81, 83, 100, 106n1
Barthes, Roland, 10, 24, 29, 31, 96
Bazin, André, 7, 10, 19, 20, 23, 26, 31, 33, 69, 184
Beckman, Karen: on the car crash, 14, 130, 137, 141, 143, 149–51; on cinema and new media, 19, 22, 183
being-there, 5, 43, 45, 50, 181
being-with, 5, 43, 45, 50, 181
Benjamin, Walter: on film, 13, 58, 59, 83, 87–88, 111, 128–30; on history, 153–54
Berlant, Lauren, 12, 86–87, 102, 104, 113, 133, 154, 184
Berlin School, history and context, 2–6
Berlin Trilogy, 87, 89–90, 93, 95, 98, 99, 101. *See also specific titles*
biking/cycling 12, 99, 110, 160; bicycle, 99, 108, 139, 149, 160, 163, 165, 166

209

Bildnis einer Trinkerin (*Ticket of No Return*, 1979), 98
Bitomsky, Hartmut, 35, 108, 108n1
Blau, Herbert, 132
Blow-Up (1966), 30
Blue Steel (1989), 100
Blumenthal-Barby, Martin, 37
body: body turn, 12; "body without organs," 83; cinematic body, 78, 80, 184–87; corporeality, 12, 60, 64, 66, 74, 78, 185; embodiment, 6, 75, 80, 83, 87, 89, 105, 145, 185, 186; embodiment of the film space, 80, 93; as spectacle, 6, 64, 68, 70, 73, 87; traumatized body, 173–75, 178; urban embodiment, 92, 96. *See also* fugitive body
Bodies in Dissent: Spectacular Performances of Race and Freedom, 1850–1910 (Brooks), 161, 176
boîte à regarder (gazing box), 13, 124
Bonitzer, Pascal, 31
Bordwell, David, 97
Böse Zellen (*Free Radicals*, 2003), 68
Braidotti, Rosi, 83
Brandstetter, Gabrielle, 60
Brannigan, Erin, 60, 70
Breger, Claudia, 54–55
Brinkema, Eugenie, 12, 63, 78, 85–87, 100, 105, 106n1
Brombach, Ilka, 4
Brooks, Daphne A., 9, 15, 161–64, 171–72, 174, 178
Bruchner, René Thoreau, 137, 146, 148
Bulgakowa, Oksana, 9, 158, 163, 169–71

Caché (*Hidden*, 2005), 37
Cage, John, 61
Cahiers du cinéma, 3
Camera Lucida (Barthes), 23, 27, 29
car crash, 13, 108, 109, 111, 128, 130–34, 136–41, 143–54, 186; sexuality, 148-153; as worldmaking, 14, 131, 133, 147, 154. *See also* death
Carlson, Marvin, 6
Carnival of Souls (1962), 17, 141
Caro Diario (*Dear Diary*, 1993), 79, 112
"caught in the act," 38, 40, 42, 44
Cavell, Stanley, 17, 139, 147

"cinema of attractions," 11, 57–60, 66, 75, 76n5, 130, 134, 183
"cinema of consensus," 4
Cinema 1 (Deleuze), 60, 94, 138
Cinematic Body, The (Shaviro), 80
Clover, Carol, 80
Conversation, The (1974), 38
Cook, Roger, 4, 144
Crafton, Donald, 137, 140
Crary, Jonathan, 81
Crash (Beckman), 130
Crash (1996), 153
Cruel Optimism (Berlant), 86–87

dance, 11, 52, 54–76, 76n2, 77n8, 79, 99, 146, 156n15, 182, 184; dance film genre, 60, 79
Das Fahrrad (*The Bicycle*, 1982), 99
Dealer (1999), 12, 89, 93–95, 96
death: through the car crash, 13, 103, 130, 140, 143, 145, 146, 151, 154; of cinema, 9, 187; death and media, 10, 17, 21, 22, 23, 32, 33, 36, 37; as transit zone, 144, 150
Death 24x a Second (Mulvey), 19
de Certeau, Michel, 91, 102–103
Deleuze, Gilles, 60–61, 84, 94, 110, 138, 139, 146–47, 183; Deleuzian, 12, 162
del Río, Elena, 9, 56, 73, 95, 106n1, 174–75
Der einsame Weg (Schnitzler), 54, 57, 179n1
Der Himmel über Berlin (*Wings of Desire*, 1987), 102
Der Räuber (*The Robber*, 2010), 11, 22, 37, 48–49
Derrida, Jacques, 21, 69
Der schöne Tag (*A Fine Day*, 2001), 12, 89, 95–98, 155n3
deterritorialization, 131, 133, 136, 146–47, 153
dffb, 2
Die Ehe der Maria Braun (*The Marriage of Maria Braun*, 1979), 174
Die innere Sicherheit (*The State I Am In*, 2000), 14, 22, 37, 40–44, 51n13, 134–37, 142, 143
Discipline and Punish (Foucault), 42
Doane, Mary Ann, 8, 29, 39, 168
Dogma 95, 3, 72
Dorfdisko (village disco), 69
Dreams of Black (2009), 53

Dreileben (*Three Lives*, 2011), 45. See also specific titles
Dyer, Richard, 157

Easy Rider (1969), 111
Eidinger, Lars, 57, 71–73, 77n16
Eine Minute Dunkel (*A Minute of Darkness*, 2011), 11, 22, 37, 45, 47–48, 76n5
Elsaesser, Thomas, 15n1, 41
Enders, Sylke, 76n2
Enemy of the State (1998), 38
Eschkötter, Daniel, 38
"excess of appeals," 11
eXistenZ (1999), 121

Factory of Gestures: Body Language in Film, The (2008), 163
Fallen (*Falling*, 2006), 68
Falsche Bewegung (*Wrong Move*, 1975), 112
Falscher Bekenner (*I Am Guilty*, 2005), 14, 111, 130, 148–153
Farocki, Harun, 35
Fassbinder, Rainer Werner, 57n4, 59, 77n4, 79, 166, 174
Feuer, Jane: musical, 11, 59, 60, 61, 74; television, 20
Film Language: A Semiotics of Cinema (Metz), 24
film studies, 12, 78, 84, 86, 120, 130, 185, 187; German film studies, 4; performance in 5, 6, 8, 9
film theory, 8; affect in, 12, 78–79, 83, 106n1; Deleuzian film theory; 12, 80–81, 85, 94, 110, 162; materialism in, 12, 24, 58, 82-83, 87, 128–29; phenomenology in, 62, 78, 81–83, 84, 129, 184. See phenomenological
Fischer-Lichte, Erika, 7, 52–53, 59, 61–62, 75, 132, 184
Fisher, Jaimey, 4, 15n3, 123, 124n13, 131, 143, 154n13, 164, 179n5
flanerie, 12, 104–106; flaneurs/flaneuse, 88, 103
Foucault, Michel, 41–42, 162, 164
French New Wave, 93, 133
fugitive body, 7, 15, 157–64, 168–69, 171–73, 178, 186; fugitive performance, 15, 158, 160, 172
Funny Games (1997), 135

Gansera, Rainer, 3, 16n4
Gemunden, Gerd, 4, 76n1
German national cinema, 2
Gespenster (*Ghosts*, 2005), 13, 22, 29–32, 37, 43, 89, 121–23, 125
Geschwister-Kardeşler (*Siblings*, 1997), 12, 89–94, 96
Ghost Trilogy, 11, 22, 37, 40, 134. See also specific titles
Gleber, Anke, 103–104, 124
global art cinema, 2, 5, 16n3, 99
Goffman, Erving, 75–76, 88, 171
Göktürk, Deniz, 89–90, 92, 106n6, 107n11
Gold (2013), 14, 108, 155n3, 158, 161–63, 167–71, 178
Goodman, Nelson, 132
Grisebach, Valeska, 2, 62–68, 76n2, 150–51, 179n7
Guattari, Félix, 83, 90, 94, 139, 146–47
Gumbrecht, Hans Ulrich, 7, 52, 62
Gunning, Tom, 11–12, 38, 58, 130. See also "cinema of attractions"

Halberstam, Judith [Jack], 144
Halle, Randall, 110, 112, 115
Haneke, Michael, 105
Hansen, Miriam Bratu, 11, 58, 129
haptic, 27, 53, 62; Thomas Arslan, 88
Haraway, Donna, 83
Hauck, Elke, 2
haunt/haunting, 1, 10, 17, 38; Avery Gordon's definition of, 21, 34; hauntology, 21
Heidegger, Martin, 5
Heimatfilm, 64, 77n11, 150
Heisenberg, Benjamin, 2, 3, 48
Hessel, Franz, 103
historical reenactment/performance, 7, 9, 161, 162
Hochhäusler, Christoph, 2, 3, 46, 80, 105, 116, 121, 151–52
Hollywood Musical, The (Feuer), 59–60
Horkheimer, Max, 54
Hoss, Nina, 3, 14–15, 17, 25, 33, 157–79, 186; in theater, 57, 157, 179n2

Il sorpasso (*The Easy Life*, 1962), 61, 112
Im Juli (*In July*, 2000), 79–80, 112, 115

Im Lauf der Zeit (*Kings of the Road*, 1976), 110, 112, 156n20
In den Tag hinein (*The Days Between*, 2001), 12, 87, 89, 97–101, 156n17
indexicality, 23, 33, 36, 38
interactivity, 1, 5, 53, 123, 184, 186; interactive spectatorship, 1, 7; affective interaction, 12, 109
Iranian New Wave, 2

Jameson, Fredric, 86
Jerichow (2008), 122, 134, 137, 139–41, 144–45, 156n20, 156n22, 179n1

Kammerer, Dietmar, 38
King, Alisdair, 4, 55n1
Klassenfahrt (*Class Trip*, 2002), 77n10, 108, 110, 112–15, 118–19, 156n17
Knörer, Ekkehard, 3, 4, 89
Koch, Gertrud, 51n9, 106n1
Koepnick, Lutz, 4, 91, 121, 131, 141, 182
Köhler, Ulrich, 2
Kopp, Kristin, 4, 112, 115, 119, 155n2
Kracauer, Siegfried, 58, 83, 97, 129–30
Krauss, Rosalind E., 50
Kroko (2003), 89
Krüger, Jan, 70–71, 73–75, 112, 117, 152, 155n6, 156n17; in the Berlin School, 2–3, 76n3
Kutzli, Sebastian, 3

Ladri di biciclette (*Bicycle Thieves*, 1948), 99
La Jetée (1962), 35
La Notte (*The Night*, 1961), 71
La peau douce (*The Soft Skin*, 1964), 61
Lefait, Sébastian, 37, 39
Le gamin au vélo (*The Kid with a Bike*, 2011), 99
Lehmann, Hans-Thies, 132
Le Mépris (*Contempt*, 1963), 71
Leningrad Cowboys Go America! (1989), 79, 112
Lepecki, André, 11, 66, 70
Les yeux sans visage (*Eyes without a Face*, 1960), 173
Levin, Thomas Y., 10, 20–21, 37, 38, 39, 42–43, 47
lines of flight, 15, 90, 147, 174; Deleuze and Guattari's definition of, 162
Lisbon Story (1994), 79, 112

live experience, 1, 5, 8–9, 27, 49, 184
liveness, 7, 32, 45, 47, 50, 50n1, 52, 53, 132, 177, 178, 183, 186; Auslander's definition of, 18; effects of, 1, 7, 21, 29, 54; in film and media studies, 10, 11, 18–19, 21; José Esteban Muñoz's definition of, 18; in performance studies, 8, 18–19; televisual, 36, 39, 40, 49
Lola rennt (*Run Lola Run*, 1998), 79
Lost Highway (1997), 122
Love, Heather, 153
Lowenstein, Adam, 8, 53, 121, 172
Lumière brothers, 60

Ma, Jean, 17
Mach die Musik leiser (*Turn Down the Music*, 1994), 77n10
Madonnen (*Madonnas*, 2007), 98
Marks, Laura, 12, 16n9, 52, 81, 82, 106n1
Marnie (1964), 101
Marseille (2004), 13, 23, 103, 108, 121, 124–26
Massumi, Brian, 12, 61, 86, 104, 109
mediatization, 8, 12, 18, 50, 51n2, 53, 84; mediation, 7, 18–19, 21, 50n1, 51n2, 54, 127, 132
Meek's Cutoff (2010), 168
Mein langsames Leben (*Passing Summer*, 2001): automobilized gaze, 121, 124–25; dance, 56, 68–70, 75; photography, 22, 32-33
Mein Stern (*Be My Star*, 2001), 11, 56, 62–65, 69, 75, 89
Méliès, Georges, 60
Merleau-Ponty, Maurice, 7, 12, 42, 44, 80, 93, 94. *See also* phenomenological
Metropolis (1927), 102
Metz, Christian, 7, 10, 32, 34, 69, 70, 120
Migrant Trilogy. *See specific titles*
Milchwald (*This Very Moment*, 2003), 108, 110, 112, 114–19, 156n17
Montag kommen die Fenster (*Windows on Monday*, 2006), 13, 121, 124, 126
movement: being-as-movement, 60, 131; bodily movement, 6, 60, 63, 68, 75, 91, 183; car travel, 108–31; diegetic movement, 5, 11, 12, 79, 87, 99, 105, 159, 181, 183; movement as performance, 157-78; movement-image, 110, 138, 183; movement over stasis; 1,

24; movement-spaces, 90; quotidian movement, 88, 89, 96; urban movement, 88–106. *See also* automobility
Mulholland Drive (2001), 138
Mulvey, Laura, post-cinematic, 8, 10, 19, 22, 31, 35–36; visual pleasure, 64, 81, 162, 176
Muñoz, José Esteban, 8, 9, 14, 70–71, 111, 137, 144, 152, 153; disidentificatory performance, 14, 131–32, 147, 154; mediation, 18–19.
musical, 2, 7, 11, 18, 58–61, 63, 66, 74–75
My Own Private Idaho (1991), 112

Naremore, James, 75, 158, 171
neo-neo-realism, 2; derivation of, 15n2
Nessel, Sabine, 4, 57–58, 68, 77n8, 96, 96n18, 107n18, 143
New Argentine Cinema, 2
New German Cinema, 3, 134, 174
New Turkish Cinema, 2
Ngai, Sianne, 87
Nicodemus, Katja, 3, 169
Nord, Cristina, 3
Nouvelle Vague Allemande, 4
Nyong'o, Tavia, 18, 20

Oberhausen Manifesto, 3, 134
ontology of cinema, 7, 20
Orly (2010), 76n1, 108

Pantenburg, Volker, 7, 13, 108–109, 111, 120, 155n1, 155n7, 185
performance: definition and derivation of, 6; diva performance, 171, 172, 177; hybrid form, 20; live performance, 1, 2, 5, 12, 25, 34, 50, 53, 54, 60, 81, 127, 132; performance studies, 6, 8, 9, 18–19, 50n1, 128, 132, 183, 187; performance turn, 2, 80, 187; performance within performance, 75, 171–72, 177. *See also* reenactment
performative turn, 6
Permanent Vacation (1980), 98
Peters, Katrin, 23
Petzold, Christian, 2, 131, 139, 141, 146, 147, 150, 159, 166, 176; on the automobilized gaze, 121–22; on cinema and the Berlin School, 133–34; on genre, 17; 24–25; on media, 17, 29–30; on surveillance, 37, 44–45, 51n12; on theater, 54–55
Peucker, Brigitte, 7, 17, 61–62, 96, 105
phantom ride, 13, 118, 121, 122, 126, 127
Phelan, Peggy, 27, 128, 132, 156n16, 156n18
phenomenological: phenomenological experience, 143, 147; phenomenological perception, 5, 24, 88, 89, 104, 147; phenomenology, 12, 24, 42, 44, 45, 78, 79, 80, 83, 175, 185. *See also* "vitalist phenomenology"
Phoenix (Petzold), 33–34, 124, 161–63, 171–78, 179n1, 180n14, 180n15
photograph, 10, 19, 20, 22–36, 39, 183; computer-generated photograph, 31, 32; *On Photography* (Sontag), 36; "The Ontology of the Photographic Image" (Bazin), 23; the photographic, 10, 20, 22, 25–27, 30–32, 34–35, 38, 51n11, 182; photography, 10, 19–24, 29–39, 49–50, 54, 73, 183; "Photography and Fetish" (Metz), 23, 34, 69
Pickpocket (1959), 94
Pierrot le fou (*Pierrot the Madman*, 1965), 112
Piscator, Erwin, 53
Plätze in Städten (*Places in Cities*, 1998), 11, 56, 66–68, 75
point of sense, 12, 78, 82, 93, 95, 99, 103, 105–6, 127; definition and derivation of, 7, 87, 184
post-cinematic, 1, 8–9, 15n1, 19, 84, 184; *Post Cinematic Affect* (Shaviro), 84, 85
postclassical cinema, 58, 75
Postman Always Rings Twice, The (1946), 144–45
presence: presence effects, 53, 70; absence and presence, 17, 21, 26, 32, 69, 70, 130, 132, theatrical presence, 59, 70, 75; sensation/sense of, 11, 62, 69, 75, 79; copresence, 82, 182, 183
"primal accident," 14, 148–49, 151, 156n23

queer performance, 9, 14, 70. *See also* performance

"reality bleed," 7, 61
reality effect, 11, 38, 45
reenactment, 7, 24, 25, 28, 29, 31, 32, 34, 35, 36, 73, 161; restaging, 27

Reichsautobahn (1984–1986), 108
relationality, 5–6, 9, 50, 79, 157, 181, 187
remediation, 7, 8, 19–24, 36–40, 44, 49–50, 53, 54, 183; Jay David Bolter and Richard Grusin's definition of, 10, 17, 20, 53; remediation of photography, 24, 29
Rentschler, Eric, 4, 39, 57–58, 76n5
Revolver magazine, 3
Roach, Joseph, 132, 161, 161n3
road movie, 13, 79, 86, 109–13, 115, 117–20, 124, 127, 156n20
Roy, Rajendra, 4, 163
Rückenwind (*Light Gradient*, 2009), 108, 110
Rutherford, Anne, 81, 93, 106n1, 111, 158, 182, 186

Sans toit ni loi (*Vagabond*, 1985), 98
Sartre, Jean-Paul, 38, 42
Scener ur ett äktenskap (*Scenes from a Marriage*, 1973), 71
Schanelec, Angela, 2, 56, 57, 61, 66–70, 94, 124–26, 155n10; on portraying death in film, 32–33
Schick, Thomas, 4, 16n4
Schläfer (*Sleeper*, 2005), 37, 155n8
Schlafkrankheit (*Sleeping Sickness*, 2011), 108
Schneider, Rebecca, 21, 29, 36, 49, 132, 161
Séance (2010), 10, 22, 34–36,
Seel, Martin, 33, 51n9
Sehnsucht (*Longing*, 2006), 62–64, 67, 75, 77n11, 111, 130, 148–151
Seidl, Ulrich, 105
"sensation of movement," 110
Shaviro, Steven, 6, 12, 55, 62, 80–81, 129, 106n1, 136, 162, 184; on accelerationism, 14, 131; on the post-cinematic, 8, 84–85, 105
Simmel, Georg, 88
slow/slowness, 5, 14, 53, 55–56, 75, 106n3, 154, 159, 181–182
"slow cinema," 16n8, 56, 159; Karl Schoonover's definition of, 55. *See also* stasis
Skladanowsky brothers, 60
Sobchack, Vivian, 6, 12, 36, 51n11, 62, 80–82, 84, 89, 117, 125–27
SOURCE, THE (2014), 53

spectacle: of the body, 6, 68, 70, 178, 182; cinematic spectacle, 57, 64; dance spectacle, 11, 55, 58, 59, 75, 79; live, 27; performance spectacle, 34; theatrical spectacle, 55, 174
Specters of Marx (Derrida), 21
"spectrum," 23
Speth, Maria, 2, 12, 76n2, 80, 87, 89, 97–99, 156n17
Spinoza, Baruch, 78; "Spinoza and the Three Ethics" (Deleuze), 85
star studies, 14, 157, 179n2
Stasi, 51n12, 164, 167
stasis: driving as, 108, 110, 120, 127, 130; freedom from, 60, 96, 159, 178; in "slow cinema," 69, 75, 181; against stasis, 1, 5–6
States, Bert O., 6, 158
Stewart, Garrett, 22, 37
Stimmung, 83, 87
Strathausen, Carsten, 39
Suchsland, Rüdiger, 3, 4, 16n4, 70, 76n3, 88, 93, 106n3, 134, 136
surveillance camera footage/CCTV, 10, 11, 20–22, 36–40, 42–50, 54, 76n5; surveillance, 41–43
Sweet Hereafter, The (1997), 150
synesthesia, 82

Tactile Eye, The (Barker), 83
Taylor, Diana, 8, 25, 29, 86, 87, 186
television, 2, 18, 37, 38–39, 40, 47–48, 50; Philip Auslander's definition of, 39, 49; Mary Ann Doane's definition of, 39
Teorema (1968), 73
theater, 11, 16n5, 21, 29, 52–55, 57, 76n4, 104, 157, 179n1; theater studies, 18, 80
theatricality, 5, 52, 54, 55, 57, 59, 61–62, 75, 185; of dance, 55, 70; Erika Fischer-Lichte's definition of, 59, 61, 184; theatricality bleed, 7, 11, 62
Thelma & Louise (1991), 112
Titanic (1997), 59
Torlasco, Domietta, 22
Toter Mann (*Something to Remind Me*, 2001), 10, 22, 24–26, 28–31, 165, 179n1
transcendental off, 21–22, 39

"travel movies," 110
Trigg, Dylan, 83
Trois couleurs: bleu (*Three Colors: Blue*, 1993), 100, 150
Turkish German Cinema, 89–90, 106n6
2001: A Space Odyssey (1968), 59–60

Uccellacci e uccellini (*The Hawks and the Sparrows*, 1966), 61
Unmarked: The Politics of Performance (Phelan), 26, 128
Unter dir die Stadt (*The City Below*, 2010), 26–27, 29–31, 87, 89, 97, 98, 101–5
Unterwegs (*On the Road*, 2004), 70–71, 73–75, 76n3, 108, 110, 112, 117–19
utopian, 9, 61, 132–33, 154, 186; utopianism, 154

Vertigo (1958), 34, 175–76
Viaggio in Italia (*Journey to Italy*, 1954), 112
video game/virtual reality game, 1, 13, 53, 120–21, 155n8
Virilio, Paul, 120, 148
"Visual Pleasure and Narrative Cinema" (Mulvey), 162
"vitalist phenomenology," 83
vitrification, 102–103

Vogel, Shane, 177
Vorschneider, Reinhold, 3
voyeur/voyeurism, 27, 42, 49, 71, 102, 103; voyeuristic, 11, 27, 42, 46, 59, 64, 96, 103, 123, 151

Wadjda (2012), 99
walking, 12, 93, 102, 108
Watkins, Megan, 127
Weekend (1967), 14, 112, 133–34, 141–42
Wenders, Wim, 79, 110
What Is Cinema? (Bazin), 23
Williams, Linda, 6, 60, 78, 80
Winckler, Henner, 2, 113–14
worldmaking, 14, 131–33, 137, 146–47, 154
Wolfsburg (2003), 14, 32, 134, 137, 139–42, 145, 165, 179n1
Worthmann, Merten, 3, 16n4, 68

Yella (2007), 51n13, 81?; automobilized gaze, 121–24; car crash, 134, 137–45, 150, 165; Nina Hoss, 179n1; surveillance, 1

Zimmer, Catherine, 37, 38, 40
Žižek, Slavoj, 34
zones of indiscernibility, 90

OLIVIA LANDRY is Assistant Professor of German at Lehigh University.

www.ingramcontent.com/pod-product-compliance
Lightning Source LLC
Chambersburg PA
CBHW061938220426
43662CB00012B/1953